MW01671281

A GOOD FRIEND WHO UNDERSTANDS THE SACRIFICE MADE BY OUR PARENT'S GENERATION WHEN OUR HOMETOWNS WENT TO WAR.

7/16/96

BEST —

A Hometown Went To War

A Hometown Went To War

Remembrances of World War II

Rolland E. Kidder

SANDY BOTTOM PRESS

A HOMETOWN WENT TO WAR

 Address all inquiries to Sandy Bottom Press, PO Box 1442, Chautauqua, NY 14722.

ISBN 0-9652842-0-4

This book is dedicated
to the veterans of World War II.

THE WHITE HOUSE
WASHINGTON

TO MEMBERS OF THE UNITED STATES ARMY EXPEDITIONARY FORCES:

You are a soldier of the United States Army.

You have embarked for distant places where the war is being fought.

Upon the outcome depends the freedom of your lives: the freedom of the lives of those you love—your fellow-citizens—your people.

Never were the enemies of freedom more tyrannical, more arrogant, more brutal.

Yours is a God-fearing, proud, courageous people, which, throughout its history, has put its freedom under God before all other purposes.

We who stay at home have our duties to perform—duties owed in many parts to you. You will be supported by the whole force and power of this Nation. The victory you win will be a victory of all the people—common to them all.

You bear with you the hope, the confidence, the gratitude and the prayers of your family, your fellow-citizens, and your President—

Franklin D Roosevelt

Contents

Foreword

World War II was a watershed event in American history, a defining moment that set a new direction for the nation and the world. Only two other events in our history have ever come close to the impact of World War II—the Revolutionary War, which established the country, and the Civil War, which defined the extent of freedom for our citizens and confirmed the unity of the states under the Constitution. World War II went beyond national boundaries. It defined how the entire world would live and be structured: democratically or under dictatorship, with freedom or under force of arms.

Today it is difficult to conceive of a world dominated by Hitler and Hirohito, but that world was a real possibility in 1941. The Japanese controlled a large portion of Asia, and Hitler had run roughshod over most of Europe. The free and open society that we take for granted today would likely not have survived if these forces had not been stopped.

Another World War had been fought in 1914-1918, but it was not a "world" happening in that sense. It was essentially a conflict between the major powers in Europe. The war that broke out in 1939 was different in magnitude. It consumed the whole globe. From Murmansk to Capetown, from London to Manila, from New York to Berlin, and San Francisco to Tokyo–everyone alive was affected. Unknown islands in the Pacific, sand dunes in the Sahara, mountain ranges in New Guinea, nondescript beaches in France became household words at home and battlegrounds for American troops.

I was reminded of all of these things again as I walked between the rows of white crosses at the American Cemetery at Omaha Beach in Normandy during the commemoration of the 50th anniversary of D-Day, June 6, 1994. Buried there were many who had made the difference in the great world conflict of 1941-1945. I knew that the World War II veterans still living wouldn't be around much longer; most were in their seventies.

What had the war been like for them? Where had their travels taken them? What had motivated them to join the military and enter the fight?

Our hometown was not different from most. Nestled in the hills of upstate New York it helped provide the manpower and womanpower for this war. Young men out of high school found themselves fighting for their lives in equatorial jungles or in the mud and snow of Europe. Women would leave their homes to join the military or to work in factories to help feed and equip a military machine operating on every continent on the globe. Millions of American young people would be forever changed by this national commitment to turn back the forces of dictatorship and repression which threatened the world.

Some of the individuals I interviewed lived in our town at the time they entered the military. Others came from similar communities, but settled here after the war. All of them served in one capacity or another overseas during World War II. Most of them had never been outside small town America. Their upbringing had been relatively sheltered. To most of them a trip to New York City or Washington, DC was something they only dreamed of doing. They, like their mothers and fathers, anticipated moving into a job after high school graduation. A few were headed for college. Some had already found jobs and occupations.

The bombing of Pearl Harbor and America's entry into World War II was to change all of those plans. Everyone in the country was being called upon to help defeat the Axis. One thing for sure...their innocence and rather limited view of what the world was like would be forever changed.

My generation has a dim memory of what happened back then. We can remember the end of the war. We remember the prosperity of the postwar years. But we have forgotten the battlefields, the sacrifices, and the experiences of our parents' generation. If we have forgotten, our own children, because of their age, have no remembrances and most of them take for granted the free world and America's dominance on the international stage for the past 50 years. All that we have known since 1945 would have been impossible had the previous generation not responded when the world was threatened by the darkness and evil of that time. We owe our world today to those who made it happen then. As President Clinton so aptly put it during his D-Day speech at Normandy, "We are the children of their sacrifice."

This is a story about some young men and women from our hometown who were plunged into this conflict, the most cataclysmic event the world had ever seen. It tells about the war from their personal experience but attempts, through background and commentary, to tie that to a historical description of the entire undertaking that was consuming the world from 1941 to 1945.

The book should not be read as a definitive history of World War II. It is a compilation of oral histories told to me in the privacy of my office by 28 World War II veterans. Each story was then typed and submitted to the veterans for their approval before being included for publication. Sometimes I include parenthetical comments where the interviewee laughed or made side comments. Aside from framing the stories so that they flowed sequentially, the words are essentially those of the veterans—even if that meant bad language or poor choice of grammar. It is their story, not mine.

Most chapters begin with a poignant, memorable experience in the veteran's own words and printed in italics, which attempts to capsulize one key event in his or her war experience. In some cases, a letter to home or a citation from a medal or award is used. The remainder of the interview is printed in regular type and usually progresses from the beginning of the war experience to the end.

The "BACKGROUND AND COMMENTARY" following the individual stories reflects some of my own feelings and opinions and is an attempt to describe the "big picture" of what was happening during the war. The references used for my research were sources available in most public or college libraries. Obviously, many aspects of the war were overlooked since these veterans represent only a small group involved in what was truly a global conflict.

The book was written primarily for the children and grandchildren of these veterans, many of whom have little recollection or knowledge of this epochal period in American and world history. It is intended to be a primer for them; not a detailed historical treatise.

Essentially, this is a book from the heart—an open, honest and sometimes emotional retelling of fifty-year-old experiences. It is meant to bring alive, for those who may have forgotten, the defining event for America in the 20th century—the defeat of fascism and dictatorship through the efforts of a democratic nation, united in a just and common cause.

INTRODUCTION

JAMESTOWN, NY
CHAUTAUQUA COUNTY, 1941

It was a small industrial town in upstate New York: nondescript by big-city standards but a good place to raise kids, a good place to get started. The Erie Railroad wound through the city on its way from Hoboken to Chicago. It was an eight- or nine-hour ride to travel to either place, but most folks went west toward Chicago. They preferred to be known as Midwesterners. They resisted the complexity and liberalism of New York City and the East.

From the bleak days of the depression, factories and jobs were now on the rebound. Furniture manufacturers and sheet metal shops were strung along the railroad and river valley like sausages on a string. Business had first been powered by the labor of Swedish immigrants, then later by immigrants from Italy. "Natives," descendants from the first English settlers, were scattered throughout the area, and small farms dotted the countryside. It was a mini melting pot. At the local high school there was a good cross section of what America was and of what it was becoming: rich kids, poor kids, good kids, bad kids. It was all there and fun to be a part of.

There were conflicts. The Swedes lived on Swede Hill and the Italians in Dago Valley. The hill folk went to Lutheran churches where Swedish was still spoken. Valley residents went to mass where Italian and Latin were the primary languages. The sons and daughters of these immigrants were at the high school, mixing it up, falling in love, cutting their own swath in their own America. A family crisis would occur when a Johnson married a Galati, or a Cusimano a Carlson. But people were learning that they had more in common than their differences. By 1941 the barriers were breaking down.

It was a time before malls and shopping centers. Downtown was vibrant, the bus system was busy, trolleys ran up the lake, and the city was the center of activity. On Saturday morning the Federal Market was clogged with vendors. You could buy a live chicken or a butchered one, oysters fresh from Boston, buttermilk in the old waxed paper, megaphone-style containers.

Saturday afternoon was a time to go to a movie and watch a Roy Rogers and Gabbie Hayes double feature. Sometimes big names like Glenn Miller or Tommy Dorsey would come to town. There were two bowling alleys and one was on the second floor. High school kids worked there setting pins; no one had heard of automatic pinsetting machines. There was no TV nor video games, but there was bobsledding in the winter and going to the lake in the summer. It wasn't a place where people thought much about what was going on in the rest of the world: why look further?

Yes, you went to church. It wasn't your choice. You had to go. On Wednesday afternoons after school, the Lutherans had confirmation classes and the Catholics went to catechism. On Fridays there was fish and no meat for the Catholics. The Protestant kids couldn't understand why. The Catholic kids just accepted that this was the way things were. But on both sides, right was right and wrong was wrong. Cheating was wrong. Talking back to an adult was wrong. Swearing was wrong, done only under your breath. Being dressed well was right. Being on time and working hard was right. Respecting your elders and your teachers was right. These were simple times. Sex outside of marriage was a "No." Everyone expected to go to work after high school. There were no "free lunches" being offered by the government.

Where was Japan? It was a place you may have read about but it wasn't a household word. Germany? Your father may have fought in World War I and you had heard the stories of the mustard gas and artillery barrages. But now Germany was a past memory and America was where the action was. Most people wanted to forget about the problems of Europe and the past war. "Overseas" was a place where missionaries went to preach the gospel.

Some things were imported. Bananas and coffee came from South America, but no one imported cars and radios. They were American made! There was really no reason to be much concerned about what was happening outside the USA. Hopefully, the problems of the world would go away.

The draft board was located at the Post Office, and the young men went down and reluctantly signed up. In 1940, President Roosevelt had sought an extension of the draft in order to provide manpower for the Army, and it passed the House of Representatives by only one vote. People didn't want a war and they had sent politicians to Washington who reflected that view. Small-town America didn't want to go to war. They didn't even want to think about it. Our town was no exception.

Things changed in our hometown on December 7, 1941, the day the Japanese bombed Pearl Harbor. Everyone knew immediately that the easy days, the simple days were over. The parochialism of 1941 was swept away with one radio announcement, and with it went whatever plans for the future the young people of the town had been making. Wars are always fought by the young, and this would be no exception. Nineteen-year-olds would be bayoneting German troops, twenty-year-olds would be dogfighting with Japanese Zeros over islands in the South Pacific, old-timers in their 30s would be operating hospitals behind the frontlines in France and flying B-17s north of the Arctic Circle. Many young kids who had never traveled more than a hundred miles from home would find themselves on the other side of the world.

Our hometown was just a microcosm of what was happening then. Though some may conclude that the accounts told in this book are only of local interest, they should realize that similar experiences happened to similar young people in their own communities and neighborhoods. From all across the country, America's towns were sending their youth to war, a war that would forever change them and their country. From 227,000 in 1939, the Army, by 1942, would grow to 5.4 million.[1] It was a civilian Army, recruited from the grassroots, and it would win the war.

One thing hasn't changed since 1941. Our town still sponsors a Memorial Day parade, and every year taps is played and a speech is made at Soldiers' Circle in the cemetery. Only now, it's those kids from 1941 who are being buried in Soldiers' Circle, and every year a few more headstones appear with the inscription "World War II Veteran." Those veterans still living are now talking more about the war. To most of them, 1941 remains a vivid memory, and what happened during the following four years has never been forgotten. As one woman said of her husband, "You know, it was his big show." For most of these young people, now in their 70s, it was their "big show"...the most monumental experience of their lifetime. As they look back now, they realize that they were involved in a historic undertaking which defined the world as we know it. They are getting old now but their memories of the war are still fresh and alive. We can learn from what they did. Their story is one that should not be forgotten.

I. The Day The War Began

I heard something that sounded like bombing or gun fire. "That's strange," I said to myself, "usually there's no gunnery practice on Sunday." Sunday was a day when most sailors slept in, just like they were doing that day on my ship. Then I heard the roar of an engine and here came a fighter plane right over me. I could see the pilot and he smiled at me as he flew by. He was flying so low that I could have hit him with a potato! It was then that I noticed the rising sun painted on his plane. I rushed to the other side of the ship, looked across the harbor and saw planes diving on the big ships over at the piers. Fires had started and black smoke was going into the air. That's when it hit me that the Japs were over Pearl Harbor and were bombing our ships. I ran forward to the Captain's cabin and yelled, "Captain, you'd better get up. The Japanese are bombing Pearl Harbor!" He bounded out of his stateroom and ran to the bridge. It was December 7, 1941, and World War II had just started.[1]

Joe Panebianco
Machinist Mate 2nd Class, U.S. Navy

[Joe Panebianco's destroyer was anchored in Pearl Harbor the day of the Japanese surprise attack. He talks about this in the following story and also about his experiences on his ship during action against the Japanese in the South Pacific.]

I graduated from the high school in 1937 but wasn't ready to settle down. My father had immigrated from Italy in the 1920s and had started a window-washing business, but I wasn't ready to commit to that kind of work. Instead, I listened to my Uncle Joe. He had been in the Navy and he encouraged me to enlist. He thought that it would be good for me to get away from home, grow up a little bit, and at the same time see the world. It sounded like a good plan, so in 1938 I enlisted in the Navy. I did my basic training at Newport, Rhode Island, and went from there to Norfolk to pick up my ship. It was an old World War I, four-stacker destroyer/minesweeper called the USS *Trever* (DMS 339). It was an old junker but reliable and it was going to be my home for the duration of the

Joe Panebianco's ship, the USS Trever (dms 339)

war. It actually had been built primarily as a torpedo ship and so didn't carry any antiaircraft guns. It also had two small 3-inch artillery guns, one forward and one aft. Because of our shallow draft, we could also be used as minesweeper if need be.

We left Norfolk and, for awhile, cruised around the Caribbean doing training exercises and visiting island ports, but then, sometime in 1939, we were sent through the Panama Canal and to our new home port of San Diego. From there, we periodically went on training cruises to Pearl Harbor and that is where I was when the war started. That Sunday morning we watched helplessly as the Japanese bombed and torpedoed our ships. Our own torpedoes were of no use and we had no antiaircraft guns. I was just lucky to be on a small ship and anchored at some distance from the piers. The Japanese went after the big ships and left us alone.[2]

Of course, the bombing of Pearl Harbor changed everything. Although I prayed pretty hard that day, I ended up missing church (laughs). I also ruined my dress whites. I wore them down into the boiler room where I helped get the engines fired up so that we could get underway. As you could imagine, things that day at Pearl Harbor were in absolute chaos since the attack had been a complete surprise. For a couple of frustrating hours that morning we waited for orders and did nothing but watch what was going on. We finally got underway and went outside the harbor to look for Jap submarines. Needless to say, we didn't find any. (Although we found out later that some mini-subs had tried to penetrate the harbor defenses.)

It became apparent after the Pearl Harbor attack that our old destroyers needed to be spruced up and rearmed with antiaircraft weapons, so we were sent to Mare Island, California, to have that work done. There, in drydock, we were converted to a two-stack destroyer, got rid of our torpedoes, and had four sets of 40-mm "pom-pom" antiaircraft guns installed on the ship. While we were in drydock, I got leave to visit home. I hadn't been home for three and a half years and, with the war on, I would probably be gone another three or four years, so it was good to get the chance to visit Mom and Dad.

With the retrofitting of the ship completed, we headed back for Pearl and then in the summer of '42 we were deployed to the South Pacific. Our first major operation was in supporting the invasion of the Japanese-held Solomon Islands. I'll never forget that sight as we moved on Guadalcanal, one of those islands. There seemed to be hundreds of ships as far as you could see. At the time, we didn't know where we were going–that was kept a secret. But, when we saw all the ships, we knew that something big was up. After the Marines had landed on Guadalcanal and had taken the little island of Tulagi across from it, we began operating out of the small port at Tulagi. Sometimes we would work with the PT (Patrol Torpedo) boats and at other times we assisted the Marines with ground-fire support from our 3-inch guns. This was a contested area with the Japanese and so we saw a lot of Jap planes and even had a battle with some of their destroyers.

The fight with the destroyers was memorable. We got a hurry-up message that some Japanese destroyers were coming down the channel between Tulagi and Guadalcanal and we were sent to intercept them. However, our 3-inch guns were no match for their larger guns, and they were faster than we were. The Japanese shells were exploding around us and the captain kept zigzagging the ship to try and throw them off. We were supposed to stay in a deep channel, but the Japanese were moving on us so fast that the captain decided he had to turn early and we went right over part of a coral reef. I vividly recall this one big sailor we had from Kentucky or Tennessee picking up depth charges by himself and heaving them off the ship so that we could reduce our draft and get over that reef. Another ship was with us, and the Japs did hit one of the guns on it and killed some of their guys.[3]

Another big battle for us in the Solomons involved some Japanese bombers. There were several of our ships in the channel and some enemy bombers came in low, expecting us to hold fire because of the chance that we could have hit each other in a crossfire. But they miscalculated and we all opened up. That day we counted 21 Japanese bombers that went down. After they had been shot down, we were ordered to go out and pick up the crews that had made it out into life rafts or were floating in life jackets. We fished them out and then put them on the forecastle of the ship until we got back to Tulagi where we could transfer them. There must have been twenty or so Japanese that we picked up that day.

Earlier, before the Guadalcanal action, we had also been indirectly involved in another naval engagement between our forces and the Japanese. We could see lights and flashes in the sky at night but the battle was quite a distance away. We were called in the next day to pick up survivors from that battle. We thought that we would be picking up our own men but, instead, found that most of them were Japanese. Most of them were Japanese sailors who had been on ships that had been sunk by our forces. Some were in rafts and others were just hanging on to oil cans and anything that would float. When we came alongside these men, our boatswain mates would stand by ready with a rifle in case any of them were armed. The first group resisted coming aboard. One of them said, "Tojo say 'No!'" Our captain replied, "Roosevelt say 'Yes!'" But they wouldn't come aboard so the boatswain mates shot them. There wasn't time to argue. The next group, who had seen this, didn't argue, although it must have been difficult for them to "lose face" by being rescued by the Americans. Some of them asked us to shoot them once they were on board, but we refused.

Most of the military action that we saw was in the early years of the war in the South Pacific. Probably because we were an old ship, the Navy decided to keep us in that area for the rest of the war, so we didn't move farther north toward the Philippines and Japan as the war progressed. We stayed in the South Pacific and operated around the New Hebrides, New Zealand and Australia, primarily escorting supply and troop ships and doing antisubmarine warfare. The farthest west that we got was Port Moresby, New Guinea.

We did have a couple of close calls because of bad weather. One day in stormy seas we almost got torpedoed. Periodically, we would come across a Japanese submarine and would try to sink it with depth charges. They would sometimes fight back but, because we had a shallow draft, the subs had a hard time setting the proper depth on their torpedoes. It was even more difficult in rough weather. That particular day one torpedo went under us and another porpoised right out of the water and went over the ship. We were in the bottom of a big swell and the thing just came out of the water, went over us, and then plunged right back into the water!

Joe Panebianco with his parents while home on leave after the Pearl Harbor attack

Another big scare came during a typhoon. We were escorting a convoy and one of our boatswain mates was out on deck in the storm trying to secure something when a davit holding one of the lifeboats swung around and knocked him into the water. It was at night, but somehow the captain got the ship turned around and we came alongside and picked up the guy. He probably figured he was a sure goner, but we found him and got him back aboard. However, he was never the same after that. Somebody told me that he finally went nuts. I guess the whole episode must have pushed him over the edge.

As I look back on those days, I suppose that Pearl Harbor was the most memorable event. In 1991, which was the 50th anniversary of the attack, our congressman sponsored a meeting in his district for the survivors of Pearl Harbor. I couldn't make the meeting, but the fact that it was held brought back a lot of memories. I was one of the lucky ones. I could just as well have been on one of those cruisers or battle wagons tied up at the piers.

Someday I want to take my wife out to Hawaii and show her where it happened. I want to visit the USS *Arizona* Memorial where over 1,000 sailors are still entombed in the waters of Pearl Harbor. I want to go to that cemetery in Honolulu where many more who died that day are buried. That's holy ground for me. I hold those fellows who died at Pearl Harbor in reverence. It could have been me.

[Joe Panebianco came home from the war and went into the window washing business with his father. Eventually, he went to work in a tool-making plant in town where he was employed for fifteen years. He is now retired.]

Background and Commentary

[1]The Japanese attack on Pearl Harbor, December 7, 1941, came as a complete surprise to Americans like Joe Panebianco who were stationed there. Tension between the United States and Japan had been growing because of Japan's invasion of China and its insistence on establishing an "East Asia Co-Prosperity Sphere"—which essentially meant an Asia dominated by Japan. Although talks continued between the two countries, Japan deemed war with the United States inevitable and began its plans for

a surprise attack on Pearl Harbor.

When the first Japanese planes came over Hawaii that morning, it was quickly apparent that they had caught the Americans flat-footed. One of the squadron leaders radioed back to the Japanese fleet the words "Tora, Tora, Tora!" which was the Japanese word for "tiger" and was the code word to indicate that the attack had been a complete surprise. There wasn't even one American plane in the air. They were all lined up in rows at Hickam, Bellows, and Wheeler Fields. The battleships were tied up next to each other at the deep-water piers on Ford Island. By sheer luck, the American aircraft carriers were out on maneuvers, a fact that was to come back and plague the Japanese. Joe Panebianco was lucky that his ship was anchored out in the harbor and was not considered a primary target by the Japanese.

For the Japanese, the Pearl Harbor attack was a great tactical victory. Eighteen warships were either sunk or damaged beyond repair; 188 planes were destroyed on the ground, another 159 were damaged, only 43 aircraft in Hawaii remained operational, and 2,403 American servicemen were killed and another 2,000 wounded. However, for the Japanese, it was also the beginning of the end. On December 8th, President Franklin Roosevelt made his famous "day of infamy" speech before a joint session of congress, and war was declared with only one dissenting vote. The bickering in the United States between Republicans and Democrats, isolationists and internationalists was over. The country came together. Young men rushed to the recruiting centers. Factories stopped making cars and started making airplanes, tanks, and trucks. Rationing soon went into effect so that all available supplies could be shipped to the fighting fronts. The American youth of 1941 were suddenly thrust into a four-year hiatus that would eventually lead them in victory to the heart of Germany and to a surrender ceremony in Tokyo Bay.

[2]One of the battleships that was sunk on the morning of December 7, 1941, with great loss of life, was the USS *Arizona.* For those who visit Hawaii, a visit to the *Arizona* Memorial is a must. The Memorial looks down on the deck plating and guns of the mammoth warship, which entombs the bodies of some 1,000 sailors who were killed on that morning. One of the bombs or torpedoes dropped by the Japanese hit the ship's magazine, and the ship virtually blew apart. As you look down into the clear waters of Pearl Harbor at the rusted hulk of the *Arizona,* periodically

you can see small oil slicks that still rise from its remains.

Many other ships were also sunk or damaged during the attack. A nearby battleship, the USS *Oklahoma,* rolled upside down when it sank. For two days, divers and salvage teams tried to free 400 men who had been caught in an air bubble in the capsized ship. Only 30 were saved, the rest died before the rescue teams could get to them.

[3]During much of 1942, the war news for the Allies was not good. The Germans under General Rommel were moving quickly across North Africa toward Egypt and the Japanese were moving swiftly south, heading toward Australia. The first major battle between Japanese and American naval forces took place in May 1942 in the Coral Sea off the east coast of Australia. Although there was no clear victor in the battle, it did slow the Japanese advance. A decisive victory over the Japanese occurred about a month later in the famous battle of Midway. Through the sacrifice and bravery of American Navy pilots, four Japanese aircraft carriers were sunk. The tide had begun to turn against the Japanese in the Pacific.

The land battle between American and Japanese forces was joined on August 9, 1942, when U.S. Marines disembarked on the Japanese-held islands of Guadalcanal and Tulagi in the Solomon Island chain. Joe Panebianco and his shipmates were sent to help support this invasion. Although the initial landing went relatively easy, the fighting on Guadalcanal became desperate. For a while, things looked so grim that Admiral Frank J. Fletcher withdrew the aircraft carriers that were supporting the Marines. This action was soon reversed with the assignment of Admiral William H. "Bull" Halsey to command U.S. Naval Forces in the area. Halsey became known as the "Patton" of the Navy in the Pacific because of his eagerness to take the fight to the enemy.

The area between Tulagi and Guadalcanal became known as "iron-bottom sound" because of the tremendous number of Japanese and American ships that were sunk there. The route from Rabaul (a Japanese stronghold to the northwest) to Guadalcanal became known as "the slot" and, at night, Japanese destroyers and cruisers would move into the area to supply their troops and shell the Americans who had landed. On October 25th, the USS *Trever* and a sister ship, the USS *Zane,* were sent on a mission to resupply the American PT boats, which were operating on iron-bottom sound. During this mission they encountered the Japanese destroyers.

Being slower and outgunned by the larger Japanese vessels, they escaped over a coral reef in an area called the Neggela Channel.

This diversion took the Japanese warships away from their original mission of shelling Henderson Field, the embattled American airstrip on Guadalcanal which had been named for a Marine pilot killed earlier in the Battle of Midway. This dirt airstrip, with its Marine and Navy fighter pilots, had held out since August, experiencing daily attacks by Japanese aircraft and naval gunfire. By the time the Japanese destroyers chasing Joe Panebianco and his fellow crewmen got turned around and headed for Henderson Field, the field had dried out from earlier rains and the fighters were able to get airborne. They pounced on the Japanese ships and sank or disabled all three of them. This was the last serious threat to Henderson Field in the Battle for Guadalcanal.

The Solomon Island area is also where President John F. Kennedy was wounded during World War II. In 1943, Kennedy was assigned to command a PT boat operating northwest of Guadalcanal in support of landings being made by the Marines on the island of New Georgia. It was there, one night on a combat mission, that his boat was intentionally rammed and sliced in two by a Japanese destroyer. Kennedy was injured but saved himself and a fellow crewman by swimming for four hours until he reached a nearby island. Kennedy's heroic action and the story of PT-109 became widely known when he began his race for the presidency in 1960.

2. Around The World

Commentary

For America, World War II started in the Pacific but the ensuing conflict was worldwide. Shortly after the attack on Pearl Harbor, the United States declared war on Japan. In a matter of days, war against Germany had been declared. Thus, the United States was confronted by having to wage war in both Europe and the Pacific. Under "lend-lease" policies enacted before its entry into war, America had been supplying the Soviet Union, Britain and China with military equipment. Now, the country would need to continue that effort as well as arm and supply its own military forces.

Some American troops would end up fighting in both theaters of war. This was the case with Sam Price. His ship, the USS *Ancon,* was the command ship for most of the allied landings in the Mediterranean. After that, the ship moved to England and ultimately became a part of the command organization for D-Day in Normandy. With the major amphibious landings in Europe complete, the *Ancon* was next sent through the Panama Canal to assist in the operation to take the Island of Okinawa from the Japanese. In his travels during four years in the Army, Sam Price nearly circumnavigated the globe.

The same can be said of Tony Mangine, a pilot in the U.S. Army Air Corps. Mangine started his Army life as a pilot in the Ferry Command. Airplanes had to be transported to the front and the quickest way to get them there was to fly them. As you will see from his account, sometimes Mangine would fly to South America, then across to Africa. From there he would go either across the African continent to Khartoum and on to Cairo and Karachi in India, or he would head north through Morocco and into Italy or Corsica. At other times, he took the northern route delivering planes through Labrador and Greenland into Scotland. At war's end, Mangine was sent to fly "the Hump," over the Himalayas from India into China. Travel maps showing the extent of global travels for Tony Mangine, Sam Price and others interviewed for this book have been included to give some understanding of the extent of the worldwide commitment of the United States during World War II.

The world became a small place for everyone who fought overseas during the war. Some saw places they would never want to see again. For others, it was an adventure that would never be equaled. For the United States, it was a mind-boggling logistical effort, a challenge which no country had ever before tried to master. For those men and women who were involved in it, it was a new experience unparalleled and unknown by prior generations. Americans were on every continent and on every ocean taking the war to the enemy. That it could all be done and brought to a successful conclusion in four years is a record that will probably stand unbroken in human history.

Sam Price's ship, the USS *Ancon.*

[The following letter was sent by First Sergeant Samuel Price to his family as his ship, the USS *Ancon,* was enroute from Europe to the Pacific. He was on a command ship which was responsible for landing troops during the many amphibious landings of the war.]

28 December 1944
Underway

Dear Family,

Christmas was as enjoyable as it possibly could be under the circumstances, due mainly to the thoughtfulness of you and others at home who took time out to insure that at least one aspect of the Yuletide spirit was not missing. There was no snow, there was no Christmas tree, but there were plenty of presents—and all wrapped the way they should be wrapped on such a day. Those of us who did have packages gathered them all together Christmas morning and opened them in a more-or-less community fashion. I thought of you at home, opening your presents at about the same time, and I wished that I had been more tangibly represented at the festivities...

On December 1st, I was promoted from acting to honest-to-goodness First Sergeant: the most significant difference being that I draw $138 base pay per month instead of the ordinary Sergeant's $78. It is quite a jump, financially speaking. With 20 per cent additional pay for overseas duty, I am now drawing approximately $160 per month (insurance subtracted)...

I took my last shore liberty on Christmas day. I had no idea that it would be my last, but I wanted to give you a phone call and, if nothing else, at least say "Merry Christmas." But telephone connections were so poor, the lines so full of traffic, that it was a hopeless proposition. The operator informed me that I would be lucky to get my call through in six hours. It is tough enough on ordinary days, on holidays three times as bad. It was a disappointment, especially so when I learned that I wouldn't have another chance to call.

My love to all—and let's hope that this will be not only a "Happy" but a "Homecoming" New Year.[1]

Sam.

Samuel P. Price
First Sergeant, U.S. Army Reserve

I graduated from Amherst College in December, 1942, and, of course, the war was on. We were all going in, it just depended on when and where. Actually, I had tried to join the Navy V-7 program earlier that year but I flunked the physical because of high albumen in my urine. It's something I'd had in the past from time to time but it had always gone away. But the Navy said, "Sorry, we won't accept you for enlistment." So I kept going to school and waited for my draft notice. In the meantime, I accelerated my program at Amherst so that I could graduate in 1942. When the notice for my draft physical came, my doctor put me on a diet so that the albumen problem would go away and I passed the physical with flying colors.

While at Amherst, I had taken a course in cryptography which had been offered because of the war-related need for cryptographers. It was a fascinating thing for me. I had always liked puzzles and making and breaking codes was something I became good at. I cracked that course and got my best college grades in that subject. Hell, with that, I figured I'd hold out and at least make Major! (laughs) Well, it didn't quite work out that way. I went to Fort Niagara with all of the other recruits from our hometown and from there got special orders to report to Vint Hill Farms, Maryland, near Washington, DC. It was a training facility for cryptography and most of us were enlisted men. I was put in an enlisted man's barracks and found that there were Ph.D.'s sleeping on all the bunks around me. It quickly became apparent that I was with an educated group of people who were not destined to become officers. Most of us would remain enlisted men throughout the duration of the war. One of our instructors there was McGeorge Bundy who later became a major figure in the Kennedy and Johnson administrations. In addition to training in cryptography, we had seven days of basic training, learned how to shoot a rifle, and then we were sent to our duty stations.

Although I was in the Army, I was assigned to a ship and went to Hampton Roads, Virginia, and boarded the USS *Ancon*, a former cruise ship that had sailed in the Caribbean prior to the war. It had been named after a mountain in Maryland, had been converted for use as a communications and command ship, had already been in the North African invasions and was now headed back to the Mediterranean for the Sicily and Salerno landings. On June 8, 1943, we left the east coast for North Africa and dipped south in order to avoid the German submarine wolf packs. We were given the option of sleeping on deck, just in case we were torpedoed, but most of us said: "Oh, to hell with it..." and took our chances and slept about four decks down along with the rest of the enlisted men. The only incident that took place on the crossing was that one of the cruisers in our convoy lost a scout plane. It went out looking for submarines and never came back.

The *Ancon* was an unusual ship since we always had an admiral and usually other field grade officers on board. Because of all the brass, even eating became a hassle. We actually had seven mess halls on the ship. There was a mess for the Filipino stewards, one for the enlisted men, a third mess for the noncommissioned officers, another for warrant officers, a fifth mess for junior officers, a sixth for the senior officers and a top-of-the-line mess for the field grade officers. Nothing like the military when it came to complicating things. But it was an exciting place to be. We were at the center of the action in Southern Europe and were the Command Ship for the Commander of the Allied Amphibious Force, Admiral H.K. Hewitt. Eventually, we would participate in the Sicily, Salerno and Anzio landings and later be involved at Normandy. After that we would be sent to the Pacific and participate in the invasion of Okinawa. In many ways, we saw the whole war and were able to view the "big picture" as things developed both in Europe and in the Pacific.

We arrived in the Mediterranean on June 22, 1943, at Mers-el-Kebir, a port city near Oran, Algeria. This area had been taken by allied troops in the fighting against Rommel in 1942 and was now a training area and embarkation point for the upcoming Italian campaign. We arrived off Sicily on July 9th, the night before the invasion. During the invasion we quickly became informed of a tragedy when American Navy ships began firing on our own planes while the airborne troops were being landed. It was unfortunate, but one of those disastrous things that happens in war. The *Ancon* had some armament but did not fire. We knew that something was wrong. We were quite close to the beach and it was at night. There were fireworks like the 4th of July, and I saw a plane go down. Later, we found out that it had been one of our own, shot down by friendly fire. [2]

Our job during these invasions was to send and receive messages to and from the forces on the shore, and then to communicate with the over-all Commander who, in the case of Sicily, was General Alexander whose head-

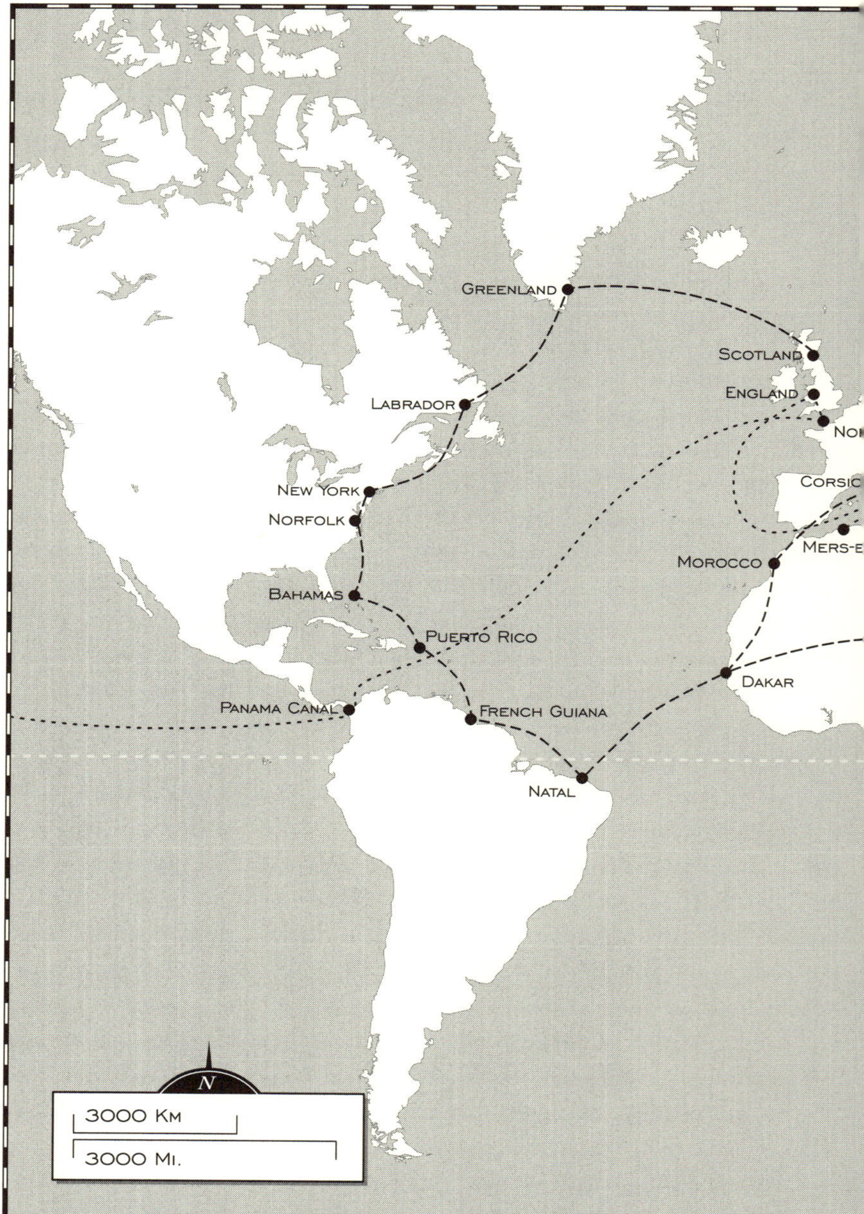

Travels of Tony Mangine and Sam Price

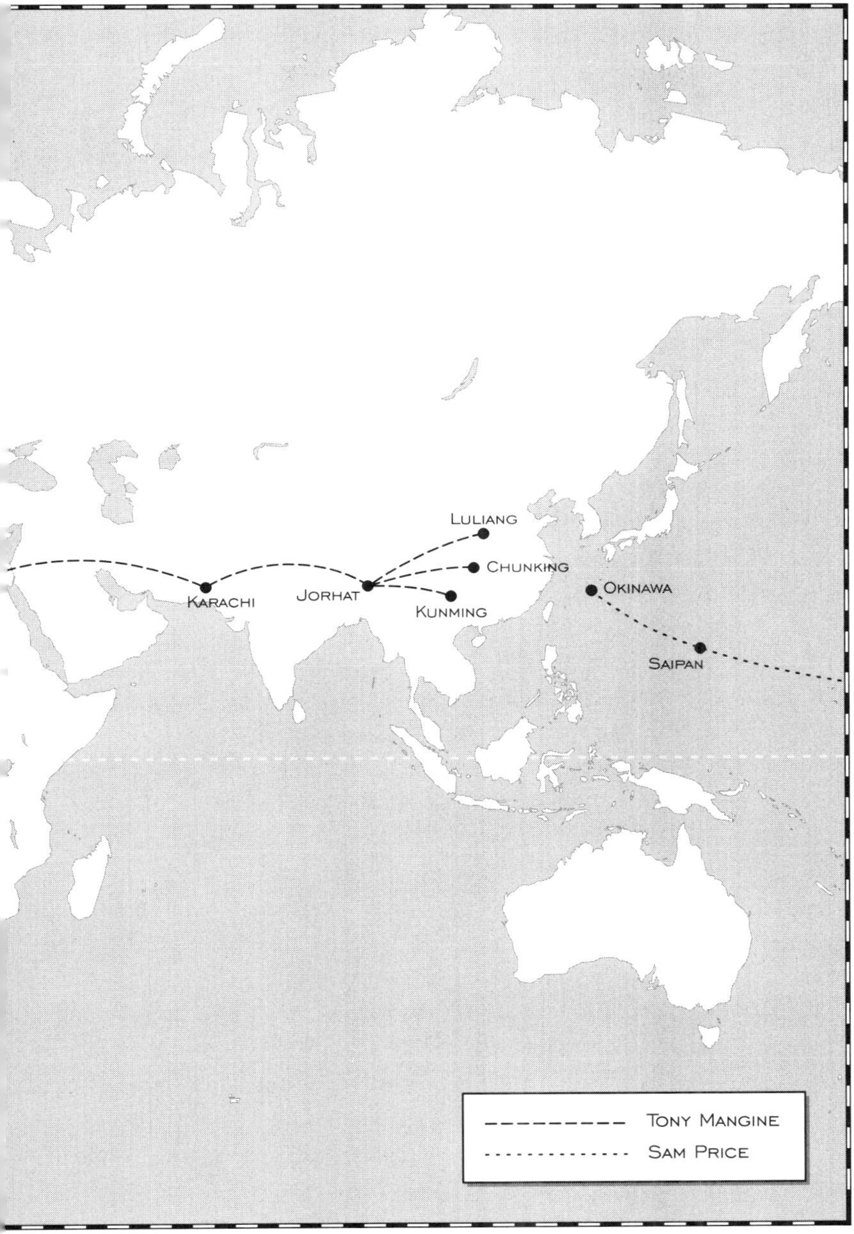

Luliang
Chunking
Jorhat
Karachi
Kunming
Okinawa
Saipan
Tony Mangine
Sam Price

quarters was in North Africa. Once our troops had a foothold, the field command would shift to the beach, but until then, the combat command was on the *Ancon.* It was always a very intense time for us. We would be four hours on duty and four hours off until the beachhead had been secured. It was also a time when the seven mess halls on the ship would actually shut down. We would be issued K rations or C rations and the ship would stay at GQ (General Quarters) until the troops were ashore and the command had shifted to the beach. The job of our unit was to encode and decode classified messages, many of which were "top secret" and "urgent." The high-speed radiomen we had on board would then key the messages over the air to other command centers. I guess my biggest contribution to the war effort was some practical advice I suggested. It took time to encode and further delays to decode at the other end, and you were never sure that the message had been encoded correctly until you received an acknowledgement from the other end. I suggested that we have one guy encoding and another decoding at the same time on the *Ancon* and that way we would be sure the message was correct when it went out. That procedure was then adopted for the duration of the war.

We saw a lot of action on the beach at Sicily, but it was later at Salerno before we saw much that affected us. By the time we got to Salerno in September of '43, the Germans had figured out that the *Ancon* was the nerve center of the operation and they attempted to bomb us. For protection at night, we would be sent away from the beachhead under the protection of a couple of destroyers, so that, hopefully, German planes wouldn't find us. Well, one night at Salerno, some Stuka dive bombers did find us. The destroyers escorting us threw up a smoke screen to try and hide us, but you could hear the screaming sound as the Stukas came in on their bomb runs. It was scary as hell, frankly, because you knew that the bomb was going to be dropped and you might be nothing in another second or two. There was no place to run or hide and no foxhole to get into. You just had to wait until it was over. Some of the bombs that night fell about 25 yards from us. You could see the geysers go up but we were lucky. We never got hit. The only casualties we had were guys who got hit by our own antiaircraft flak dropping down on top of us.

Of course, the time between invasions was a lot different. War, they say, is characterized by moments of terror and then days of boredom. That was certainly true on the *Ancon*. To help pass the time, we organized a bridge group in the enlisted man's mess and I became quite proficient at the game. There were also some memorable liberty experiences. My brother Charlie [see his story in Chapter 14] had introduced me to an Army friend of his by the name of McCloskey who also went by the name of Harry Lyness. (Why two names? I don't know.) Lyness was supposedly well-connected with the international society set, and when he found out that we were going to be going to England to prepare for the invasion of Europe, he suggested that we contact some of his lady friends. Among those he suggested we call were Bebe Daniels, the actress; the Dowager Marchioness of Milford-Haven; and Lady Mountbatten.

Well, when we got to London, a friend of mine, Jack Wilson, and I got tickets to *Panama Hattie*–a show then playing in Picadilly Circus. We went to the show and during intermission I asked the usher to take a note backstage to Bebe Daniels. I mean, what the hell, we're in the Army with nothing better to do...we might as well take a shot and see if we can meet her. I'll be damned if she didn't invite us backstage and we had a nice conversation. Then I mentioned to her that Harry Lyness had suggested we make contact with her and she had this blank stare as if to say "Who'n the hell is Harry Lyness (laughs)?"

We had also sent a letter to Lady Mountbatten using Lyness's name but had not given her a London address because, at the time, we were still on the ship at Plymouth. Well, she contacted the ship after we were in London, tracked us down at our hotel, and invited us over. Just before we went to her apartment, we stopped by the Red Cross Center in London and while we were there we met Fred Astaire's sister, Adele. She did volunteer work at the center, had married an English guy, Lord Cavendish, and was now known as Lady Cavendish. I remember her complaining about what a drunk he was. I also remember being impressed that I had met Fred Astaire's sister (laughs)! While we were there, we met an American girl and when she found out that we were going to Lady Mountbatten's, she wanted to go along. So, Jack and I took her along and what a night that was. It was a real fancy flat and quite a party was going on. Lady Mountbatten was very cordial to us and we had a delightful conversation about her work during the war. At one point she said, "Excuse me, I need to talk to the Air Vice Marshall. He's just back from India and has some words from my Dicky." (Apparently, "Dicky" was the nick-name that she gave her husband, Lord Louis Mountbatten, who was British Commander in the China, Burma, India theater.) In any event, she never brought up Harry Lyness's name so we were never sure if Harry Lyness knew any of these people. Maybe he put the whole thing on. We were unable to make direct contact with the Dowager Marchioness of Milford-Haven, and so never met her.

D-Day at Normandy was, of course, an incredible event. I had been on three previous invasions but none of them compared to Normandy. There were ships as far as you could see. Your only thought was that no enemy could withstand this firepower and incredible assault force. It was just too big. We were the command ship for Omaha Beach and Admiral John Hall and Major General Leonard Gerow, Commander of V Corps (the 1st and 29th Infantry Divisions), were on board. Although we knew there was a lot of action on the beach, we didn't actually receive any shelling that morning. The sea was rough and we had quite a few men on board who had to be landed. The boats were bouncing and men were jumping from the nets trying to get in. It was when the boats came back though that we knew that the fighting was bad. As soon as our boats off-loaded troops on the beach, they would load up with the wounded and bring them back to the ship. It wasn't a pleasant sight. On the night of D-Day we got strafed by a German aircraft and our gunners returned fire. John Hicks from NBC News was on our ship at the time, and I still have the live account he gave over the radio that night as the German planes came over and our machine guns and anti-aircraft guns were shooting at them.[3]

After Normandy, we were sent to the Pacific via the Panama Canal. We stopped at Saipan, which had been taken earlier by U.S. forces, but then moved on to Okinawa for the invasion. We were the command ship there for the Seventh Amphibious Force and for the Second Marine Division. The landing actually wasn't too bad. It was later, as the Marines pushed inland, that the fighting really got intense. The big thing about Okinawa, of course, was the Japanese kamikaze raids. Those planes came right over us several times but they were heading for the bigger ships, like the battleships and cruisers, and pretty much left us alone. I remember it being very hectic with the radio messages flying back and forth ferociously during those kamikaze raids. When we were off duty, we would go topside and you could see those suckers coming in. Once again, we were scared to death, because you knew that if they ever hit you it would be all over.

After Okinawa, those of us on the *Ancon* were beginning to wonder how much longer our luck could hold out. I had been on four invasions in Europe and one in the Pacific and the ship had not been hit. It was with some relief then when we heard about the dropping of the atomic bomb on Japan. It was apparent from the fighting in Okinawa that the invasion of the Japanese homeland would be a bloody operation, and we were all worried about it. It wasn't long after the second bomb was dropped that Japan announced its surrender. Because of the length of my time on board, I was almost immediately relieved and sent back to the States. The *Ancon* was sent to Tokyo Bay for the surrender ceremonies without me, but I never felt that I missed anything. I was getting out of the Army and was on my way home!"

[Sam Price went to law school after the war and then returned home and joined his father's law firm. He is retired now, but still practices law from time to time.]

GENERAL ORDERS: HEADQUARTERS, ARMY AIR FORCES
INDIA BURMA THEATER
NUMBER 149 A.P.O. 671, 27 June 1945

II. AWARDS OF THE AIR MEDAL.

1. Pursuant to authority contained in Army Regulations 000-45, War Department, Washington, D.C., dated 22 September 1943, the Air Medal is hereby awarded to the following named officer(s) and enlisted men of the India China Division, Air Transport Command, for meritorious achievement by participating in more than two hundred fifty (250) hours of operational flight in transport aircraft over the dangerous and difficult India-China air routes, where exposure to enemy interception and attack was probable and expected. Flying at night as well as by day, at high altitudes over impassable, mountainous terrain through areas characterized by extremely treacherous weather conditions necessitating long periods of operation on instruments, often encountering severe icing conditions and mechanical difficulties requiring courageous and superior performance of their respective duties to overcome, they accomplished their missions with distinction. Their achievement in the face of the hazards and difficulties faced regularly and continuously with steadfast devotion to duty, reflects much credit on themselves and the Army Air Forces of the United States…

ANTHONY MANGINE, 0508921, First Lieutenant, Air Corps, as pilot and co-pilot, from 26 February 1945 to 19 May 1945.

As a young man, you don't think about it, but in retrospect that was some pretty tough flying. You know, we only had LF (low frequency) beacons for navigation and we had to squeeze between those peaks through mountain passes in order to get to China and then back to India. Plus, I was only a Lieutenant and they gave the Captains and higher the better planes...what do you expect, it was the Army way. That's what happened to me that stormy night we had to bail out in India on the way back. The engines in that old B-24 were worn out and used a lot of fuel...we just didn't have enough fuel to get back. But, hey, I made it and since then I've been flying for almost 40 years.

Tony Mangine
Lieutenant, U.S. Army Reserve

[Tony Mangine flew "the Hump" between India and China during the war. The language of the Air Medal graphically portrays the risks involved in this type of flying. Like Sam Price, he also nearly circled the world–only his travel was done as a ferry pilot for aircraft being delivered to the fighting fronts.]

I've been flying almost my whole life. When I started, the airport at home just had a turf strip, the runway was all grass. Mom and Dad owned the restaurant and tavern called Ma's and Pa's at the bottom of Airport Hill. Heck, I could walk up the hill to the airport for flying lessons and did. I got my pilot's license in 1932, when I was 18, and have been flying ever since. Back in those days, I flew primarily single engine airplanes and did a lot of the early commercial flying in town. One of our big customers was the President of the local telephone company. He really liked to fly. I also became an instructor and so had quite a few hours in airplanes by the time World War II rolled around.

I figured I would be called up anyway, so in early 1942 I went to talk to the Army...they needed pilots. For the first few months, I was assigned as a civilian pilot with the 4th Ferrying Group in Wilmington, Delaware. We were basically ferrying planes around the United States. The CO of the outfit was Colonel Barry Goldwater who later ran for President, a good pilot and well-liked fellow. Because we were right near the Glen Mitchell Aircraft Company in Baltimore, we did a lot of ferrying of B-25s and B-

THE TAIL OF THIS B-24 WAS DESTROYED WHEN ANOTHER AMERICAN BOMBER IN FORMATION WAS SHOT DOWN AND CRASHED THROUGH IT AS IT PLUNGED TOWARD THE GROUND. THE PILOT WAS SOMEHOW ABLE TO MAKE AN EMERGENCY LANDING ON CORSICA.

26s. A lot of our pickups would be at the factory and we would fly the planes all over the country: Arizona, California, the midwest...wherever they were needed.[4]

I'll never forget one of my early trips. I was sent down to Washington, DC, to Bolling Air Base, right across the Potomac from Washington National Airport. We were supposed to pick up a B-25 there and fly it to Tucson. I was under orders never to fly a plane unless it had been flown in the last 30 days. When I went inside to check the paper work on that particular plane, I found out that it hadn't been flown in almost 90 days. Then I checked out the brakes and the accumulators were shot, and when I tried to move the throttles they were stuck. The Colonel in charge said, "I can get this stuff fixed in a couple of hours," so my copilot and I left to kill some time in a drug store. He was quite a lady's man and there were usually girls hanging around the soda fountains at drug stores.

When we got back to the field, the Colonel said the plane was ready to go. I asked, "Has anybody flown it?" and he said "No." My response was that we weren't supposed to fly it until somebody had test flown it. He was

Mangine standing between two of his crew members at the pyramids in Egypt.

a young Colonel, 25 or 28 years old, and he started getting porky with me and told me to take it. "I can't do it," I said, "until somebody takes it up and flies it." So finally he said, "OK, I'll do it," and he took with him a couple of friends who were around the hanger looking for a plane ride.

When we got back to the field, the Colonel and his buddies were up flying, checking out the plane, so my copilot and I went out on the ramp and waited for them to return. Suddenly, my copilot turned to me and shouted, "Tony, they're in trouble!" And sure enough, the plane was approaching the airfield and an engine was smoking. The approach was too high and one engine was out. When the Colonel saw he was going to overshoot the field, he gunned the good engine to try and reach a runway across the river at Washington National Airport. But he hit the power too hard and it flipped the plane over. The plane spun right in on the field and everyone on it was killed. When I got back to the Ferrying Group in Wilmington, were they ever happy that I had stuck to my guns and not taken that airplane! That plane was not ready to fly.

Things went okay in 1942, but more and more they wanted military pilots. So in January, 1943, I received my commission as a Second Lieutenant in the Army. Now that they had made me an officer, I guess they had to try and teach me what that meant and so they sent me off to an Army Air Forces Officer Training School in Miami Beach, FL. That was a lot of fun, and I graduated on May 1, 1943. From there I went to the 2nd Ferrying Group operating out of Birmingham, AL.

One of the planes we flew a lot was the A-30. It was a heavy, twin-engine fighter/bomber and we had to deliver a lot of them to the British. We would fly them out to Nassau in the Bahamas and turn them over to the RAF (Royal Air Force). I couldn't believe how cheap the booze was out there. You could buy Scotch for two or three dollars a bottle! It was hard to get good booze in those days, so I would load up with it and eventually get it back to my parents' restaurant. One day, a Colonel in our command asked, "Tony, how are you getting all of that booze home?" I told him how I did it. "Take the silk out of your parachute, and fill the bag with booze. It's heavy, but it works!" At first, he was worried about what would happen without a parachute, but I reminded him that if he had to parachute into the Atlantic Ocean he probably wouldn't live anyway (laughs). From then on, he started scheduling himself for more ferrying trips to the Bahamas (more laughs)!

Sometimes we would have to ferry planes to Karachi, India. The British had a big base and factory there. Hundreds of Indian women worked in it and they would retrofit things into the planes that the British wanted. That was always quite a trip. We would fly to Puerto Rico and gas up. The next stop was usually French Guiana on the coast of South America and then we would follow the coast down to Natal, Brazil. From there, we would start the big hop across the South Atlantic to Ascension Island and then on to Dakar, Africa. Our next stop would be Khartoum, in the Sudan, all the way on the other side of Africa. You talk about a long hop over nothing. Most of it was over desert. If we went down, we figured nobody was coming out! How would they ever find you? From Khartoum, we would fly up to Cairo. That's one place I never thought I'd get to, but here we were in the land of the pyramids! From Cairo, we would make another big jump to Karachi; and then, of course, we would have the long ride home, hitchhiking back to the U.S. on other airplanes so that we could pick up another aircraft to ferry someplace.

A couple of times we had to fly planes to Europe and would take the northern route through Labrador and Greenland and on into Scotland. I'll never forget one ride back on a MAT (Military Air Transport) plane. We always played craps to kill time and we had one helluva crap game going in the back of the plane. It was a pretty smooth ride. We were at about 10,000 ft. and all of a sudden the plane hit some severe, clear air turbulence. In all of my years of flying, I've never seen anything like it. Boom, clear as a bell, we're all up on the ceiling, all of us! Then crash we're back on the floor, and boom were back on the ceiling! The cards, dice, money, everything flew all over the place. I'll never forget that crap game!

I remember one trip, sometime in 1944, when we had to take a B-25 to Italy. It was the usual run down through Puerto Rico, South America and then to Dakar, Africa. We stopped and fueled up at Dakar and headed for Casablanca. By this time the Allies had invaded Italy and they needed more planes in that part of the Mediterranean. When we lifted off at Dakar, everything seemed to be going okay. We flew over mountainous and desert terrain as we headed north and the weather was good. All of a sudden, the port engine started smoking and then the oil pressure fell off. I feathered the engine to keep it from freezing up and headed back toward Dakar. The B-25 was an amazing ship! Those 1,800-h.p. Pratt and Whitneys were powerful and you could trim the plane out on one engine so that single engine flight could be maintained without losing altitude. That's how we limped back into Dakar.

The U.S. had a major repair facility there and I figured we could get the engine repaired quickly. Right after we landed, I ran into a buddy who was heading back home and I told him, "Hey, tell my wife I'll be a little late getting back from this trip. I don't want her to worry." Well, I was a "little" late...about a month late. They didn't have the right parts for the engine and so we had to cool our heals in Dakar for about three weeks. Needless to say, I caught hell from my wife for being late when I got home (laughs).

We finally got airborne again and flew the plane up to Casablanca, Tripoli, and then across to Naples. Finally, we landed at our destination in Corsica, which at the time was still close to where some of the fighting was going on. Periodically, the Germans would come over and bomb the field, so the night we were there we had to go up into the hills away from the field as a safety precaution. Sure enough, that night the Germans bombed the field. You could see flashes in the sky and hear the bombs exploding and the next morning, when we went back, we found that a lot of the planes had been damaged. Christ, we took over 20 airplanes and they must have wrecked half of 'em! I saw a B-24 there that was truly amazing. Part of the tail was gone and I was told that it had been severed by another B-24 flying above it in formation that had been brought down by enemy flak. The aircraft above had come crashing down through the formation, cut off most of the tail and killed the tail gunner. But the bomber still had enough tail left to make an emergency landing at Corsica. Those B-24s were great airplanes and could take a helluva beating!

In the fall of 1944, I got myself checked out in B-24s and shortly thereafter got my orders to report to India in order to fly the Hump. Our job was to take as much aviation fuel and bombs as we could into China. The Chinese were building air bases so that we could land our B-29s. From those bases, the B-29s could bomb Japan. We would fly in, land, and those Chinese would unload us in nothing flat. I was always amazed by those Chinese. Here they were 1,000 miles from nowhere, coolies pulling huge rollers to pack down those runways...and they had dollar bills! We used to bring in cartons of cigarettes, and some boss or "papa-san" in charge of the roller crews would come over and pay us $10 a carton for American cigarettes. Where did they get that money? Who knows?

I flew copilot until April 1945 and then was checked out as a pilot. It was difficult flying. We lived in a hot, tropical climate in Jorhat, India. We actually lived in small tent-like hooches called "bashas" and had Indian boys who would take care of the places and keep things cleaned up. We had a lot of fun and played a lot of cards. But you would leave that hot climate, climb fully loaded to 15,000-20,000 feet on oxygen where it was below freezing and fly through those passes in the Himalayas. The weather was brutal: freezing rain, ice, headwinds, turbulence...none of us liked the trips. The toughest route was the "Able" route to the north, only 20 miles from Mount Everest. But that was also the safest route because it was farthest away from Japanese-held territory.

The night we bailed out was something. It was May, during the monsoons, and there were a lot of thunderstorms around that night in India. I had an old ship that was hard on gas. The engines ran all right but the rings

Tony Mangine (far right) and crew in front of a B-25.

and valves were shot and it used a lot of gas. I told the Operations guys in Kunming that with the weather and head winds, we didn't have enough fuel to make it back. "Tough luck," the officer on the line said. "You know the rule, we keep all of the fuel and ammo you bring in. We aren't authorized to give you any fuel. Go see the Chaplain!" With that we took off and headed back over the hump.

Sure enough, in India the weather was brutal. Thunder and lightning all over the place. We only had LF (low frequency) radio communications and you couldn't hear anything with the static. I held over Jorhat at about 17,000 feet hoping that the weather would break and we could get in. It wasn't long before the #3 engine quit; we were running out of fuel. I told the boys, "Bail out!" and they all ran for the cargo hatch. It was jammed and so they had to go to the escape hatch near the tail. I made one more procedure turn and got the plane trimmed up with only three engines so that it was flying straight and level. We didn't have an auto pilot so all I could hope was that I could make it to the hatch before some turbulence got us or another engine went out and the plane flipped. You never saw anybody run as fast as I did for that hatch and out I went!

Now, you've gotta realize I had never used a parachute before. I counted and pulled the rip-cord and I had this handle in my hand with nothing attached. I thought I had screwed up or the equipment had failed. I didn't realize that once you pulled it, the rip cord handle separates from the chute. Just then, snap! The chute opened and I started down. As I came out from under the first layer of clouds I saw the lights of the plane. It was out of control, had turned around and was coming at me! "I'll be a son-of-a-gun," I thought, "I got through this whole thing and now the plane is going to kill me!" But at the last minute, it peeled off and headed down out of sight. As I got nearer the ground, I saw through the lightning something that looked like a road, but I also saw what I thought was the Brahma Putra River. It wasn't a river, it was a fog bank. I went into it and then Wham! I hit the trees in the jungle.

The Army had taught us in survival school to always get our chute down and use it as a blanket. I did that, pointed a branch in the direction of that road that I thought I had seen, and then went to sleep. The next morning I started out by compass toward what I thought had been a road. The only problem I had were some jungle leeches that I had to burn off. I used the machete, followed some trails and, would you believe it, around nightfall I came across that road. It actually wasn't a road, it was the one rail line that went from Calcutta to Jorhat. I flagged down the train and within a few hours was back at the base. What were the chances of that happening? In that whole jungle I found the only way out of there. It wouldn't happen again in a million years!

We got back to our base in the opposite order that we bailed out. I bailed out last, but got back first. The radioman was back by the second day and my copilot, the third day. But the engineer didn't have as much luck. He got screwed up. He made a big mistake and tried to start a fire. Why would you try to start a fire in the monsoon rains? It was dark out and while trying to start the fire, he lost his parachute. After three weeks in the bush, he finally stumbled down a stream in the Naga Hills and got to a British outpost. He was really sick, almost died and had been eaten alive by the bugs and leeches.

Of all the flying I have done, the Hump was the toughest. When you've been through something like that, you are never the same. I'm a member of the Hump Pilots Association. There are fewer of us every year, but what happened to us over there in the China-Burma-India theater forever changed our lives. It was an experience that still keeps us close to each other even after all these years.[5]

[Tony Mangine still flies. He is 83 years old and lives with his wife, Evelyn, on a farm on Airport Hill.]

Background and Commentary

[1]Mail is what kept most of our fighting men in World War II on an even keel. Nothing was more eagerly anticipated than "mail call"–receiving mail from home. All outgoing mail was censored by the military so that no adverse information on the war would fall into enemy hands. Letters sent home were not supposed to have any information as to where the writer was and what operations he was involved with; therefore, most letters were quite general in nature. This letter was sent by Sam Price to his family just after Christmas 1944, as his ship was enroute from the European Theater of War to the Pacific where he would participate in the invasion of Okinawa.

The "insurance" referred to in the letter was a payroll deduction for life insurance. All U.S. military personnel were required to carry $5,000 to $10,000 worth of life insurance and the premium was deducted from their paycheck.

[2]The incident described by Sam Price was the unfortunate tragedy that occurred when naval gunfire opened up on the aircraft that were landing the 504th Regimental Combat Team by parachute near Gela, Italy. 145 paratroopers and airmen were killed by friendly fire that night and 23 planes were shot down. It was one of the first major attempts at using paratroopers during the war and, obviously, planning and coordination had gone awry. The U.S. military took steps after that tragedy to improve communications between ground, air and naval forces, and so at least some lessons were learned at Gela. However, waging war is not a perfect science, and deaths by friendly fire would continue to plague U.S. and Allied forces throughout World War II.

[3] During the amphibious landings in the Mediterranean at Sicily, Salerno and Anzio, the USS *Ancon* was the command ship and coordinat-

ed overall operations of the landings prior to command being established on the beachhead. During those operations, such luminary figures as Generals Patton, Mark Clark, Ridgway and Bradley were aboard Sam Price's ship. These were the field commanders who had to await the establishment of command headquarters with communications on the beach before they could disembark and begin leading their forces on land. At Normandy, the *Ancon* became the command ship for General Leonard Gerow, who was the Commanding General of V Corps, the force made up of the 1st and 29th Infantry Divisions that assaulted Omaha Beach. (See the story of Anthony Constanzo of the Big Red One, First Infantry Division, chapter 4.)

[4]On December 29, 1940, in one of his "fireside chats" on the radio, President Franklin Roosevelt told the American people that they must become "the great arsenal of democracy" to help supply those fighting against German aggression. Though the U.S. was not yet in the war, President Roosevelt realized that the British could not hold out against Hitler alone. Thus, he began to sell war material and aircraft to the British and finally instituted "lend-lease" which was a means of sending equipment to the British in return for the American use of certain British bases in the Caribbean. The aircraft, of course, had to be transported to Britain and, for the larger multiengine planes, this often meant they were flown to England. The initial 2,700-mile northern route from Bolling Field in Washington, DC, via Montreal and Newfoundland to Scotland, was named by the British the "Arnold Line," in honor of General "Hap" Arnold, the commander of the U.S. Army Forces. Prior to the end of 1941 and before the entry of the United States into the war, 2,400 planes had already been flown over the Arnold Line and into England.

Initially, a Ferrying Group was set up to do this and the Army Air Force would enter into contracts with commercial pilots to do the piloting. Pan American Airways was enlisted in the effort and other commercial airlines cooperated. Tony Mangine was initially one of these "contract" pilots. However, after war broke out, it became necessary to bring this function directly into the military. A Ferrying Command was formed which eventually became the famous ATC, or Air Transport Command. This was the organization that gave Mangine his "Lieutenant bars" and for whom he worked until the end of the war.

The southern ferrying route, as decribed by Mangine, was truly a monumental undertaking. Extra fuel tanks often had to be installed for planes to make the long jump from South America to Africa. Airfields for refueling and repairs were quickly built and can still be seen today in places like Antigua, Saint Lucia and Jamaica in the Caribbean. The distance from Miami to Cairo was 10,000 miles: it was 4,000 miles to Brazil and then another 6,000 miles to cross the Atlantic and the African continent to Cairo.

Interestingly, ATC was also an organization where women were able to make a mark in World War II. Though not allowed in combat, women were brought in to assist in the ferrying operation. Primarly through the efforts of a famous female pilot of the time, Jackie Cochrane, Arnold created a special force called the "WASPs" (Women Airforce Service Pilots). For the 27 months they were in existence, this group of female pilots completed some 12,650 ferrying missions and flew over 9,000,000 air miles. Commanders in the field would often request that a WASP pilot ferry air-

Tony Mangine in front of his "basha" in India, with his Harley Davidson motorcycle and his pet monkey.

craft, because the planes that they flew generally arrived two or three days earlier than aircraft flown by men. When asked why this was so, "Hap" Arnold replied, "Because she doesn't carry an address book with her!"

Though thousands of airplanes were ferried by the ATC, the greatest number were sent by ship. This was especially true of single-engine fighter aircraft which just did not have the range capability of making these long flights. However, the movement of aircraft to the fighting front, by whatever means, was one of the great logistical feats of World War II. From July 1940 through August 1945, the Army Air Corps took delivery and transported over 230,000 airplanes to places all over the world.

[5]The pilots who flew "the Hump" were engaged in some of the most difficult flying of World War II. The weather conditions included everything from icing at high altitudes to thunderstorms and monsoon rains. Navigational aids were primitive and were limited in most cases to low-frequency radio beacons which did not provide the kind of precision aerial navigation that we have today. After the Japanese cut the Burma Road, all supplies to the Chinese had to be flown in from India. An incredible system of air supply developed which, at its peak, reached over 71,000 tons per month, a rate three times greater than had ever moved over the Burma Road. On its peak day, August 1, 1945, the Air Transport Command of the Army Air Corps flew 1,118 trips and 5,327 tons of air cargo over the Himalayas. The aircraft used in flying "the Hump" were primarily C-47s (which became the famous workhorse DC-3 that built the American airline industry), C-46s and the four-engine C-54. Converted bombers were also flown, like the B-24 that went down in India with Tony Mangine and his crew.

For part of 1944 and into early 1945, a great deal of the tonnage was going to advanced air bases for the new B-29 which could bomb Japan from China. However, after the United States had established air bases on islands like Tinian (see Carl Lenz's story in Chapter 22), it became more efficient to operate the B-29s out of the Central Pacific and so they were withdrawn from the China area of operations. By the time the war ended, a total of 777,000 tons of supplies had been flown over the Hump, at the cost of 910 American flyers who gave their lives to make it happen. The difficult lessons of totally supplying China by air did prove valuable after World War II when, in 1948, the United States was forced to supply Berlin by air after Stalin cut off all road and rail transportation to the city.

3. Fighting In The Arctic

I guess you could say that I spent most of my time in World War II in the Arctic. God, was it cold up there! Our first duty station was in Greenland, at BW-8, an outpost on the west coast. What I remember most about it was that it was 728 miles from the North Pole! Can you believe it? After that, we still stayed in the north, but did so by flying out of Prestwick, Scotland. We would cross the North Sea looking for German submarines and then fly up the coast of Norway looking for German ships in the fjords. Talk about godforsaken country. It was just mountains, trees and snow. Fortunately, we never went down because nobody would have ever found us.

Most of the time we would fly across the top of Norway and Sweden and land in Murmansk, Russia, to refuel. It was a huge port and a lot of our lend-lease equipment to Russia was coming in there by ship. It was cold there, but the port didn't freeze in and could be used most of the year. Our outfit, part of the 4th Bomb Wing, was called "Balchen's Bastards" after our CO, Colonel Berndt Balchen.[1] The Air Corps would send us out wherever there was a shortage of personnel. I guess we did everything that nobody else would do (laughs). One time we even went to Russia to assemble airplanes for the eastern front!

Norm Skinner
Master Sergeant, U.S. Army

[Norm Skinner got an early start in the Army Air Corps by enlisting in the Army in the 1930s. He has seen a lot of life and recently celebrated his 87th birthday.]

I got interested in flying back in 1920. I went to the county fair and paid for an airplane ride with a barnstormer. It was an old Curtiss Jenny biplane. What a thrill! I decided then that I wanted to fly. I kept my eyes open and in 1923 found an ad in *Popular Mechanics* about the Heath School of Aviation in Chicago. I responded, was accepted and went to Chicago to learn to fly. It was sort of a crazy program. Because I didn't have any money, I had to work in a factory run by the school. For every hour I spent in the plant, they would give me one minute of flight time. After three hours and

35 minutes of flight instruction, I soloed. I finally graduated from the Heath School with about 50 hours of flying time and got a certificate. Back in those days you didn't get a license from the federal government. You just flew until somebody thought you knew what you were doing and then you became a pilot (laughs).

In 1927, I got my first flying job with Robinson Aircraft in Maywood, Illinois, a suburb of Chicago. We were flying the U.S. mail between Chicago and St. Louis in open-cockpit, Curtiss D-12 biplanes. When I got there, I was supposed to replace a pilot who was leaving and he flew with me four times so that I would know the route. He was leaving for bigger and better things. His name was Charles Lindbergh and he was leaving to make his flight over the Atlantic. Actually, Lindbergh wasn't a very friendly guy. He was a loner and nobody really liked him. When he was done with a mail flight, he would park the plane, not even go into the operations shack, jump in his Model-T and leave the field. I can't say we were sorry to see him go.

I flew the mail for about a year, until Robinson Aircraft lost the U.S. Mail contract and that put them under. It was fun flying that route. We had no radio navigational aids. We would fly the "iron-beam," following the railroad that ran from Chicago to St. Louis. I got to know every farm field and house along that route! The only memorable event was the crash landing I had to make one winter day. The engine quit and so I landed in a farm pasture near the railroad. The farmer came out, we loaded the mail in his truck, drove it to the nearest train station and put it on the next train for St. Louis. The next day I disconnected the fuel line and, sure enough, it had frozen and was full of ice. We thawed it out in the farmhouse, I put it back on, started the plane, took off from the pasture and flew back to Chicago. Just another day flying the mail!

After Robinson Aircraft folded, I came back home. My Mom was sick and needed me. That was 1928. I had saved some money and bought an old Jenny with that grand old OX-5 engine in it. The OX-5 was an eight-cylinder, water-cooled, very dependable, 80-h.p. engine manufactured by Glen Curtiss and used in World War I and in the early days of aviation. (I later became a member of the American Pioneer OX-5 Association. You had to have flown a plane with that engine in it or worked as an OX-5 mechanic in order to be a member.) I did some barnstorming of my own around western New York, but needed a job, so I ended up working for Curtiss-

Wright in Buffalo. It was a factory job—metal testing the airplanes. But at least it involved airplanes and so I was happy.

In 1932, I decided to join the Army Air Corps. The Army was starting to get more serious about aviation, but they still didn't have basic training for aviation cadets. So they sent me to Madison Barracks in Watertown, New York, for basic training in the artillery. (Thank God, it was the last time I saw the artillery. It wasn't my cup of tea.) In July 1933, I was transferred to Kelly Field in San Antonio; at least I was getting back toward aviation. One day we were sent out to a big cotton field outside of town. There was nothing there but some tents where we slept. "Stick around," they said, "This is going to be an airfield." And sure enough, bulldozers started to roll in and we watched while they built us an airfield. It became Randolph Field and the Army started training pilots.

My problem was that I was an enlisted man and didn't have a college education. (At that time, all officers had to be college-trained and all pilots were supposed to be officers or college-trained cadets.) The Army, though, didn't have enough officers to fill all of the classes and I had flying experience; so Colonel Estabrook, a World War I ace, said, "Skinner, you can get your wings and we'll make you a pilot, but you can't get a commission!" That was good enough for me and that's how I became an Army Air Corps pilot.

I loved those early days in the Air Corps, but they were soon to end. The Army was small, there wasn't much commitment to aviation, and so in 1936 I was discharged to the reserves and sent home. I went to work in a factory, Empire Case Goods, but flying never got out of my blood. I yearned to get back to it and it finally happened. In 1938, things had started to heat up in Europe and the government had decided to start beefing up the Army again. I got recalled and was first sent to Mitchell Field on Long Island and then to Westover Air Base in Massachusetts. At Westover, I became a part of the 4th Bomb Wing.

In 1941, the U.S. had begun a major program in lend-lease with the British. This was before the war really started for us. We were not really "lending," but in fact were giving the British millions of dollars worth of military equipment, including airplanes, so that they could keep fighting the Germans. Obviously, we needed a way to fly these planes to England and that meant there was a need for refueling and repair stations along the way. In the summer of 1941, a part of our outfit was sent to Greenland to set up one of these bases. We went by ship in a convoy escorted by British corvettes, small destroyers. We were to establish a base called Bluie West 8 (BW-8) just north of the Arctic Circle on the west coast of Greenland, located on the Sonderstrom Fjord. On the way though, we had to stop at BW-5 and clean out some Germans. They were there guarding a cryolite mine (a mineral used in making aluminum) and had taken it over when they invaded Denmark. Because we weren't at war with Germany, it was British commandos who actually did the work of rounding up the Germans. There wasn't much to it, and in a couple of days we headed on up to BW-8. As I mentioned, it was located 728 miles from the North Pole![2]

It's hard to describe how barren Greenland is. You can only see rock and soil up to one or two miles from the ocean's edge and then you run into the ice sheet. Sometimes the ice sheet comes down to the water's edge, especially along the fjords. When you fly over it, it looks like a white sea; it looks like the clouds do above a solid overcast when you are flying. There are no landmarks except for the mountains which periodically poke up out of the ice. This was to be my home for over a year. While I was there, war broke out and this changed everything.

Our main mission in Greenland was to be a weather-observation station and to act as a refueling and supply base for airplanes being flown to England. Needless to say, the weather was brutal. The winds would often exceed 100 m.p.h. and temperatures would fall to 80 degrees below zero. It was nothing to see an oil drum or some big box go flying over your head if it wasn't tied down. To avoid the wind, we built most of our buildings in shallow ravines to stay out of the direct blast of the weather. We would tie the buildings down with cables and cover them with dirt. It was the only way to insure that we wouldn't be blown away. Our airfield was actually five miles from the base because it was the only flat area around. You didn't want to have to walk that on a cold day!

Most of the time I was in Greenland, I flew a YAC 64 Norseman, a Canadian-built plane. We also had a couple of P-40 fighters there. We flew mostly for weather observation and sometimes for search and rescue. There wasn't much liberty way up there either. There were a few Eskimos around but no town to speak of. Sometimes, to kill time, we would go out to the glaciers for target practice. Just the crack of rifle fire would often cause enough reverberation to get chunks of ice to fall off. One day we were doing that and one of the guys saw something dark on the glacier, caught in the ice. He fired and a big chunk came down and, would you believe, there was a frozen prehistoric caveman in it. He was dressed in fur and there wasn't a mark on him. We told the base commander and the doctor back at camp about him and they wanted to take a look. So back we went to the ice block and the Doc said, "You'd better chip him out, this is a real find!" So we did, brought him back and supposedly he was shipped later to the Smithsonian. We never heard. In typical GI fashion, we stood him up outside one of the hootches and the guys would flick up his animal skin to see his privates. The Doc finally put a stop to it (laughs)!

We were supposed to be relieved in six months, but our relief crew never made it. Their ship was torpedoed just outside the fjord and all 800 men went down or froze in the water. The ship that went down was the USAT *Dorchester*, a coastal steamer from Boston that had been converted for use in the war. It was a sister ship to the two ships, *Chatham* and *Fairfax*, that had brought us to BW-8. What a tragedy that was. We all knew that it could have been us on the ship. At the time, we had a real happy-go-lucky chaplain by the name of Father Sullivan. Everybody liked him and he loved to play poker. He had been a missionary in Greenland once and so knew the people and the area very well. When they brought those frozen bodies in from the *Dorchester*, they stacked them like cordwood on the pier. Father Sullivan stayed there all day and all night until the last body was brought in, and he gave all of them, Catholics or not, the last rites. Within a month of that, his black hair had turned white. It had a terrible effect on him and eventually he had to be medivaced back to the States for mental help.

Late in 1942, we finally got relieved and were sent to Prestwick, Scotland. The 4th Bomb Wing was getting back together, though we never would totally. Initially, we flew B-17 missions over Norway. (Major Carl Russell was our Flight Commander.)[3] Most of the time, I was a gunner but because of my pilot training, I would also fill in as an extra copilot. On most of our flights we would take off from Scotland, fly across the North Sea and then go up the Norwegian coast. The Germans would hide ships in the Norwegian fjords and they also controlled some cryolite mines. If we didn't find shipping, we would usually drop our bombs on the mines, railroads or port facilities. By the time we got to northern Norway, we probably had been in the air five or six hours and would be in need of fuel. So we would fly over the top of Norway, Sweden and Finland and land in Murmansk to rearm and fuel-up. Believe me, if we had ever gone down up there, no one would have found us. That country was truly the end of the world!

In the spring of 1943, we got one of our "fill-in" assignments. In the battle of North Africa, the British had lost most of their photo and reconnaissance aircraft and more photos were needed. So, about 20 of us were shipped off to North Africa. We flew on a B-17 out of southern England at about 100 feet off the water to avoid German radar. It was a direct shot, probably a six-to-eight-hour flight, and we landed at Oran, Algeria. By that time, the Germans had been squeezed into a small area around Tunis, and we and the British were pounding the hell out of 'em. My job was to pilot an old, single-engine, YAC-64 Norseman (like the one we had in Greenland), with a photographic officer in the back seat, to try and get photos after the bombers had finished bombing a target. We flew alone and weren't armed so our best defense was to fly low. That old barnstorming experience came in handy and a few times I brought that officer back with branches and leaves still stuck to the plane. I swear the guy's white socks had turned brown (laughs)!

We operated out of Bizerte on the Tunisian coast but also flew to the British side on the east and operated with them. Our final missions were over Pantelleria, an island off the coast of Tunisia, located between North Africa and Sicily. Eisenhower wanted it taken before the start of the Sicily invasion because it was an observation point for the Germans and had an airfield. The Air Corps bombed the hell of out it and we took pictures of the bombing. The Navy also shelled it from ships and finally the infantry made an amphibious landing. It wasn't much of a battle and the Axis troops, primarily Italian, surrendered without a lot of fighting. It seemed like a long time then, but we were probably only in North Africa for a couple of months before heading back to Scotland for more of our Arctic flying.

As I mentioned, during the summer of 1943, about a hundred of us went on a mission to Russia to assemble P-40 fighter planes for the Russians. We landed in Murmansk and were taken by ship to Archangel, another Russian town along the arctic coast. The pier at Murmansk was an incredible structure and stretched way out into the harbor. It was jammed with supplies from the States. Everything from jeeps to planes to food rations were piled up on that pier. The GIs there said that at one time there was a pile of blood plasma on the pier, but that the Russians either didn't need it or didn't know what to do with it, and they finally bulldozed it all off the pier and into the ocean. The Russians also thought that our butter was grease. They used it to grease their equipment and then ridiculed us when we put it on our bread. What a place! [4]

Archangel was another godforsaken place, exposed to the elements, out on the tundra up there on the Arctic coast. We were put in tents on one side of an airfield and our job was to uncrate P-40 fighters, put the wings on them, get them ready to fly, make one test flight, and then give them over to the Russians. It was strange the way it worked. The Russian soldiers were told to have no contact with us, and so after we had tested an airplane, we would park it out in the middle of the field and turn the engine off. Then a truck would bring out a Russian pilot and he would start it up and take off for the eastern front to use it against the Germans. The Russians were supposed to be our allies but you would have never known it. They almost acted like we were the enemy. I guess we should have realized then that we were bound to have trouble with them after the war.

In the fall of '43, I was sent back to Prestwick for more of the northern B-17 patrols over Norway. None of us had much time for the Swedes because of their neutrality in the war. Although they were supposedly neutral, the Germans regularly went through Sweden on their way to Norway and we knew that. We weren't supposed to fly over Sweden but who was to stop us? Besides, we were flying the Norway/Sweden border and periodically we would just drift into Sweden. I recall one day when we spotted a Swedish patrol boat down below us. The boat radioed and warned us to get out of Sweden. The skipper got mad and said, "Watch this, we'll show them yellow-bellies!" And sure enough we did. We had a portable toilet in the plane and one of the guys put it on one of the bomb racks and we opened the bomb bay doors. Down we went on the deck, just a-screamin', and right over that Swedish gunboat we let 'er go. You should have seen those guys head for cover (laughs)!

It was one of those flights along the border that finally ended my career in the U.S. Army Air Corps. We were cruising along the Norway/Sweden border and saw a troop train heading for Narvik, Norway. The captain circled and waited for it to get into a tunnel and then we flew down to seal up the tunnel. We came in below the level of the mountain tops because we

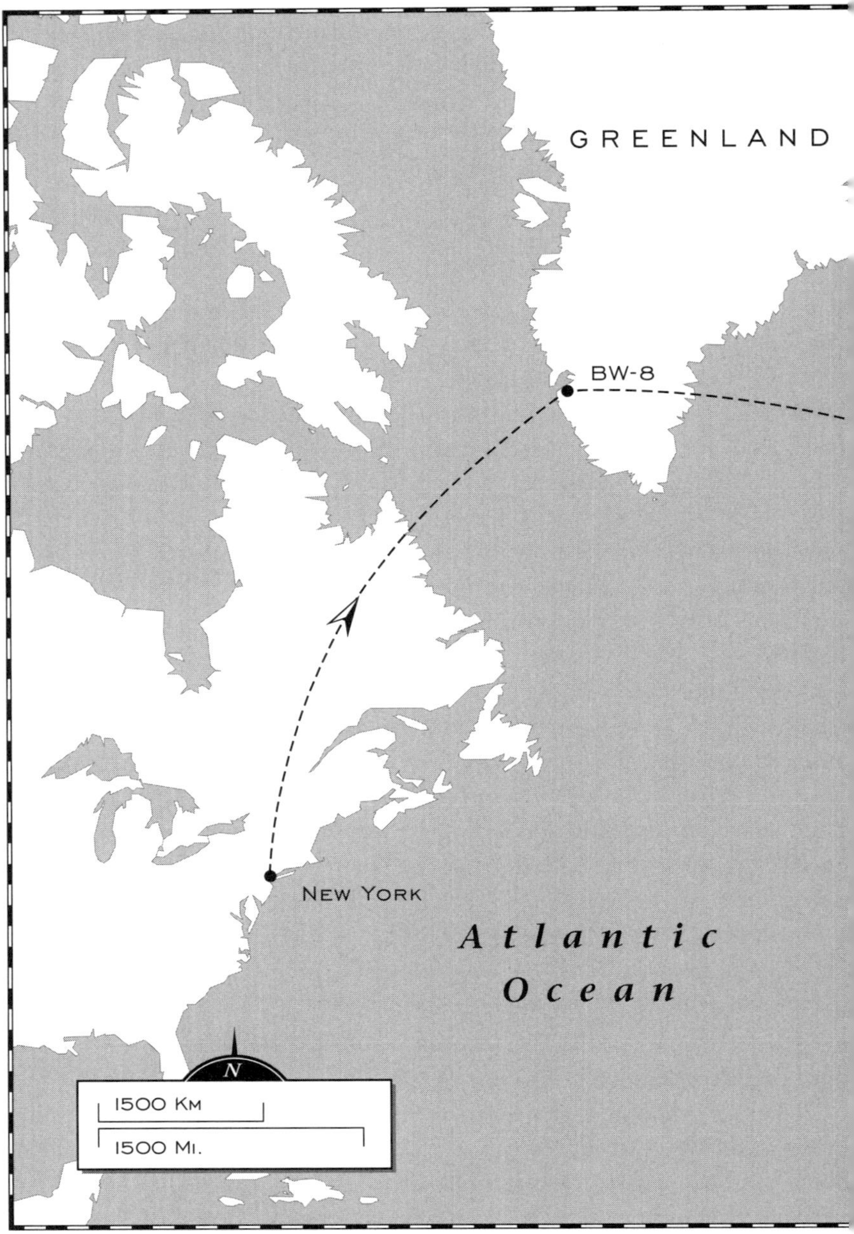

TRAVELS OF NORM SKINNER

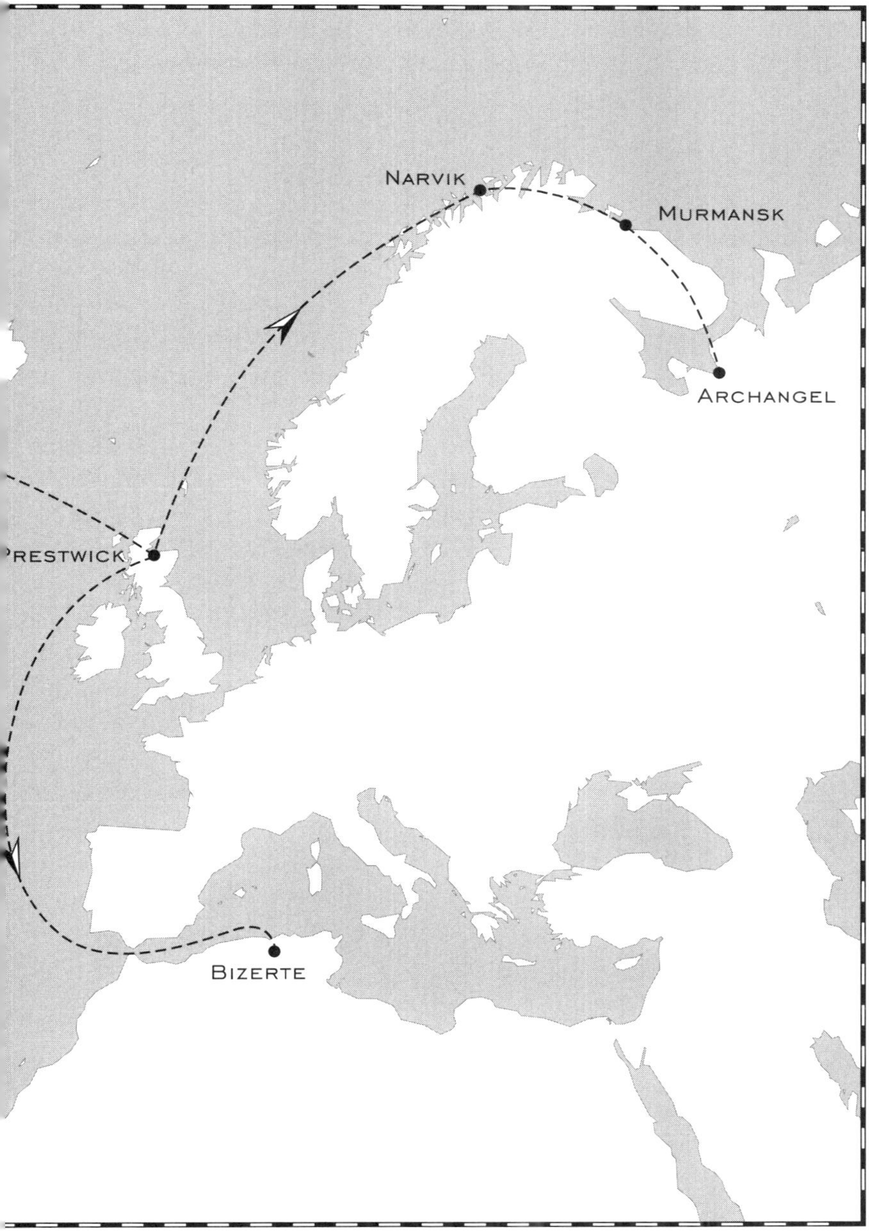
NARVIK
MURMANSK
ARCHANGEL
PRESTWICK
BIZERTE

knew that our only chance was to skip one of our bombs inside the train tunnel to try and destroy the train. We came in hot and the bombardier did a good job—he put it right in that tunnel. But we were so low that the German gunners on the heights really got us zeroed in. We were flying through flack, machine gun fire and everything. I was in the waist gun and got hit. Both the nose gunner and the tail gunner were killed. Somehow the old man kept it flying and we limped back to Aberdeen. I couldn't move. The shrapnel from the flack had come through the side of the fuselage. Some of it had hit me in the back and another piece hooked me through the leg holding me tight against the fuselage. I couldn't move. I was fish-hooked to the side of the plane. I had to stand up all the way back to Scotland, but made it okay because of the morphine the crew gave me. My boot was full of blood when we got back but the ground crew soon had me cut out and on the way to the hospital.

I never flew after that. The shrapnel injury in the back had somehow severed or damaged enough of my nervous system that it upset my sense of balance. I could never trust myself again with flying a plane. In a way, I guess I got home the easy way. No more flying, but also no more war. I got back to the States in early November 1943. There's not much more to tell. I spent the next 29 years in the shop at Dahlstroms and Dawson Metal and have spent the last 18 years since retiring making wrought iron products here at our place on the lake. By the way, look at those birds out there on the feeder! There's been a lot of them there this winter. They remind me of flying. There's nothing like the freedom and excitement of being up there in the clouds, even if you're being shot at once in awhile. It's been over 40 years since I've been in an airplane, but in my own mind that's what I always was and always will be, whether in a Curtiss Jenny or a B-17...a pilot, and one helluva good one I might add.

[Norm Skinner was awarded the Purple Heart for his wounds incurred in the war. He also holds a 1923 Aviator Certificate from the Heath School of Aviation. He returned home prior to the end of the war, but because of his war wounds, he never flew a plane again. He worked in a metal manufacturing plant before retiring, and now constructs custom-made wrought iron products in a shop he has next to his house.]

Background and Commentary

[1]Norm Skinner's commanding officer, Berndt Balchen, was a legend in Arctic flying. He was from Norway and had been involved in early attempts at reaching the North Pole by air. In 1927, he made history by piloting Admiral Richard E. Byrd on his nonstop crossing of the Atlantic Ocean in a Ford Tri-Motor (a high-wing airplane with three engines). They made it across, but Balchen had to crash-land the plane in the water along the coast of France. Everyone on the plane survived and Balchen became one of the flying heroes of the day. In 1928, he and the famous flyer Floyd Bennett went to the aid of a German plane, the Bremen, which had crash-landed on the Labrador coast. Bennett contracted pneumonia and died, but Balchen was successful in rescuing the downed German flyers. The next year, 1929, he was again in the news when he piloted Admiral Byrd on his famous flight across Antarctica and the South Pole.

From 1940 to 1941, Berndt Balchen ferried planes for the British from San Diego to Singapore, but three months before Pearl Harbor, he accepted a Captain's commission from the U.S. Army Air Corps and led the expedition to BW-8 that Norm Skinner was on. When the BW-8 group went to England, Balchen formed an ad hoc flying group that, as Skinner describes, did a lot of different things. He was most famous, however, for the secret, wave-top shuttle flights that he flew between Sweden and Scotland carrying people interred or trapped by the war back to Allied territory. He also flew secret flights into Norway to supply the Norwegian underground. On one occasion, he is purported to have secretly gone to Oslo, postmarked a letter to the local German Gestapo chief, and then left the country. After the war, Balchen became controversial when he alleged, based upon what Floyd Bennett had told him, that Bennett and Admiral Byrd never made it to the North Pole during their famous flight in 1927. Norm Skinner obviously had met quite an unusual individual when he was assigned to Berndt Balchen's Air Corps flying group.

[2]Construction of the BW-8 air base in Greenland started in late September 1941. Situated halfway (775 miles in either direction) between Goose Bay, Labrador, and Iceland, BW-8, with its one 5,000-ft. gravel runway, became a stopping point for aircraft being ferried to Britain. It was also used as a weather station in predicting the weather that could affect military operations in northern Europe.

[3]The B-17 is probably the American bomber that most people would identify with World War II. It was a rather homely, bulky 4-engine bomber that had actually been built by the Boeing Corporation before the war. It was relatively slow, had a tail wheel instead of a nose wheel, but was known for its dependability. It is most identified with the European war and with the attacks on Germany made by the U.S. 8th Air Force from air bases in England. It is also the plane that became famous in the movie *Memphis Belle,* a film which realistically depicted the chaos and carnage that took place on these bombers when they were hit either by flak or by German fighters while on their bombing runs. Over 12,000 B-17s were built and used by the Army Air Corps during the course of the war.

[4]When Americans discuss World War II, they don't often discuss the Russian front. This is probably due to the fact that after the war, the Soviet Union became our Cold War enemy. It is also probably related to the reality that we had very few troops on the eastern front fighting with the Russians. (From Norm Skinner's experience, it does not appear that the Russians really welcomed our presence, although they did need our equipment and supplies in fighting the Germans.) Americans, though, should not underestimate the importance of the Soviet Union in contributing to the final defeat of Hitler. It is doubtful that the war in Europe could have been won without the tremendous sacrifice made by the people of that country.

In a surprise offensive, on June 22, 1941, German forces attacked the Soviet Union and swept across the Russian plains toward Moscow. After great initial success, the German war machine finally bogged down, in large part helped by the severe Russian winter. For three years, the Russian people experienced incredible suffering. In Leningrad (St. Petersburg) alone, during the winter of 1941-'42, while nearly surrounded and cut off from food supplies by the German Army, 3,500 - 4,000 people a day were dying of starvation. Russian estimates are that a total of 632,000 men, women and children died in Leningrad during that blockade. It is estimated that, in total, 25 million people in the Soviet Union died as a result of the war with Germany, two thirds of these civilians.

4. D-Day: The Invasion Of Europe

When I went over the side of the assault boat, I almost drowned. My god-damned helmet strap was snapped and the water was deep. I went under, the water crashed up into the helmet, the helmet yanked my chin strap and I almost strangled (laughs)! That was just the beginning. I'd gone over the side because the landing craft we were in had broached and was going sideways. The seas were rough and I thought we might tip over. I said: 'Bull-shit. I'm gettin' outahere. Sink or swim!' and over I went. The landing craft never did make it back. It got stuck on the beach.

All hell was breaking loose on Omaha Beach. I was in the Big Red One, (First Infantry Division), 16th Infantry Regiment. I was a BAR Man (Browning Automatic Rifle). Fortunately, those of us who were still around after North Africa had learned from the other invasions. A lot of the guys now were new and had never been through it. There were all kinds of screw-ups, just like in every operation. We had been blown off course by the wind and waves and weren't exactly in the right place. (I didn't know exactly where we were, to be honest.) What I did know was that there was a lot of fire coming from the beach: machine-gun fire, rifles, artillery and 88s.

You had to improvise and stay low. A lot of the new guys were getting killed by standin' up and moving upright toward the beach. They were bigger targets. I crouched and stayed low in the water, sometimes pushing a body ahead of me for concealment and protection. (The bodies floated because of the packs that we all carried.) It's hard now to think about that. They were my buddies and I wish they were covering me with fire during the advance. But they were dead and now they were helping me get to shore alive. They were my guiding angels. It could have been me. But they were still helping me. For cover, I got behind one of those steel obstacles or girders that the Germans had placed to hinder our landing. I rested the BAR in the cross bars of it and started firing at places high on the bluff where some of the fire was coming from. Slowly, I worked in, moving from obstacle to obstacle, staying low.

When we got to the base of the bluff, we hunkered there trying to keep some cover between us and the Germans. Finally, somebody got through, had gotten to the top, and more of us followed. By nighttime, we had beaten the Germans and were in good shape on the high ground. It had been a much tougher amphibious assault than we had either in North Africa or Sicily. The beach itself was a mess: bodies, wrecked boats and vehicles were all over the place. But I wasn't to stay in Normandy long. I got out of there before the big fight at Saint-Lô.

Tony Costanzo
Corporal, U.S. Army

[Tony Costanzo was at Normandy on D-Day, but he also fought in North Africa and Italy. His story, which follows, tells it all from the point of view of a foot soldier in World War II.]

I went in early, you know. I was in the Army eleven months before the Japs bombed Pearl Harbor. My buddy, Alex Laska, and I went down to the Post Office at the same time. He had graduated from high school, but I never did. I needed to work to help my folks during the depression, so I joined the CCC, the Civilian Conservation Corps. They put me at Allegany State Park building roads and stuff. We had military instructors and were paid $30 a month; $25 of it went home to help my folks. When I got out of the CCC in 1940, things were heating up in Europe with the Germans, so I talked Alex into going down with me and signing up. We actually wanted to join the Navy, but I couldn't...I hadn't graduated from high school. Hell, we were born on the same street, Water St., and we wanted to stay together. So we joined the Army.

We were sent to Fort Jay, on Governor's Island in New York City, and became a part of the First Division, the Big Red One. God, that island was cold as hell in the winter time and we had to take the ferry back and forth to New York when we went on liberty. I could see the Statue of Liberty from my barracks window. After basic, the whole division was sent to Fort Devens, Massachusetts. At Fort Devens they had a pecking order. We were in wooden barracks, behind the brick barracks. But way out back, in some other buildings, were the colored barracks. The whites and the colored weren't together then, you know. It was at Fort Devens that we got a lot of training in hand-to-hand fighting, how to use a trench knife, how to bayonet a guy, and stuff like that.

I was on KP the day that the Japs attacked Pearl Harbor. I was laying on

Soldiers of the 1st Infantry Division on maneuvers before heading for North Africa.

my bunk almost asleep when some Sergeant yelled, "Hey, the Japs just bombed Pearl Harbor. Anybody gettin' discharged Monday? Nobody's gettin' discharged Monday!" He was right. "Holy shit," we all thought, "OK, I guess nobody is going to get discharged on Monday!" Immediately, almost, we went on some big maneuvers down in North Carolina, near Greensboro. After that we went down toward the ocean near Virginia Beach. Hell, we were on board ship more than the Marines were. All we did was climb down nets and make beach landings, day after day.

After that, we went back to Fort Devens and guess what?...the whole division packs up and heads out for Camp Blanding, FL. (It was somewhere near Jacksonville, 'cause that's where we all went to get laid.) And guess what again? There isn't a camp there at all; just trees, jungle, snakes and swamp. We had to cut down trees and make tent stands for our tents! They issued us jungle gear, stuff for the tropics. We figured we were going to the Pacific to fight the Japanese. But guess what? Right after that they sent us to Indiantown Gap near Harrisburg, PA and we turned all of our tropical stuff in (laughs)! Then we were issued typical military stuff, heavy woolens, coats, etc. Now, nobody knew where we were going. The one good thing

1st Infantry Division soldiers practicing climbimg down nets to embark in assault landing craft.

about Indiantown Gap was that I was only about four hours from home, and so I got a three-day pass to go home and see my Mom and Dad.

What a surprise when I got back to the camp. There were guards all over the place. We weren't allowed to make any phone calls. Then we were ordered to go down to the tracks and board a train. My parents had no idea that I was leaving and going someplace. The whole division got shipped out overnight to New York and the next day, the 16,000 of us boarded the *Queen Mary* and headed out to sea. Nobody knew where we were going. We were all stacked up like cordwood, but I got to know a few guys better. I became good buddies with Johnny Kasperik and Earl Ruggles. (A few months later Earl was dead...he got it in the head on Messerschmitt Lane or Stuka Valley in North Africa...can't remember which. You know, the Germans would come over and strafe us. When that happened, we would dive into the field next to the road and hit the deck, but it was desert, no place to hide. It was the luck of the draw whether you got hit or not. Earl's luck ran out.)

A few days later, the ship arrived in Scotland and a train was waiting for us. The Army was wasting no time. We were on our way to England. I think we ended up somewheres near Salisbury, not sure, anyway it wasn't too far from London. It was called Tidworth Barracks. We started maneuvers again, scaling walls, bayonet practice, etc. Oh, yeah (laughs), I got into trouble, too, at Tidworth Barracks. We used to go on "harvest runs," we called them. We'd load up a bunch of guys and go help farmers bring in their crops. The Sergeant said, "Hey, Costanzo, you go drive the truck, hang around and then drive 'em back." I said "OK" and we left for a farm. On about the third trip to this farm, the farmer's wife came out and she was young, you know. Not bad-looking either. She said, "Hey, you gotta nice looking lorry there," and said she would like to take a ride in the truck. So we took this truck ride and she kept giving me directions on where to go and we ended up at a deadend in the woods. Finally she said, "Let's go, nobody comes through here", and so we started to do it and I was hammerin' her (laughs). For the next few days, I kept going back to that farm (more laughs). Then this other girl I was going with in the village, she squealed on me and the farmer found out. Hell, I thought he would kill me and so I went to my CO with the problem and told him I couldn't drive the truck no more. Well, he solved the problem by restricting me to the base and that's where I stayed until we finally shipped out for North Africa.

I always liked women and being in the Army gave us our opportunities. One time, before I got restricted to the base, we got a three-day pass and went to London. Hell, there was bombing and blackouts all the time while we were there. The GIs would wait until all the girls went down in the bomb shelters and then we'd go down. It was always dark in there and after a few minutes we'd start monkeyin' around with our hands (lots of laughs). We scored a few times there too. I got busted once in North Africa for this kind of stuff when I took our squad into a cathouse in Algeria someplace. I had been told not to go but I found out some of the officers were going so I said, "What the hell, let's go." Well, they busted me for doing it. I got reduced from corporal to lance corporal. But what the hell, I didn't want command responsibility anyway (laughs)! I didn't want to give orders. I mean, Jesus, some of our guys were from New York. If they didn't like an order, they'd be apt to shoot you! They were only paying me $21 per month. Maybe I shouldn't be saying all of these things, but, god damn it, these were the good times. Things like this happened to us during the war.

We shipped out from Liverpool in them limey ships. Man, was the food lousy...mutton and fish. God, it was awful. I didn't even know we were headed for Africa until we were halfway there and they told us where we were going. One officer got on the PA system and advised us all to get a short haircut because it would be easier to fix a head wound if we didn't have much hair. That made everybody real antsy, but we all went and got our heads shaved. We went through the Straits of Gibraltar at night with the ship's lights turned off and then landed at Arzew beach, near Oran, Algeria. It was just at dawn and we headed toward shore. The P-38s were zooming over us firing at the beach as we got close. What I most remember is that I was scared as hell. I didn't know what to expect and my knees were shaking so bad I could hardly move. Our first contact was with the "goons," as we called them. These were tall, black Senegalese guys who were fighting with the French. Our first fighting was against the French because the Vichy French government had sided with Hitler. After just a few days, the North African French came over to our side and so that eased the fighting in that area.[2]

One day around Oran, we were moving down this road, and here came a jeep going like hell with a .50-cal. machine gun on it. I said, "Those guys 're crazy, they're going to get killed out here." Well, we were running short on rations, and one of them asked, "You guys need any food?" Guess who that was? It was General Teddy Roosevelt III, our Commanding Officer. He was a great General, liked being out with the troops, and everybody liked him.[3] He threw us a case of C-Rations and we loved him for it. We used to carry those cans from the C-Rations in our packs and a lot of guys were saved by that when shrapnel would hit those cans instead of the guy. *Mingia*, [Sicilian slang] did we have a lot to carry! Everything we owned was in them packs, and I was a BAR man so I was also loaded down with clips and bandoliers of ammunition.

We found our first winery somewhere near Oran. Hell, most of the time in North Africa we were half loaded (laughs)! Everybody carried wine in their canteen instead of water. Anyway, at this winery some of us were down below filling up our canteens around the wine press, and one of our guys went berzerk or bananas or something. He started opening fire on us from up on top! A couple of our guys got hit in the leg. I think his name was Shapiro. Somebody said, "Shoot 'im!" But the Sergeant said "No," and some guy finally got up behind him and tackled him. He had gone bonkers, never recovered from it, and was sent home. I never seen him no more. That happened sometimes to guys. Most of 'em could handle combat, but sometimes a guy would trip out.

We learned not to monkey around with those Arab women. The ones with just a half a veil were okay. They'd pull it aside and smile at you and give you a wink. But the ones totally covered with just a little hole to see through...you didn't mess with them. There was always an Arab guy following them. One day, we found one of our guys dead and totally naked. The Arabs had sliced him open in three places and his guts were hanging out. He had been monkeyin' around with one of those women and they'd killed him.

After we cleared out Oran, they sent me and few other guys out by train toward Tunis. We didn't know why everybody wasn't going but soon found out. They needed gunners for the tanks and so we were put on "detached service" and sent up to the front. Hell, I'd never been in a tank before and these were lousy pieces of equipment. They were the old General Grant tanks with that stinkin' 75-mm gun and a turret that could only turn 45 degrees.

Tony Costanzo with a buddy from the Navy in Sicily near the end of the war

It was in those tanks that we took up positions in Kasserine Pass, and we found that we were no match for those German Tiger tanks. When Rommel came through, he made mincemeat out of us. We were going up this "wadi," a dry river bed, and the Germans were coming from the top. Our tank got hit in the ass-end by an 88, and three of the five guys in the tank were killed.[4] Me and the driver were in the front, got out the trap door on the bottom, crawled out from under the tank and then moved away from the German tank keeping our destroyed tank as cover in between. It was hard to find cover because it was all desert and rocks. We finally hid behind a small sand dune. We were lucky we didn't get killed or captured. We were cut off, but after the enemy left we were able to work our way back to our own lines. The Germans didn't know it, but if they'd hit us once more, the war would've been over in Africa. We really got licked at Kasserine Pass.

Of course, we didn't get General Patton until after we got slaughtered at Kasserine Pass. He was a helluva good General. I'm glad we had him. Things changed after we got him. We started winning and away we went.[5] Another thing we learned at Kasserine Pass was how to fight better against the German tanks. Before that, we'd been taught to dig slit trenches or long, narrow foxholes. But we found out that the German tankers would put a track down into those trenches and crush guys. After Kasserine Pass, we started digging round fox holes. If they came over you, the tank would just pass on over without crushing you.

I got hit once more in another tank before I finally got back to the infantry. It was up near Gafsa someplace and we took this direct hit with AP (armor piercing) right in front of where I was. But the armor plating deflected the shell up and over the tank. (We were in a Sherman tank by then, a much better tank.) When the shell deflected up, it cut that 75-mm gun barrel in two, so we only had half a gun. When I got back out of that fight and looked at the tank, right where the AP had hit it was like someone with a big ice cream scoop had taken a bite out of the steel in the front of the tank. We were lucky that time.

Somehow, our Lieutenant found out that I could speak Italian and he decided to put it to use one day. We were dug in somewhere up close to Tunis in a defilade position with only the top of the tanks and the turret showing. We was slugging it out with the Germans about a mile away and the Italians were caught in between. (It was near where Captain Johnson was killed. He was on top of the tank and took a direct hit, blew his head off. We had to dump him off the tank and stuck his dog tags in his jacket so that the "graves guys" could identify him.) Anyway, all the Italians had were small arms and every once in a while some of them would pop their heads up and look over the situation. The Lieutenant thought that they wanted to surrender, so he said, "Costanzo, get out of that tank and crawl out there and try to talk those guys into surrendering!" So I crawled out toward them, waved something and said, "Hey, compare...!" and started talking to them in Italian. At first they thought I was one of them, but I told 'em I was American. "You guys better surrender," I said, "If you don't, we're going to overrun your position and then you'll have to move back toward the Germans and they'll kill you." Well, in a little while, we saw a white flag waving, and about 200 of them came over. We gave 'em to the goons to take 'em back, but I told the Sergeant, "I wouldn't do that. The goons are apt to

Tony Costanzo's grandmother in Sicily, 1945.

shoot 'em before they get back and there are some colonels and majors in there who could give some good intelligence." So he sent 'em back with four GIs. I think maybe I saved those guys' lives with that advice because we'd had experience before with the goons killing the prisoners.

After North Africa we were put on ships again and, when we were at sea, they told us we were going to invade Sicily. I said, "Sicily, Jesus Christ, my grandma lives in Sicily!" And sure enough, later on, after we'd pushed the Germans out of Messina, I got a three-day pass and went to see her. What a great time that was. I'd never seen her before; she was my father's mother. (Later, after Normandy, I was sent back to Sicily as an MP to help with the occupation forces and I saw her again. She had it all set up for me to go underground and not report back to the Army. "Grandma, I can't do that!" I told her, "That'd be desertion, they'll shoot me" (laughs). She was something. She didn't want her grandson to get killed and so had it all set up for me to hide in that little Sicilian town.)

We hit the beach in Sicily near Gela and then moved up the coast to Palermo. [See Chapter 14 for Bob Putney's story. He went on the same general route through Sicily with the 45th Division.] The fighting here wasn't quite as bad as North Africa because the Germans had decided not to make a big fight of it. They were withdrawing from Messina and pulling back to Italy. Our biggest thrill was waiting for Montgomery and the British once we got to Messina. Monty had told everybody that the British would get there first. Well, we said "piss on 'em"...we were waiting for them when they finally got to Messina. I don't think people ever really appreciated what we did in Sicily and North Africa. Montgomery always tried to take all of the credit. After Sicily, we were sent back to England to get ready for the Normandy invasion.[6]

As I mentioned before, D-Day was the toughest invasion. The water was so damned rough that we got pushed way off our god-danged course. But we made it, we made it. We was gettin' pounded, though; it was no picnic. We tried to take the new guys under our wing and teach 'em what we knew...but there's no way you could prepare them for something like Omaha Beach. A lot of them got killed that day. Things are still muffled in my mind. I mean, you're scared shitless at the time. I got to hand it off to those ships too; they just kept pounding that one side until they finally got that big German gun. That's what helped us get the opening we needed.

As soon as we had a chance, we got off the beach. People were scattered all over the place. But by night time, we had begun to get together in our old outfits. It was one helluva fight. We moved into the hedgerow country but right after that I was pulled out and sent back to Italy to be an MP. The fighting in Normandy around Saint-Lô really got tough after I left.

Today, you know, I'm on the VFW firing squad. Whenever I fire that gun at some ceremony, I do it in honor of my buddies that I left behind in that war. I was one of the lucky ones that made it home.

[Tony Costanzo was awarded two Bronze Stars, a Purple Heart, and a Combat Infantryman's Badge. He came home from the war and worked for forty years in one of the local furniture plants before retiring. For the past ten years, he has been a dedicated member of the VFW (Veterans of Foreign Wars) color guard and firing squad. This group of former soldiers dress in uniform, parade the colors, and perform as an honorary firing squad, when requested to do so, at special events and at the funerals of veterans who have died.]

Background and Commentary

[1]It is hard to know exactly where Tony Costanzo came ashore on D-Day. Most of the assault force on Omaha Beach got swept toward the east by the wind and tides. He was supposed to go ashore at Easy Red or Fox Green Beach. If he did, he came ashore at or near the American Cemetery at Normandy. If you have the chance sometime, you should visit this incredible memorial which impresses upon you the sacrifice of the 9,386 who are buried there and who are only a part of the thousands who died in the battle for western France. As you stand on the edge of the cemetery, at a point 200-300 feet above the beach, and look out at the English Channel, you can visualize the struggle that day. You are standing on the high ground, you have the weapons and firepower, and you are firing down on those thousands of men and hundreds of landing craft. It would be like shooting ducks in a barrel. But they wouldn't stop coming. They were determined to succeed. Many of them would die, but by the end of the day they would hold the high ground upon which you are now standing.

[2]Initially, in Algeria and Morocco, the Americans were fighting primar-

ily the forces of Vichy, France, the collaborationist government that had capitulated to Hitler. Although the French generals in North Africa disliked the Germans, they were soldiers first and felt compelled to take orders from the Vichy government. Finally, General Eisenhower was able to convince Admiral Darlan, Commander of French Naval Forces, to issue an order to the French armed forces to stop fighting and to join the allied cause. By mid-November 1942, most of the Vichy French forces in North Africa had ceased opposing the landings and were now working with the American and British troops.

[3]Tony Costanzo was right. The troops loved General Teddy Roosevelt III, son of the former President and war hero who had charged up San Juan Hill during the Spanish-American war. Generals Eisenhower and Bradley didn't believe he had strong administrative skills for command but they did recognize his natural leadership abilities with the troops. For that reason, on D-Day, he was assigned to be with the 4th Infantry Division at Utah Beach. He landed on the first wave and realized that the wind and tide had pushed him nearly a mile from his intended landing point. However, he was not experiencing significant German opposition and the causeway to the interior right in front him was open and could handle vehicle and troop movements. He is purported to have said to those around him, "Hell, we're not in the right place, but we'll start the war from here!" He personally stood at the beach entrance to the causeway and directed hundreds of vehicles and thousands of soldiers to move inland while they had the chance. For his courage and quick thinking on Utah Beach that day, he was awarded America's highest military honor, the Congressional Medal of Honor. About a week later, he was dead of a heart attack. Teddy Roosevelt's brother Quentin was killed in France in World War I. They are buried next to each other, with adjoining white marble crosses marking their graves, at the Normandy American Cemetery overlooking Omaha Beach.

[4]The German 88 was probably the most feared and respected weapon used by the German Army in World War II. The gun itself weighed five and a half tons and could throw a 22-lb. projectile up to 16,000 yards. It was very effective against tanks and personnel and was initially introduced to the American Army by General Rommel during the fighting in North Africa. It could also be mounted on the German Tiger Tank, thus making the German Panzer Divisions an especially feared force during critical bat-

tles. Everyone who came in contact with the 88 never forgot it. It could pump out 15-20 rounds per minute of incredible destruction and was an effective weapon for the Germans right up until the end of the war.

[5]Tony Costanzo, like all of the others interviewed who served with Patton, nearly worshipped the man and credited him with the turnaround in North Africa and later with the successful assault across Central France. General Patton was always around the front lines, cussing and swearing with the men, bringing them food and ammunition. Perhaps his own view of the American soldier explains why he was so beloved by many of the men who fought under him:

> *"The soldier is the army. No army is better than its soldiers. The soldier is also a citizen. In fact, the highest obligation and privilege of citizenship is that of bearing arms for one's country. Anyone, in any walk of life, who is content with mediocrity is untrue to himself and to American tradition. To be a good soldier, a man must have discipline, self-respect, pride in his unit and in his country, a high sense of duty and obligation to his comrades and to his superiors, and self-confidence born of demonstrated ability."* [7]

[6]The British General, Bernard Montgomery, was a good leader but a pompous person. He always reveled in the glory of his victory over the Germans at El Alamein in North Africa and would forever sign his name thereafter: "Montgomery of El Alamein." He was not well-liked by the American GIs. However, his British 8th Army had some of the toughest fighting in Sicily. As they moved up the east coast of Sicily toward Messina, the British were confronted by the natural roadblock caused by the volcano, Mt. Etna. At that point, there was only a narrow plain squeezed between Mt. Etna and the sea. It provided the German Army with a natural defensive line. The British suffered heavy casualties fighting against well-entrenched German positions in that area.

5. The Breakout From Normandy

On June 25, 1944, we were bivouacked in Exeter, England, awaiting our orders to move to France. Eisenhower and Patton came by to see the 35th Division to be sure we were ready to go. Ike was especially interested because the Division was made up primarily of units from the Kansas, Nebraska and Missouri National Guard and he was a native of Kansas. He was looking for guys from Kansas and my squad leader, Sgt. Hill, was from Clay Center, Kansas. He talked with Hill a while and then asked me where I was from. When I told him upstate New York, he asked, "How'n the hell did you get into this outfit?" I told him I had absolutely no idea (laughs). We fought under Patton later in the war and so I saw him several times, but this was the first and last time I would see Ike.

Shortly after Ike's visit, we were loaded on ships and moved to France. After we'd arrived off the Normandy beaches, an LCVP (Landing Craft Vehicle & Personnel) pulled alongside and we started our climb down the cargo nets. The seas were rough and the LCVP was bobbing up and down with the waves. I waited, caught 'er as she started up with a wave, and then jumped. I was in with a full pack and no broken bones. As soon as 40 guys were in, we turned shoreward and headed toward Omaha Beach.

We were F Company, 320th Regiment, 35th Infantry Division and we were going in to join and support the 29th Division, which had made the June 6th landings. As soon as the boat hit sand, wham! down came the front ramp. As soon as the last man was off, the LCVP was backing up and hoisting the ramp, heading back for another load. We waded in. The water was about knee deep but every once in a while we would hit a deeper pocket, either scoured out by the tides or caused by an exploding shell, and then down we would go to our chests or our waists, but we kept moving. Most of us in F Company had landed together so we started scrambling up the cliffs. The first group had already pushed away from the top and were heading inland. We went by a bombed-out German gun emplacement which looked like it had been taken out by a direct hit from one of our ships. Aside from occasional artillery and mortar fire, we didn't see a lot of action. It was in the days and weeks ahead, as we pushed through the hedgerows and sunken roads of Normandy, that we would really get hammered. It was to start with the breakout at Saint-Lô.

Bob Kerr
Sergeant, U.S. Army Reserve

[Bob Kerr was an infantryman who made it all the way from Normandy to the Elbe River in Germany at the end of the war. He lived, which is something that didn't happen for many of his comrades in arms.]

I graduated from high school in June of 1943, was drafted and left for the Army on August 13th. I was mustered in at Camp Upton, Long Island and then was shipped right out to Camp Rucker, AL. There was no time for basic training. I was put right in the infantry, the 320th regiment of the 35th Division, also called the Santa Fe Division. My platoon lieutenant was Orval Faubus, who was later to become Governor of Arkansas. (President Harry Truman had also served in the 35th Division in World War I.) We went right into maneuvers around Murfreesboro and Lebanon, TN, and then were sent to Camp Butner in North Carolina for Advanced Infantry Training. Time flew quickly and in May of '44 we were loaded on a ship, the *Edmund P. Alexander*, left in convoy and on May 27th landed at Liverpool, England. There was no time for sightseeing in Britain. We were getting ready for combat and on July 5-7, 1944, we were landed off the beaches of Normandy.

After the landing in Normandy, the "fun" really began. Normandy was ideal for defensive fighting by the Germans. The French called it bocage country; the farm fields were small and divided by huge hedgerows of rocks, trees and bushes. The roads were actually sunken and were about two feet below the level of the surrounding fields. It was perfect for digging in and setting up fields of fire. It wasn't good for armored vehicles and tanks because they had to move on the roads. This was country which had to be taken by the infantry and it was slow going, one hedgerow at a time. We never really stopped. The lines were always moving. We would take 18 hedgerows, then the Germans would counterattack and take back 12. You couldn't hold the towns and terrain without the armored and they really couldn't help much because of the hedgerows. It wasn't until after the breakout after Saint-Lô that Patton and his tanks could really get on a roll.

The Normandy fighting was probably the toughest we had in the whole war. We got right into it around July 9th when we became involved in the battle to take Saint-Lô —a crossroads town where several highways intersected that were needed in order to accomplish the breakout from the beachhead. We would push as far as we could and get our brains beat out, losing men little by little. Then the Germans would counterattack and push us back a little because we didn't have the people anymore to hold everything we'd taken. The 115th Regiment of the 29th Division would then come in and do the same, as we moved back to get replacements. They would get battered up and we would replace them, etc. It was tough going but we always kept moving, leapfrogging with the 115th. Some people believe it went quickly. It wasn't that way. Sometimes we gained just a few hundred yards at a time before we ran out of steam.

One day we lost three officers: the Executive Officer of the Battalion, Captain Swanson; our Company Commander, Captain Hodeson; and a Platoon Commander, Lieutenant Potter. Captain Swanson got hit by a machine gun and was killed instantly. The other two got hit in a gap in one of the hedgerows. We were pushing through one of the hedgerows and Hodeson headed toward a cut in the embankment in order to get through. The Germans had it either mined or booby-trapped with a trip wire. As we went through the gap, I saw this big corporal by the name of Dishman who had been hit with them; he was holding his leg up with part of his foot blown off. Hodeson and Potter were down and looked real bad. The medics were already there so we kept moving up. By that time, there were only two officers left in the Company. The next day they gave our Platoon leader, Lt. Goddard, a battlefield promotion and he moved up to Company Commander. He was killed about two months later. That's the way it worked all the way across France and Germany. After ten months, when we had gotten to the Elbe River in Germany, we had been through fifteen Company Commanders. The odds weren't good.

I think the toughest weapons we faced were the German mortars. They had 50-, 80- and 120-mm mortars. Unlike artillery with the "whish-whish" tumbling sound of incoming rounds, you could hardly hear mortars. When you heard them they were exploding. You had to keep moving, that was critical. It was suicide to stop. If a guy got wounded and there was no medic around we'd stop long enough to bandage him, pour sulfa powder on the wound, wet the bandages with canteen water so they wouldn't stick, wrap him up and then move out. Sometimes the medics got killed. Our platoon medic, Paul Dwyer, got killed early in the Saint-Lô battle. Tony Morizzo and two other guys got nailed in the middle of a field by a machine gun. I looked through field glasses and they weren't moving. I told Dwyer not to go out because they looked dead to me and he was sure to get killed. He didn't listen and headed out into the field. The Germans got him too. Now there were four of our guys dead in that field.

The hedgerow fighting meant that the Germans and us were almost on top of each other. At night you could hear them maybe 200 yards away, talking and banging their mess kits around. We were too close together for any close air support and sometimes even too close for artillery. Normandy was infantry country. Our primary objective in taking Saint-Lô was hill #122. The Germans were really dug in there and had an 88 (88-mm artillery gun) and some other artillery on the hill. The 29th Division couldn't move down the road to Saint-Lô until the hill was neutralized. It was close quarters fighting. We were throwing grenades up the hill; they were tossing them down at us. We lost a lot of guys, but finally took the hill at about 10:45 p.m. at night. There has always been an argument about who got to Saint-Lô first, the 29th or the 35th Division. We had the first patrol that got into the town but the first battalion command post was from the 29th. I guess we can both take credit. The 29th had a major who was a Battalion Commander who had said hours before Saint-Lô fell, "I hope to Christ I live long enough to get to Saint-Lô." He was killed just before we took the town, but the soldiers of the 29th kept his wish and brought his body into the town. He was forever known as "The Major of Saint-Lô." The town itself was blown to bits.

One thing I'll never forget about Saint-Lô were the smells. It was farming country and a lot of cows had been killed in the bombardments. On top of that, the Germans had used horses to haul artillery and many of the horses had been killed and were rotting in the fields. For a couple of weeks, there were also a lot of dead Germans lying around turning black. Some of the bodies had split open but we couldn't stop to bury them. It all created an ugly smell and it didn't seem to change no matter what direction the wind was coming from. Anybody who was in Normandy will tell you about the smell, especially if you came up as a replacement. You'll never forget it. "Gee," one replacement said as he walked by me, "what's dead?"

"Almost everything," I said.[1]

By this time, we'd learned a lot about fighting and how to adapt our uniforms to real life in the infantry. We actually fought in a dress uniform in Normandy, but without the tie. We had those short little field jackets. It wouldn't be till later that they gave us the longer field jackets. The cartridge belts were a waste. Hell, when they got wet they would shrink and you couldn't get your clips out. It was quicker to grab a clip out of your pocket or take one off the sling of your rifle. So we used the cartridge belts for cigarettes. They were the perfect size for cigarettes. We all smoked and the Army gave us free cigarettes. The only problem was that the guys behind us got first pick and would take the good brands. We never saw Lucky Strikes or Camels. We got the Old Golds and Raleighs (laughs)! Those canvas leggings were a joke, too. Dunk 'em once in a canal and they would shrink...we threw 'em away. When we walked along with our pants

Sgt. Robert P. Kerr, north of Nancy, France - 1944.

rolled, we probably looked like Li'l Abner, but who cares? We threw away the gas masks too; they just got in the way. Besides, the gas mask pack was perfect for storing your rations. Those nets on the helmets were for camouflage but they were a hazard. If you were running under a tree or crawling through bushes, they'd get caught and pull off your helmet so most of us ripped them off. When we started out all we had on our feet were GI shoes. We didn't get combat boots until someplace near Nancy in eastern France.

On the morning of July 25th, after the battle of Saint-Lô, we made the big breakout from the Normandy beachhead. Just before we jumped off, I think about 1,500 bombers went in. I remember lying in my foxhole watching those bombers and you could see the lead plane drop a smoke bomb and then the planes following would drop on that target. Somewhere in Normandy that day, one of the bombers made a mistake and dropped its load on a forward command post killing General McNair of the 30th Division and most of his staff. McNair was off to our right. We were working again in conjunction with the 115th regiment of the 29th Infantry. Despite all of the precautions taken, we all knew that mistakes could happen. Deaths from friendly fire were always the hardest to take.

Right after the capture of Saint-Lô, we had been transferred to Patton's 3rd Army and had an immediate problem. General Von Runstedt had been ordered by Hitler to attack the invasion force and the Germans had retaken Mortain and were headed for Avranches. Patton threw us in to stop them. They hauled us off the trucks we were on at St. Halaire and ordered us to attack Mortain to relieve the 120th Regiment of the 30th Division which had been trapped there by the Germans. The 337th Tank Battalion was working with us. We started with 54 tanks and after the third or fourth day of the advance, we were down to 16. The Germans really clobbered us. First Battalion had their eyeballs shot off. They really got it! We were Second Battalion and following up; things were in confusion. The lines weren't straight and some of the German units were in between our companies. Some of our tanks were shooting both ways and I said: "Holy shit, this is going to be a dandy one" (laughs)!

Well, finally we got half-assed straightened out and started up this hill. I'll never forget it. I've got this signal corps #536 radio, a walkie-talkie type radio, and Lieutenant Goddard told me to call Sweeney to have him bring

3rd platoon up faster on the right, and guess what's on the radio? Don MacNeil and the breakfast club from Chicago (laughs)! Can you believe it? A military operation in the middle of France and I'm listening to that song: "Good morning breakfast clubbers it's time to greet you...first call to Breakfast, Philco's call to breakfast!" I said, "Lieutenant, I can't get hold of Sweeney but you oughta hear this" (more laughs). Hell, it went on for twenty minutes and MacNeil was talking to Aunt Fanny etc...must have been an atmospheric screw-up of some kind. For a second I thought we were home!

Of course, Hitler's order to attack at Mortain was really a terrible tactical decision. Once we stopped them, the Germans were in a pocket and this is what created what we called "the Falaise Gap." They had to escape and withdraw down this one road and we really nailed 'em. The British had come down from the Caen area and we had swung around below them. That's when the Air Force went in and beat on them pretty badly, strafing and bombing that road. I'd never seen as many dead horses as I saw there. They usually had six of them in a team pulling wagons and artillery and as far as you could see on that road were dead horses and bombed out trucks. Von Runstedt got out of that but took a tremendous pounding in the escape. Of course, it had been Hitler's idea to attack Mortain. Von Runstedt wanted to make a slow, well-executed retreat toward Paris. Christ, when he got the order from Hitler to attack they say that monocle almost fell right out of his eye (laughs)! Hitler was our best man on the German side because of all the stupid decisions he made.[2]

After Mortain, we were actually supposed to go to Paris, but the big "boo-hoos" decided that they should send the French in to liberate the city; so we went south of Paris. They did send the newly arrived Pennsylvania 28th Division through the city and they marched under the Arc de Triomphe with the French. After the parade, the 28th marched right out the other side of town and into combat. I think that this was the only time in the history of the US Army that something like this happened. The generals said, "Go on through and have your parade and then get into one hell of a fight" (laughs). Usually you had your parades after the fighting was over.

We had another big fight just south of Paris at Chateaudun. The Army sent us a little north of the road we were on to take this airfield that they wanted. The 137th Regiment went south and took Orleans. While we were moving up, a German Mark I Tiger tank drove right up in front of us. Lt. Peterson, another new officer, told me, "The Germans are pulling out." I said, "Lieutenant, truck tires do not squeak. That's a tank and it's coming this way." Sure enough, just then the muzzle of that damn tank came over a little rise and he parked there right on the railroad tracks in front of us. I looked at the Lieutenant and said, "Lieutenant, that is a tank" (laughs). When we saw the tank, we were in a small ditch on a little road that ran through a field full of haystacks. It wasn't even a good ditch. The good ditch to be in was down on the main road across the field. Well, this tank started taking down some houses off to our right, and then he started some of those haystacks on fire with the tracers from his machine guns.

We were in trouble at this point. Lt. Sweeney was off to our right again and the Germans had him pinned down with machine gun fire and 20-mm cannon. (The krauts were using their 20-mm A/A guns at the airfield as machine guns; shooting them at us at low trajectory.) At this point, we had outrun our artillery and so we didn't have much to throw back at them. The only thing we had was H Company's heavy mortars and so we called back and told them to throw that in. Well, that stopped the tank from going further. I don't really know if they ever hit him because I crawled down toward the main road looking for a deeper ditch (laughs). Fortunately, it was hot and humid and the smoke from the haystacks hung close to the ground, so the tank couldn't see us very good and we made it to the main road. Finally, we got our heavy stuff pulled up and the next morning we took the airfield.

Right after we took Chateaudun, the FFI (French Forces of the Interior) took over and they were dragging collaborators out and shooting them, shaving the hair of all the girls who had slept with the Germans, and generally raising hell. They were running around with these old Citroen automobiles with "FFI" and French flags painted all over them. People were clapping and celebrating all of this. They were cheering us, shaking hands, calling us buddies, etc. They were dragging people, pounding on 'em, spittin' on 'em, etc. Finally, we had to step in and stop it until the MG (military government) people got there.

By September we were in Nancy, France. This is where we ran out of gas. Patton had been moving so far, so fast that they couldn't keep up with supplies. Everything was still coming off the beachhead. Antwerp hadn't been taken, and it was tough getting the supplies that we needed all across France.[3] Finally, after we got resupplied, we had a hell of a battle in the Gremecey Forest. This is were I got my Purple Heart. The Germans were firing 80-mm and 120-mm mortars at us; they would hit the tops of the trees and the shrapnel would ricochet down on top of you. A lot of guys got hit from that. I actually thought they were using artillery and didn't realize it was the big mortars until we got to the other side of the forest and captured a couple of them. They were trigger-fired, not drop-fired like our mortars.

We broke out of Gremecey on November 8th, got into a big fight at Chateau Salins and then went across the Saar River and into the Saar region of Germany. That's where we were around Christmastime when the Germans broke through in the Battle of the Bulge. That's when Patton said that he would have two divisions pulled out, turned around and on their way within 48 hours! Well, we were one of those "48 hour" divisions. We were pulled back across the Saar River. On Christmas night we were loaded up, and in a couple of days we were in Arlon, Belgium. Our job was to relieve the 101st Airborne, which had been trapped in Bastogne. We linked up with the 4th Armored at Arlon, and headed straight north toward Bastogne. We had a ripsnortin' fight around Marve, Belgium, and another pretty good fight in a wooded area around Bisery. Cold, Jesus, it was cold! That's the only thing that made us happy: we figured the Germans had to be as cold and probably colder than we were.

It was over for all intents and purposes by the 15th of January and the Germans were in retreat, so they pulled us out and sent us south again. The 45th Division was in a helluva fight against the 10th German Mountain Division down south in the Alps, so they sent us down there for awhile to help them out. The thing I remember most is that it was still very cold and we saw lots of snow.

After that we were pulled back, separated from Patton and sent north to help straighten out the Ruhr Pocket as part of the 9th Army. This is where we ran into our first black troops. They were tankers, the 784th Tank Battalion. [See Vivian Taylor's story in Chapter 9 on what it was like to be in a segregated outfit in World War II.] They were good and I remember them well because we met them at the same place Captain Watkins got

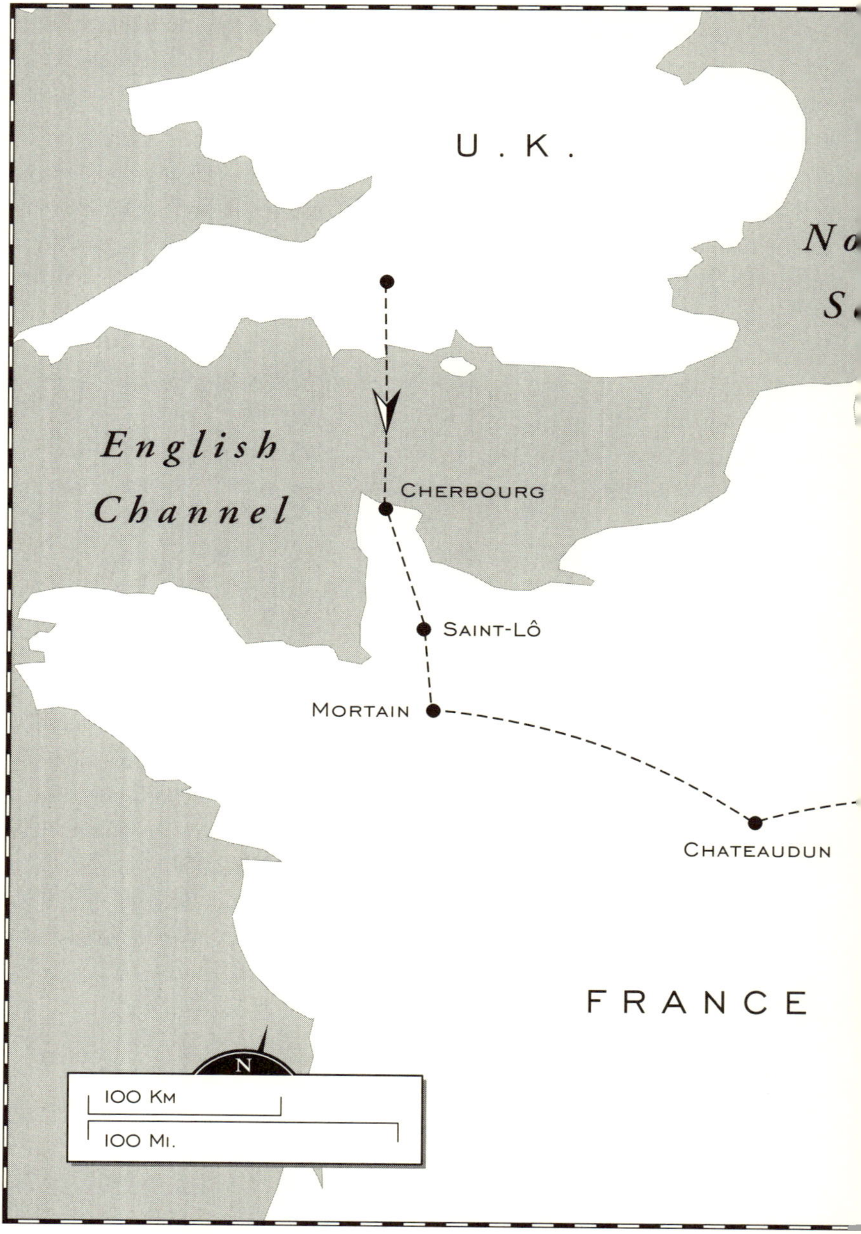

TRAVELS OF BOB KERR

NETH.
ESSEN
ZERBST
DORTMUND
G.
ARLON
GERMANY
LUX.
SAARBRÜCKEN
NANCY
SWITZ.

killed. (We called Watkins "Little Caesar" because he loved to give orders.) He also liked to ride on the tanks but that day he was shot right off the top of one of them.

At about this time, our objectives were to take Dortmund and Essen. This was March and April and Germany was starting to crumble. We moved fast across northern Germany heading for the Elbe River. We hit pockets of resistance but nothing like the big battles we'd come through. We actually crossed the Elbe River at Zerbst and were 23 miles from Berlin when they told us to stop and wait for the Russians. This was where we really got the German prisoners. Thousands of them came our way so they wouldn't be captured by the Russians. We'd just send them back down the line. They were coming in with fully armed tanks, half-tracks and whatever they had with them. The MPs got mad because we weren't disarming them but what were we supposed to do, disarm them with our rifles? We just sent 'em on back. They were finished and knew it and weren't going to give anybody any problems anyway. We figured it was going to be over soon. On May 7th, they pulled our regiment back across the Elbe and on May 8th the war ended. "Whoopee," I said, "the war's over." I guess it really didn't hit me. We'd been living this life so long that it was hard to believe it would end.

We ended up in Hamm, Germany, guarding an ammunition dump and helping out with the occupation. It was there that the First Sergeant, George Delost, called me in and said, "Hey, Bob. You and Bush are the only two original guys still with the Company. How would you like to go on leave to England?" (Dulost had been our Mortar Sergeant but became First Sergeant when our First Sergeant and Supply Sergeant were wounded at the Battle of the Bulge.) That's when it hit me as to the casualties we had taken. Some men had been transferred, but most had been killed or wounded and medi-vaced out. In that ten months of fighting, 133 out of the original 160 in F Company had been killed or wounded. I'd started as a private and was now a sergeant and the squad leader. We'd been through fifteen Company Commanders.

Well, anyway, me and Don Bush went to London on a thirty day furlough, stayed at the Columbia Club near Hyde Park and had one helluva time until the money ran out (laughs). The Army gave us a fifteen-day leave extension but we had no money. That's when we really saw England because we had no money to run around and booze it up. We hung around the Navy, Army, Air Force Institute where the girls were pretty friendly. We called them the NAAFI girls. It was quite a time. It didn't cost nothin' and they'd always treat you to a stale biscuit and some tea.

After we got back to our outfit, the Army sent us to France and put us in a tent camp near Cherbourg called "Lucky Strike Camp." There were three big camps for gathering in the troops and getting them ready to go home, all named after cigarettes. The other two were "Chesterfield Camp" and "Philip Morris Camp." Anyway, we got on the *Queen Mary,* 14,600 of us, and on September 10, 1945, we came into Pier 97 in New York City. I finally got home on September 11th, the day before my 21st birthday. Now the war was over for me. I'd done a lot of growing up by the time I'd reached 21. Hell, today, you can't even take a legal drink until you're 21!

[Bob Kerr was awarded the Bronze Star, the Purple Heart, and the Combat Infantryman's Badge while serving in the Army on behalf of his country. He came home from the war and went to work as a fireman for the local fire department. He worked there for 35 years before retiring.]

Background and Commentary

[1]Although a lot has been written about the D-Day assault at Normandy, most of the casualties in the fighting there came later, as the Allies tried to expand the beachhead and then began the breakout. Indicative of this, Eisenhower spent much more time, in his account of the war, dealing with these later developments than he did in describing the activities on D-Day. Initially, the Allies had planned to turn or pivot on the British sector at the eastern end of the beachhead, and push off through northern France and toward the lowland countries. However, Montgomery, though having promised an early breakout near Caen, couldn't push the Germans back because of their tremendous strength in that area. Thus, as often happens in war, plans were changed and the decision was made that the breakout would be made by the Americans on the western end of the line near Isigny and Saint-Lô. The fighting here was very tough. Through the ingenuity of an American sergeant, a steel device which helped some of the troops was made from the beach obstacles that the Germans had installed. It looked

like a big fork and was welded to the front of some tanks to help rip apart the hedgerows. Though this helped in some parts of the bocage country, Bob Kerr did not see it used in his area of operations.

[2]Bob Kerr attributes the leadership on the German side at Mortain to Von Rundstedt. Since Von Runstedt had been relieved in early July, it was actually Field Marshall Gunther Von Kluge who was ordered by Hitler to attack Mortain and Avranches. (Hitler tended to keep replacing Generals whenever the Germans suffered losses.) Yet, it was a major mistake by Hitler to order this attack since it resulted in approximately 100,000 German troops being taken prisoner when they were caught in the pincers movement between British, Canadian and U.S. troops. About 50,000 German troops escaped but thousands of others were killed and wounded as allied aircraft and artillery pounded the retreating soldiers in what became known as the "Falaise gap." Eisenhower called it one of the great "killing grounds" of the war. He found it to be much as Bob Kerr described it. "Forty-eight hours after the closing of the gap," he wrote, "I was conducted through it on foot, to encounter scenes that could be described only by Dante. It was literally possible to walk for hundreds of yards at a time, stepping on nothing but dead and decaying flesh."[2]

[3]Bob Kerr, as well as other veterans interviewed, were proud of their association with General Patton. (See Commentary of Chapter 4, p. 60 for more about Patton.) He was aggressive, was usually up front with his troops, and was greatly feared by the Germans. He moved so fast sometimes that fuel trucks and supplies could not keep up with him. Probably one of the greatest intelligence coups of the war was Eisenhower's decision to keep Patton in England until after D-Day. A phony Army with several non-existent divisions was established in England across the English Channel from Calais. Patton would make appearances in the area and mock-up tanks and pieces of equipment were built so that the Germans could photo them from the air. Discreet announcements were even put in English newspapers discussing weddings, births and other events supposedly happening to the men assigned to the non-existent Army. Hitler swallowed the bait and three weeks after the Normandy invasion, he was still convinced the "real" invasion would be led by Patton and that the point of attack would be in the area of Calais. Hitler's unfounded fear obviously kept thousands of German troops from moving south and joining in the battle for Normandy.

6. A Nurse's Scrapbook

I had been in nursing for several years when the war broke out. I think I was 37 or 38 when I enlisted in the Army. Many of my friends from the Nursing School at Buffalo General Hospital had already gone in the service and some of them had gone to North Africa. I felt guilty about staying home. I was ashamed that many of my friends had gone to help in the war, and that I was still at home. I thought I should go, that I should also contribute, so I enlisted. I can't remember a lot of the places and dates anymore but maybe you can get some of that from my scrapbook. Being in the Army at that time and being a part of the invasion at Normandy were probably the greatest experiences in my life.[1]

Margaret Marker,
Lieutenant, U.S. Army Reserve

[Because of Margaret Marker's failing memory, much of this story was taken from her very thorough notes and a scrapbook that she kept of her experiences. She landed with a group of nurses in Normandy and followed the infantry as they pushed the Germans back to the East. Once in Paris, she and her outfit established a hospital to treat the dying and wounded from the war.]

I remember that day when we were loaded into the boats off Normandy. It was over a month since D-Day. It was July 20, 1944, but the Germans were still active in the area. The Navy kept looking for German planes until they felt it was okay to go. We walked down a ladder from the big ship and got into this little flat-bottomed boat. It was bobbing around and there were 36 nurses all jammed in with our helmets on and fatigues with everything we owned in bags draped over our shoulders. We were in the 203rd General Hospital group and we were going ashore.

They finally dropped the front of the boat and we all got wet! It was above our waists but we waded ashore, went up a hill, and they put us in a big cow pasture in some large tents. It was pretty primitive living. We dug foxholes because German planes were still in the area. The 203rd General Hospital group had just invaded France!

Nurses of the 203rd Hospital Group prepare to depart for Normandy, July 1944

We had really been trained well for all of this. Right after I enlisted in early 1943, I was sent to Walla Walla, Washington, for training at a U.S. Veterans Hospital there.

We had basic training here with our hospital work. It was hot that summer with huge mosquitos. In our spare time, which wasn't much, we rode horses at a nearby stable and toured the surrounding countryside. In August we knew that we would all be assigned to different units all over the world. I remember a picnic we had near a beautiful pond just before we got our orders. It was a happy but sad day, because we knew that after this we would be scattered to the four winds.

After basic training, I was assigned to the 203rd General Hospital Group and we were sent to Baxter General Hospital near Spokane and were stationed there from August 16 - December 15, 1943. It was amazing where everyone had come from and how I would see some of them later. Our chief nurse, Captain Beadles (later she made Major), was regular Army and had been ready to retire when the war broke out. She knew the ropes and favored me, but her assistant, 1st Lieutenant Rose, used to give me the rides. Later, Lt. Rose became a friend and I met her again in Paris.

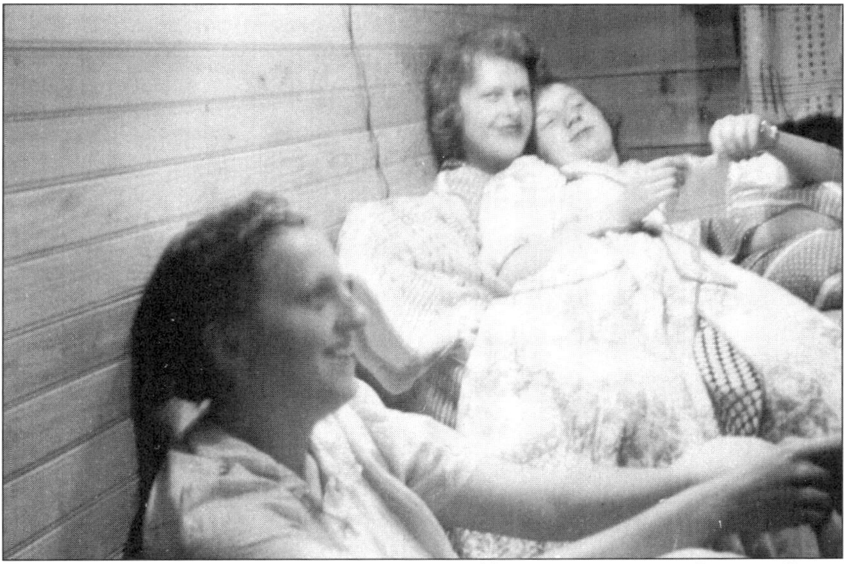

A party in my barracks room at Walla Walla. Two of these girls, Grace & Ruth, went with the 82nd General Hospital Group, and I met them later in Paris. Another was June Simpson from Buffalo.

Ready for drill in new fatigues!

I also made good friends with Larantia Campbell from Pittsburgh of the 27th General Hospital Group and we both were on the bottom of the pecking order. We got tired of filling coke machines and doing monthly inventories. At the same time we received our orders for England, Larantia and the 27th were sent to the South Pacific.

The field training continued. We had to take long hikes, dig foxholes and crawl under real gunfire. But no one complained about the food. On hikes, our mess department would put up lunches for us with more stuff to cook if we needed it. Excellent food! The girls all said that they must be fattening us up for the kill!

In early 1944 we arrived in England. We had come over in a convoy with three large troop carriers and we were on the ship *Brazil.* There were 12 girls in a room sleeping in cots, and all we were allowed to bring had to be put into two duffel bags. What a mess!

England at first was rough living. From January 14 - March 15, 1944, we were quarantined, bivouacked in tents on the hunting grounds of a wealthy British nobleman. It wasn't much fun and we couldn't travel very far. By mid-March, though, we were sent to Burford, about 20 miles from Oxford. We continued to train and it was here that we would receive our orders for France. Housing was hard to find and the English were required to house Americans in their homes. I was fortunate to have my own room in the home of a retired British Colonel. The only negative was that I had to walk a mile to our mess tent to get meals.

The invasion occurred on June 6th and in early July we were moved to a marshalling area near Winchester. For eight days we stood ready to be able to leave on 30 minutes notice for France. We were behind barbed wire and had army regulations read to us on the penalties for desertion. Thirty to a room, dirty straw mattresses, flea powder, vomit bags, rations, yuck! But for four days we were with the famous "Black Watch" troops. That was fun.

Then the trucks came and took us to Southhampton. After two rough days at sea on the channel, we landed on July 20th at a beach in Normandy just 12 miles from Saint-Lô, a town that had just been captured by the Allies on July 19th.

The Army put our big hospital tents up in that pasture near the sea and told us to expect patients within 10 days. The war, however, moved faster than anticipated and we kept moving toward Paris. After six weeks of tent

Nurses on field training, Spokane, Washington, 1943.

Our only warm day in May, 1944. It was a Sunday afternoon off and we were lapping up the sun. Our hut is in the background. Most of us had sold our bikes and so we couldn't travel far, as we had been alerted that we would be shipping out for somewhere.

From a cliff near the beach at Normandy. This village, possibly Ste. Marie-du-Mont, was peaceful and untouched.

living we found ourselves in our new home—a permanent building and hospital in a place called Garches, near Paris.

As we followed the troops toward Paris, we followed a path of the carnage and destruction of war.

Everything we did on that six week march toward Paris was done outside or in tents. The mess was a bucket over a fire, latrines were holes in the ground, the hair salon was under a tree sitting on a stump. Twenty of us at a time would line up and go into a tent for a shower which consisted of holes drilled in a pipe with water leaking down on top of us. The next group would wait outside for the next batch of water to reheat. Even our church services were outside.

Hordes of French families would swarm to our area for anything they could find: chocolates, cigarettes, cast-off clothing, food and soap. They would do our washing for us in a very crude manner. A luxury at first, but later, we preferred struggling with it ourselves.

One day the outside living got to us...we needed glamour. Carol dug out some bathing suits and long gowns. They were all wrinkled but they were all we had and we needed a change! Did it ever feel good getting out

THE BRITISH BLACK WATCH TROOPS: THRILLS WENT UP AND DOWN MY SPINE!

of those fatigues! It was time for some glamour in the middle of the war.

When we got to Garches we got right down to work. There were long hours as more and more wounded men were brought in from the field hospitals. From Sept. 1, 1944, until the end of the war we treated 30,000 patients. At one time we had a census of 4,000 patients. We had patients jammed in everywhere. As soon as they were well enough, we would send them back to the states. It was work, work, work!

It's hard to remember all that happened to you then. I do remember saving the cigarette rations that the Army gave me, even though I didn't smoke. When the wounded men came in from the front, the biggest thing they needed was just some love and understanding. And there was no better way to welcome them than to give them a cigarette. Most of them had not seen a warm bed and a heated building in a long time.[2] I also remember taking care of the German prisoners. They had been through tough times as well and we did our best to help them. Probably because I was older, they gave me the German ward to supervise and I always had to speak through an interpreter. One day one of the German prisoners balked at taking some medication. They had never heard of some of the antibi-

A destroyed Church at Valognes, France.

One of many.

Just one more of those things.

Helen playing the organ for Father Kraemer. Our Church was with us always.

otics and medicines that we had. I told him to take the medicine or we would ship him out to a German hospital. He took the medicine!

The war went fast for us after the invasion and in May 1945 the Germans surrendered. It had been a long and bloody struggle and we were homesick and ready to go home. There were 2,000 nurses waiting to go and finally on the night of November 3, 1945, we set sail for home on an Italian liner called the *Vulcania.* Someone in the Army had printed a little booklet called "The Road Back...pointers to help the returning service woman fit back into the picture of civilian customs and courtesies." There was a lot of advice on how to fit back into civilian life, but I especially liked this advice on bathing:

> *When you wish to bathe, do not throw your overcoat over your bathrobe, do not wrap your soap, washcloth, toothpaste and brush, comb, cold cream, talcum, shower cap and toilet paper in a towel, and do not grab a flashlight and grope your way outdoors. Most houses in the States have special built-in rooms called "bathrooms" where all facilities are available indoors!*

I suppose it was a life-changing experience for me. An upstate, rural kid who had never been out of the country getting thrown into that war and getting sent off to Europe. I had only heard of the Eiffel Tower and the Champs-Elysées. I never thought I would get there. And I got there in fatigues, a helmet and a uniform—a uniform I was proud of. But after it was over, I was ready to head home. It may sound corny but I really believe what I said at the end of that scrapbook:

"It's Home again, its Home again
America for me.
For my land I'm yearning
And her coast I long to see.
America! America!
God shed His grace on thee,
And crown thy good with brotherhood
From sea to shining Sea."

Patients awaiting transportation from the 203rd General Hospital.

A French family we were able to help.

It was time for some glamour in the middle of the war.

Margaret Marker driving a jeep.

[After the war, Margaret Marker came home and became a school nurse, a position that she held for over thirty years before retiring. She died on March 3, 1996, at the age of 92.]

Background and Commentary

[1]It was difficult for women to get to the fighting front in World War II. All combat roles were reserved for men, as was typical of the time. Nevertheless, many women wanted to contribute to the war effort and thousands did serve during the war. In total, 140,000 women served in the

Women Army Corps and 100,000 in the Navy. (See the Commentary to Chapter 2, pp. 33-34, for discussion of the role of women ferry pilots during the war.) Another 23,000 women served with the Marines and 13,000 with the Coast Guard. In addition to these support troops, there were 14,000 Navy and 60,000 Army nurses. Margaret Marker was one of those nurses. She and her fellow nurses followed the infantry from Normandy as it moved toward Paris. She could hear the sounds of fighting and could see the destruction of war as she passed through the countryside. Once in Garches, on the outskirts of Paris, she helped establish and became part of the staff of the 203rd Group Hospital. Other nurses worked in field hospitals closer to the front lines, but all of them saw the human destruction caused by the war as the wounded and dying were brought in for medical help.

[2]A great camaraderie developed during the war between the American nurses and the men that they treated. Many fell in love and weddings soon followed after the war. The nurses felt close to the men and the feeling was reciprocated by the combat soldier. He had tremendous respect for these women who had come overseas to help in the hospitals. During the war, those in the military religiously read the *Stars and Stripes*, the official military daily newspaper, and many would write "letters to the editor" to the paper. In 1944, near the German border, Lt. Frances Slanger, an Army nurse, wrote this to the fighting men of the U.S. Army:

> *We have read several articles in different magazines and papers sent in by grateful GIs praising the work of nurses around the combat areas. Praising us—for what?...The GIs say we rough it...True, we are set up in tents, sleep on cots and are ankle deep in mud, but you have to lie in it... You the men behind the guns, the men driving our tanks, flying our planes, sailing our ships...it's to you we doff our helmets. To every GI wearing the American uniform, for you we have the greatest admiration...Rough it? No! It is a privilege to be able to receive you and it is a great distinction to see you open your eyes and with that swell American grin say, "Hiya, Babe!"* [2]

There was a tremendous response from the GIs who read Frances Slanger's letter and one of them wrote back to the *Stars and Stripes*:

We men were not given the choice of working on the battlefield or the homefront...We are here because we have to be. You are here merely because you felt you were needed...You could be home, soaking yourselves in a bathtub every day, putting on clean clothes over a clean body and crawling in between clean sheets at night. Instead, you endured whatever hardships you must to be where you can do us the most good.

I'd better stop now, because I am getting sentimental, but I want you to know your "editorial" did not change but only confirmed my deep respect for you modern Florence Nightingales. If the world had a few more people like you in it, there wouldn't be any wars.[2]

Unfortunately, Frances Slanger never had the chance to see her letter printed in the *Stars and Stripes* or the responses to it that came in from the men in the field. On the evening of October 21, 1944, the day she wrote the letter, she was sitting in her tent preparing Christmas presents to be sent home in the mail when a German artillery shell slammed into her tent, killing her. However, because of what she stood for, before the end of the war, a hospital ship would be commissioned and named in her honor.

7. Shot Down On The Kassel Raid

September 27, 1944:

It was my 29th mission. After 30 missions you get to go home. But this day I wouldn't be going home; we got shot down over Germany. The raid was really botched up from the start. We were headed for Kassel, Germany, and somehow we split off from the main formation and got too far south. We couldn't find the primary target and finally dropped our bombs on a secondary target and headed back for England.

There were forty B-24s in our squadron but four had already aborted due to engine or equipment problems. Because we had gotten off track from the main attacking force, we had lost our fighter cover. By this point in the war, the Luftwaffe (German Air Force) had been weakened and our biggest worry was antiaircraft flak over Germany, but today it was different. I was pilot in the number two plane and all of sudden my earphones crackled, "Fighters attacking from rear!" Our gunners opened fire with their 50-caliber machine guns but they were no match for the FW-190 German fighters. The Germans had equipped these fighters with something new—a 20-millimeter cannon that would explode on impact. They stayed back, out of range, and lobbed in the shells.

The skipper's plane was ahead of me one second...and gone the next. It had been hit and the tail had broken off. Then a round hit us, right under me in the nose of the plane. The instrument panel came up at me, the glass on the gauges came off, somebody yelled "Fire!" and I knew we were going down. I ordered the crew to jump as I held the plane straight and level. For a while it was quiet. The plane was flying fine, all engines were running, it was just me and this B-24 cruising along through this beautiful sky at 25,000 feet. Then, snap! the control stick went limp in my hands. The rudder cables had burned through. As I turned and started toward the fire behind me and the bomb bay doors through which I could jump, I figured I was a dead man.[1]

Ralph Pearson
Lieutenant, U.S. Army Reserve

[Ralph Pearson volunteered for the Army Air Corps and ended up flying as a part of the 8th Airforce. He was shot down on the Kassel Raid and ended his war years as a prisoner of war in Germany.]

When you think about it, I had come a long way from home in a lot of ways. I never really should have been a pilot because I had never graduated from high school. Pilots were supposed be college men. But I was through with boot camp, had been sent to the Army Air Corps base at Jacksonville, Florida, and was tired of shoveling sand and doing all of the other grunt work that they gave to enlisted men. One day we were out on a work detail and two P-39 Cobra fighters came overhead. These were the fighters that were made in Buffalo, with the engine behind the pilot and the machine gun in the nose of the propeller. Were they ever beautiful. They did a couple of barrel rolls right over us and I said to someone, "Would I ever love to fly!"

A sergeant heard me and said that if I was serious, I could take a two year college equivalency test and that I might be accepted as an Aviation Cadet. Somehow I finagled my way on to the library staff at the base and started studying for the college equivalency test. One day, I went into Jacksonville to the Army Recruiting Office, they gave me the test, and I passed. That was in September of 1942. Then I started down the path of most Aviation Cadets: two months at classification school in Nashville, TN; two months of pre-flight training at Maxwell Air Base in Montgomery, AL; two months of primary flight training in PD-17 Stearmans at Carlstrom Field in Arcadia, FL; two months of basic flight training in BT-13s in Bainbridge, Georgia; two months of multi-engine school in Twin Beech AT-10s at Turner Field in Albany, GA; and then, finally, back to Maxwell Field in Alabama for B-24 training. It was late in 1943 when I had finally finished everything and was ready for the transition to overseas duty.[2]

I really was a pretty good pilot. About 60% of those who started in pilot training got washed out. You had to be good to make it. I liked aerobatics, too, and that helped in flight training. I recall the day that I got checked out in basic flight training. The colonel who checked me out told me to do a chandelle, which is basically a wingover maneuver, a half loop and come out on top going in the opposite direction. I did a rather mild

Ralph Pearson (far left, back row) with his bomber crew.

one and he said, "Who the hell taught you how to do a chandelle. Let me show you how its done!" He gave it the gun, hauled back on the stick and did a tight one. "Now you do it," he said. "I'll show you, you son-of-a-bitch," I said to myself, and really cranked back on the stick. The nick-name for those BT-13s was "Vibrator" and boy could they vibrate! I pulled it around so tight that I thought the wings would come off. Pulled so many Gs that I almost blacked out. It shut him right up. We flew back to the base and he passed me.

When I got to AT-10s and took the check ride, I thought I had failed. Another captain took me up for a check ride and what a frustrating day—I couldn't do anything right. Every time I did a maneuver, he said it was wrong. "Holy Christ!" he said, "Who taught you how to fly? I'm going to chew out your instructor when we get back to the base." I made a great landing and just silked it on the runway. His comment was, "Where'd you ever learn to land a plane like that!" By that time my knees were shaking and I figured I had washed out. We walked across the ramp toward the ready room and my face was as long as a mile. I was really crushed. When we opened the ready room door, all of my pilot buddies were there laughing and crying their eyes out. It had all been a "put-on" and they had been clued into it. Was I ever mad (laughs)! I had passed the flight test with flying colors.

Before we left for England, we went to Westover Air Force Base in Massachusetts for transition training. It was here that I picked up my crew that was to be with me for the duration. That really hit me. Here I was 24 years old and all of these 18- and 19-year-old guys were looking to me for the answers. I was the boss and in that plane called the shots. It sort of weighed on me. Through a fluke, we almost didn't make it to Europe. One night in March 1944 we were scheduled to take a cross-country familiarization trip. We had flight-planned a three-leg trip heading first northeast toward Bar Harbor, Maine, then a turn toward the west and Montreal, and finally back to Westover. Before we left, the skipper called me in and said, "Pearson, you will be flying but I am putting an experienced captain in the copilot's seat. He just got back from flying thirty missions in North Africa and he will be in charge of the flight. It will be good training for you."

After we took off, it started to snow like hell, and this guy told me to lower our altitude to try and get under the snow, so I let her down a few thousand feet. However, I was doing dead-reckoning navigation in my mind (as I usually did on flights) and more or less through timing and watching the compass, I kept track of where I thought we were. I said to this guy in the copilot's seat, "Captain, you know that our route will take us close to Mt. Washington in New Hampshire, and this altitude is lower than the mountain." He asked the navigator to check our location and the navigator said that he would get back to us in a minute. Suddenly, the navigator called in a panic and told us on the intercom that he thought we were very close to the mountain. Just then, through the darkness and snow, somehow I saw the mountain. We were going right into it. Instinctively, I hauled back on the wheel and put the nose almost straight up. Fortunately, this Captain was experienced and he acted just as quickly giving us ten degrees of flaps, shoving the throttle all the way in while at the same time putting the props on high rpm to give us more power. Up we went, with that bomber almost standing on its tail! After that our experienced copilot said, "I've had enough. The weather's bad. Let's go back to Westover," which we did.

We didn't tell anyone what had happened, but the next day I got called in by the colonel, our Commanding Officer. "Pearson", he said, "you've been flying low and buzzing, haven't you!?" "No Sir," I replied, "that's dangerous and against Army regulations. I wouldn't do it." "Then explain this," he replied. "How did all these branches and pine needles get stuck in your ailerons and on the tail of your plane?" That's when I realized how close we had come to crashing, and so I had to tell him the story. After I told him what had happened, he threw his hands up in the air and said, "Pearson, you're one lucky son-of-a-bitch!" Then he dismissed me and called in the captain who had been in charge of the trip. Later, I ran into that guy and asked him what had happened in his meeting with the colonel. "I came damn near being sent back to North Africa." he said. "But then I reminded the colonel of how quickly I had responded with those flaps, throttles and props and how that helped get us through the crisis. I also reminded him that we needed quick, fast-thinking pilots in the Air Corps. He agreed and told me to forget it." We both laughed. It had been a close one.

On May 26, 1944, we left for Europe via Goose Bay, Labrador, where we stopped for fuel. We got a little sleep in Goose Bay; it had been a long trip...10 hours to Goose Bay and another 10 hours to go to Scotland. It wasn't long before we were airborne again on our way to Ireland. I suppose I was a little tired, but as we flew along it seemed to me that the plane was flying nose heavy, so I woke up the crew and told them to shift some weight to the back of the plane. I guess I should have been more specific because they must have carried everything that was stored in the nose back to the tail. We landed in a place called Nutt's Corners, Ireland, and the landing went okay. But as I pulled the plane into the parking area and brought it to a stop, slowly the nose started to rise and there we were, propped back on our tail with the engines running (laughs). I got on the intercom and told them, "Every man take some weight and go to the nose of the plane." Slowly, the nose started to drop until the nose wheel hit and then I turned off the engines. Not a very grand and glorious way to arrive in the British Isles.

From Ireland, we were sent to Tibenham Air Base in England and that's where we started flying our bombing missions. We were a part of the 445th Bomb Group of the 8th Air Force and initially were assigned to the 700th Squadron. That was actor Jimmy Stewart's squadron. But after one mission, we were moved over to the 701st Squadron, and that's where we stayed for the rest of the war. Our first mission was on June 29, 1944, just three weeks after D-Day. By that time we were flying far into Germany. We were on daylight raids and sometimes there would be 800-1000 planes on a mission. We would circle and get lined up over England and then off we would go over the channel.[3]

We would usually get our first taste of flak from German A/A batteries on the French coast, but it was nothing like the flak we ran into over Germany. It was especially bad over Berlin. I remember my first mission over Berlin. There was a cloud of flak about five miles around with thousands of red explosive bursts going off inside it. One of the fighter pilots providing escort must have been on his first mission. He called his leader and asked, "Little Red, this is Little Red One, are they going to fly through that stuff?" "Yeah," the answer came back, "they (the bombers) are but we're not!" And then into the cloud we went. We lost a few planes but most of us made it back. How? I still don't know how most of us got through that stuff. You ask yourself now how you were able to keep going up and flying back through that flak two or three times a week. It's hard to say, but for most of us, we believed in the need for the war. As far as we were concerned, Hitler was a madman and we had to do our part to get rid of the son-of-a-bitch.

We had to abort on one mission. Right after takeoff, when we were rendezvousing for the mission, my number one engine started to windmill. The governor must have broken or something because I couldn't control the engine. It started whirling like a son-of-a-bitch and was vibrating the whole plane. I was so busy that I couldn't talk to the crew but they knew something was wrong. We started to lose altitude and the only way I could keep the plane under control was with full right rudder and the wheel back in my gut. My other hand was on the throttles because I had to goose the number two engine in order to keep us from flipping over. My hands were so busy that I couldn't use the mike. In the midst of all of this, the flight engineer came into the cockpit. I nodded or something and he interpreted it as an order to bail out. All of a sudden, the tailgunner called in, "Hey, there's two chutes out here!" Those guys must have thought I'd given the order to bail out.

I couldn't think much more about that problem because I was in a fight with the airplane. I figured the only way to bring the plane back was to ride it down to 10,000 -12,000 feet and see if the engine would finally burn itself out and freeze up, which it eventually did. Then on three engines we went out over the channel, dropped our bombs and headed back for Tibenham. By that time I was exhausted, but we got a clearance for a straight-in approach and I landed it with no problem. Because of the crisis, I had forgotten about Johnson and O'Keefe bailing out; and, just as we pulled in to park the plane, here they came in a jeep, carrying their parachutes and eating an ice cream cone. Can you believe it, they got back to the base before we did (laughs)! [4]

The day of the Kassel raid, though, was my most unforgettable memory of the war. Eighty percent of the planes on that raid never made it back. Twenty-five were shot down in the same area near Eisenach, Germany. There is a plaque there now commemorating the event. It was the worst group casualty event ever inflicted on the 8th Air Force. Over 118 men were killed and an equal number were captured. It goes through your mind, you know. Did you do the right thing? As skipper of the plane is there something else I could have done? We suspect that Lt. Hendricks and Lt. Stearns, our bombardier and navigator, died when the cannon shell exploded in the nose. I ordered Sgt. Johnson, our flight engineer, to jump with everyone else and motioned for him to follow me through the fire to the bomb bay doors, but I don't think he made it out. Reports say that two chutes were seen just before the plane rolled over and exploded. I'll lean on that for comfort, but we never heard from him again. As you look back at it, time slows down and you think that maybe you could have taken more time and done more. But actually, everything happened very quickly.

After the control cables burned through, I turned and headed back for the bomb bay doors. Luckily, Sgt. O'Keefe had spotted the fire early and had thought to open the bomb bay doors before we lost all of the hydraulics or we never would have gotten them open. There was a wall of flame and smoke I had to get through right behind the cockpit. When I got to the bomb bay, I hopped down on the cat walk and from there jumped out. The plane was burning and in a turn as I went out. I tumbled as I fell. We were still at 25,000 feet, without oxygen, and it must have affected my memory because I never remember pulling the ripcord. What I do remember is that when the chute opened, it jerked me so hard that

A view of the POW camp, Stalag-Luft #1.

my beautiful fleece-lined flight boots came off. As I floated down in my stocking feet I thought, "Nuts, some German kid is going to be wearing those comfortable boots."

On the way down, the fighters who had shot us down made a couple of turns around my parachute. I tried to play dead because we had heard that sometimes pilots had been machine-gunned after parachuting out. But these guys just circled and I imagine called in my position because when I landed, there were three or four soldiers waiting for me. As a matter of fact, the soldiers looked friendlier than the farmers with their pitchforks who were standing around. My face had been burned pretty bad and one of the soldiers said something and it sounded a little like the Swedish word I had learned as a kid which meant "smarting or burning." I said "Ya" because my face felt like it was burning up. My face was badly burned and all of my hair had burned off after going through the fire to get to the bomb bay doors.

Considering the bombing, the war, the hatred, the misery of the German people, I can't really complain about my treatment. The Wehrmacht soldiers put me in a motorcycle side car and drove me to a Luftwaffe hospital nearby. It was obvious that their pilots got first-class treatment. The hospital was clean and well-equipped. They put me into some kind of holding area and early the next morning took me in for treatment. I had second and third degree burns all over my face. The German doctors were careful, though, and disinfected and cauterized my whole face, covering me with bandages like a mummy. I couldn't talk but there was a small breathing hole for my mouth and nose and slits for eyes. The most I could eat were bread crumbs that I could push through the mouth hole. But I have to hand it to the German doctors, they did a good job. I have no scars today. It was also lucky that I had flung off my oxygen mask and helmet, otherwise they would have probably fused to my skin in the fire.

Most of the pilots who were taken prisoner on that ill-fated day ended up in northeastern Germany in a place called Barth. The name of the prison camp was "Stalag-Luft #1." It was a prison camp for pilots and flight crews and we were only 60 miles from Sweden across the Baltic Sea. The Germans tried to interrogate me once before I got to the prison camp, and had put me in isolation beforehand to try and loosen me up. All it did was make me mad. When I got to the interrogation room, they tried to get more information from me other than my name, rank and serial number. I told them, "To hell with you. I'm not telling you a goddamned thing. I lost my plane, probably half of my flight crew and I don't give a good goddamn if you kill me!" With that statement, one of them wrote something in a folder, and they dismissed me and sent me on my way. After the war, I found that old German folder in the archives in Washington, DC. The guy had written: "kraftig," which means "strong soldier."

There were 20 of us in that barracks at Stalag-Luft #1, in a room about 15 feet by 20 feet. It was plenty crowded and we had one small stove for heating and cooking. There wasn't much food; but, of course, by then the Germans didn't have much food either. They gave us potatoes and cabbage to eat but by the spring of 1945 that had pretty much run out. We did get Red Cross packages periodically which had food in them. Towards the end, even the Red Cross packages stopped. We figured that the Germans were starving, too, and had started to use the Red Cross food to survive. We were a close-knit group and one of our guys spoke German. We could negotiate with the guards by trading items from the Red Cross packages, and we actually bribed a camera from one of them. We took a few pictures of the place and the Germans never found out. One time, the Commandant of the Camp, who was a pretty nice guy, called me in. I think they were looking for Jews because he asked me my nationality. It was more information than I had to give under the Geneva convention, but I didn't see much harm in it and said, "Commandant, I'm 100 percent Swede and proud of it. If that information will help you, you're welcome to it!" With that I saluted and left. I never heard anything more.[5]

I think the Germans knew by then that they had lost the war, and they did their best not to mistreat us. In late April of 1945, we started to hear the artillery and guns of the approaching Russian Army. The soldiers at our camp went out and blew all of the ammo dumps around the camp. The Germans had stored ammo near us because they figured our bombers would not bomb a POW camp. After they detonated the ammo dumps, the Germans took off for the west because they wanted to surrender to the Americans and not to the Russians. It was a great day when the Russians arrived, but even greater when two weeks later the Air Corps started flying in planes to take us out. We had to march four to five miles from the camp to an airfield. Before the Army would let us in the planes, they dumped DDT powder on us to kill fleas. It made us mad, because none of us had fleas! As we hopped in the plane, there was DDT dust on the floor...we obviously hadn't been the first group to go through the process.

We flew west to France and ended up in a base called Lucky Strike Camp. One day Eisenhower came to visit the camp. The troops had been complaining about being delayed in returning home, so Ike decided to double the number of troops on the ships by having soldiers take turns sleeping in the available bunks. It was a popular decision because we wanted to get home. The day he came, I was lucky. I was standing in the front line. He reviewed the troops and must have wanted to see some of the repatriated POWs because a lot of us were in the first row. As he walked along in front of us, he would stop periodically and talk with a soldier. I was pretty thin from lack of food, and he stopped in front me and said, "Soldier, don't worry. We're going to fatten you up." The top man had spoken with me; it was a thrill I'll never forget.

Finally, we were loaded on a ship, about 7,000 of us, and we headed for Boston. Because of the large number of men, the Army brass was worried about possible pushing and shoving in the mess hall and so, since I was an officer, I had to go to the mess decks and stand there with the mess sergeant and maintain order. (As it worked out, there was never any problem with the men on the whole trip.) That's when I found out that the mess sergeant was Victor Mature, a movie actor, and a terrific guy. That was something to remember. But what I remember most about that trip is finding my brother, Vic. Two days before I was shot down, I had received word that he was missing in action. That means that he was either dead or a prisoner of war. Somehow we found each other on that ship. He was an Army ranger, had been captured in France and spent the rest of the war, as I had, in a POW camp. Was it ever great to see him! My Mom had all her three sons in the military during the war, and two of us had been listed as MIA. Needless to say, it was a happy homecoming when Vic and I finally got home.

[Ralph Pearson was awarded the Purple Heart and the Distinguished Flying Cross. He returned home and worked in auto body shops specializing in reconstructing antique cars before retiring.]

Background and Commentary

[1]On the 27th of September, 1944, the 445th Bomb Group sent out 38 B-24 Liberator bombers to hit an oil and chemical complex near Merseburg and Leuna, Germany. The planes got separated from the main attack force and were attacked by FW-190 Luftwaffe aircraft. Within three minutes, the Luftwaffe had shot down 26 B-24s. It was the biggest one-mission loss inflicted on any heavy bomb group during the war.

[2]More that 3,000,000 people served with the Army Air Corps in World War II, and of this number 190,000 were pilots. Virtually all of them were civilians, trained and prepared for this duty because of the war. When hostilities ceased, most of them, like Ralph Pearson, returned to their normal jobs in civilian life. For pilots and aircrewmen, flying against the enemy was dangerous work. During the war, the Air Corps incurred 115,382 battle casualties—the total of men killed, wounded or missing in action.

[3]The organization that General "Hap" Arnold assigned to take the air war to the Germans from England was the 8th Air Force and he appointed one of his best friends, Major General Carl Spatz, to head it up. At first,

American prisoners of war at Stalag Luft 1.

the 8th Air Force had to compete with other demands for airplanes in the Mediterranean and the Pacific, but, as the invasion of Europe grew closer, the resources were shifted to Spatz so that he could take the war to the German Luftwaffe. The bomber commands of B-17s, B-24s, B-25s and B-26s were combined with fighter commands of P-47s, P-38s and P-51s. It was a consolidated operation. Whereas, the British chose to bomb at night, the Americans believed that they had better accuracy with daytime bombing. With the addition of extra fuel tanks, the fighters were able to fly escort cover farther into Germany. Before the end of the war, there was no part of Germany that couldn't be reached by American air power. Yet the men who climbed into those planes faced death everyday from German ground and air defenses.

[4]The B-24 bomber flown by Ralph Pearson was manufactured by the Consolidated Aircraft Corporation, and was another marvel of American mass production. Unlike the B-17, the B-24 had tricycle gear with a wheel in the nose. This gave it better maneuverability and vision on the ground. The bomb bay was deep enough to store bombs vertically and the plane could haul 8,800 lbs. of bombs for 2,100 miles. The four 1,200-h.p. Pratt

& Whitney engines could move the aircraft up to 200 mph in level flight. Other than the infamous Kassel Raid, the aircraft was also used on the well-known Ploesti raids to Romania, an attempt to knock out Nazi oil refineries from air bases in North Africa. The British used a version of the B-24 which they called the "Liberator" and the plane was also widely used in the Pacific war. Pilots like Tony Mangine also flew the B-24 in the China-Burma-India theater of war. (See Chapter 2.) The first production versions of the B-24 were made in 1941, and by the end of the war more than 18,000 of them had been delivered to the fighting fronts around the world—6,000 more than the number of B-17s that had been produced. It was truly another marvel of American production on the home front.

[5]Ralph Pearson spent about eight months in the prisoner of war camp

Inside the prison barracks at Stalag-Luft 1.

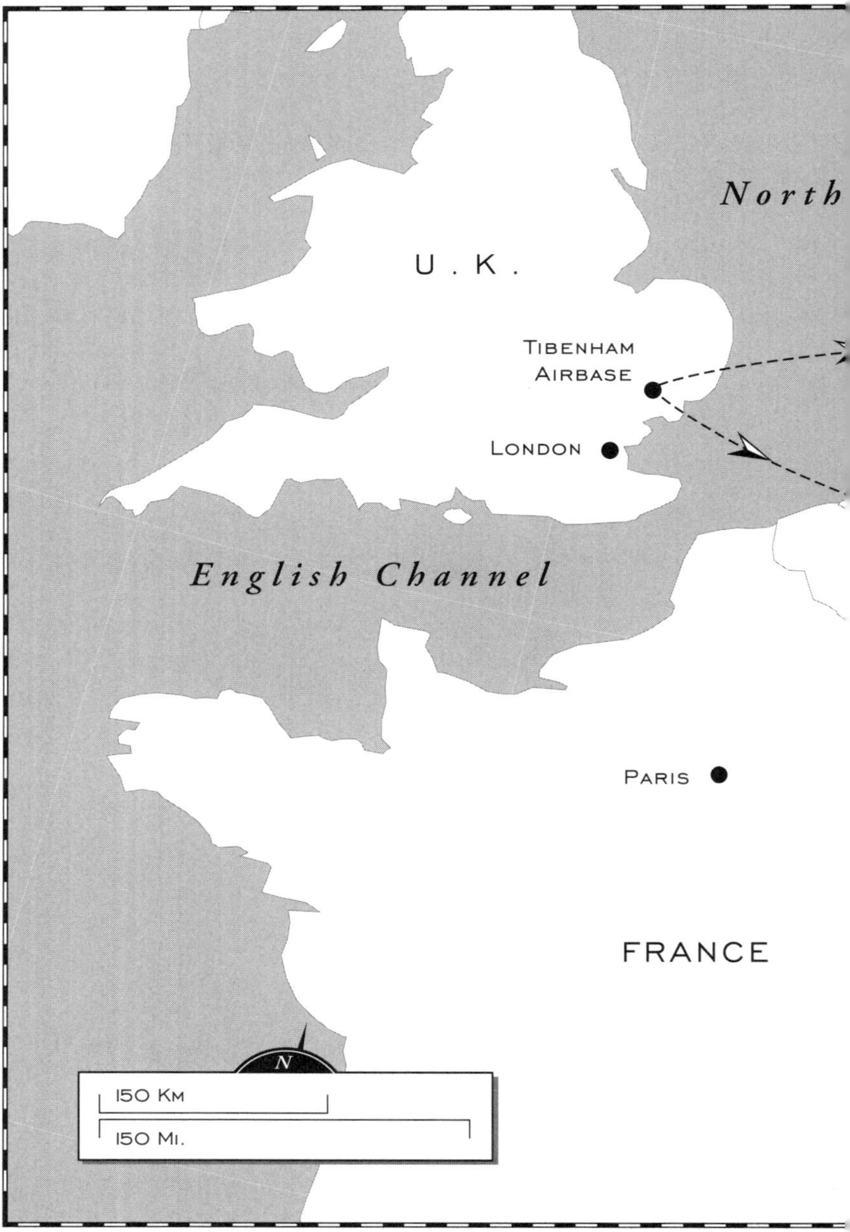

Travels of Ralph Pearson

STALAG-LUFT # I
BERLIN
KASSEL
TH.
UX.
GERMANY
CZECH.
AUSTRIA
SWITZ.

called Stalag-Luft #1. There are not very accurate statistics as to how many American POWs there were in World War II, but it is estimated that approximately 139,000 Americans were captured and imprisoned during the war years. Over 425,000 POWs (mostly German) were brought to the United States during the war and were dispersed around the country where many of them were put to work in factories or on farms. The Germans provided relatively good care to American and British prisoners, but the conditions in most Japanese POW camps were very harsh.

The Hague Conferences of 1899 and 1907 had established procedures to safeguard the health and safety of prisoners of war, and these procedures were generally complied with by the Americans and British in World War II. However, this was not the case on the eastern front in Europe. German attitudes toward the Poles and Russians were such that these prisoners were essentially treated as subhuman. Many Russians and Poles were forced into slave labor camps and others were just left to die. During the terrible winter of 1941-'42, vast numbers of Russian POWs were left in the open by the Germans with no food or shelter and thousands perished. Of the estimated six million Russians taken prisoner by the Nazis in World War II, only one million survived the war.

When the Soviet offensive of 1943-'44 began to push the Germans back, the Russians reciprocated in kind, and large numbers of German POWs were killed and others disappeared into Siberian concentration and slave labor camps. It was the fear of this happening that drove thousands of retreating German soldiers to seek refuge behind American and British lines. If at all possible, they wanted to surrender to the Allied armies coming from the west, rather than surrender to the Russians attacking from the east.

8. Rushing To The Battle Of The Bulge:
THE SINKING OF THE LEOPOLDVILLE

Part One

My experience in the war had been quite uneventful. I was a mess sergeant, a cook with the 66th Division and most of our time had been spent at an Army camp in Alabama. Then in 1944 we were sent in reserve to England. Just before Christmas, we were called up in an emergency to get on a ship to Belgium because the Germans had broken through at the Battle of the Bulge.[1] *We got underway at 2 a.m. on Christmas Eve day. At 8 o'clock that night I was jumping into the frigid waters of the Atlantic Ocean off the coast of France. Our ship, the* Leopoldville, *had been hit by a German torpedo and was sinking. It was every man for himself.*

Joe Caprino
Mess Sergeant, U.S. Army Reserve

[Joe Caprino's outfit was called up in reserve for the Battle of the Bulge. Unfortunately, on the way there, they were torpedoed off the coast of France.]

To be honest with you, I never expected to be a U.S. Army soldier. I was born here in 1919 but my Mom and Dad had moved back to Sicily when I was two years old. But there was no work in Sicily so I moved back to town in 1938, found a job and lived at my cousin Carl Cappa's house.

Things were getting bad in Europe then and Hitler was on the rise. I had joint citizenship, U.S. and Italian. Mussolini must have thought I was only Italian because in 1940 he sent me a draft notice: "Report to the Italian Armed forces. You are drafted!" it said. I laughed and threw it away. I knew from then on that I would be an American forever. My younger brothers, though, who were Italian citizens, did get drafted by Mussolini, and ended up fighting on the other side. It's a small world.

At the end of 1941, most of us had the sense that America would soon be dragged into the war. The draft board was getting busy and I was scheduled for a draft physical in Buffalo. It so happened that my physical was scheduled for December 7th. There we were, all standing like pieces of meat in a long line, when the PA system announced that the Japanese had bombed Pearl Harbor. We all knew then what was coming and most of us went down and volunteered. Early in 1942 I was sent off for basic training and my career as a cook in the U.S. Army was about to begin.

It was a fluke really: if the Germans had not broken through our lines in 1944; if I had been in another outfit; if I had been on a different ship other than the *Leopoldville*...there are a lot of "ifs" in life. Those kinds of thoughts flash through your mind when your ship gets torpedoed on a cold winter night in the Atlantic Ocean.

It was just after supper on Christmas Eve and I was laying on my bunk in the troopship. There wasn't much else to do. All of sudden there was this blast. My helmet was hanging over my head and came down giving me a bloody nose. Someone yelled, "We've been torpedoed!" and everybody started to scramble. The lights were out and it was hard to find things. I bundled up in my coat and hat but couldn't find my life jacket. Finally, I found one in the corner all covered with puke and I said, "What the hell!" and put in on anyway.

Out on deck things were in confusion. You could see the lights of Cherbourg, France, but the ship was obviously not moving and it was starting to list. They kept telling us not to worry, that everything was okay, that we wouldn't sink, but the ship kept tilting more all the time. We heard that the Belgian crew had left the ship. Some of our guys started to try and lower life boats. However, they had no experience in it. One end would get lower than the other and most of the lifeboats never got released.

Another ship came alongside and guys were trying to jump aboard. But it was tough because the seas were rough and the ships were moving and the decks were bobbing up and down. Some people jumped and missed. Others were crushed between the two ships because the heavy seas were causing the ships to bang against each other. Finally, the rescue ship was forced to move away.

Two hours must have gone by since we had been hit and now the ship was really listing to one side. We knew now that it was going to sink. Other ships had started coming out from Cherbourg, but it was Christmas Eve and a lot of crewman and harbor workers had gone home or were celebrating.

There was another big explosion. It could have been a boiler, I don't know. Finally, I decided I had to get off. I couldn't swim but had the life preserver on. I started climbing down the cargo net strung over the side in order to get to the water. My only hope was to get in the water, try and stay afloat and move away from the ship so I didn't get sucked down with it. But the man ahead of me on the net froze, he wouldn't move, he couldn't force himself to keep going down. Then I saw a line hanging from the top of the ship, heading for the water. I grabbed it, and shimmied down toward the sea...and jumped.

I'd never been so cold, but I was afloat and knew that I had to get away from the ship. I had never learned how to swim, so I moved my arms like I'd seen other people swim and gradually I moved further away from the ship. I was probably 100 yards from the ship when it went down. The water went down and I felt like I was inside a huge bowl with water on all sides. But it never crashed over me. I bobbed back up and there were ships around and men in the water.

I was lucky. A small wooden raft made like a pallet drifted by and I grabbed it. I was too wet and waterlogged to get on board, and there was a duffel bag on it. Every time a wave came along, the duffel bag would hit me in the head and put me under. So I moved around on the other side and grabbed onto a line tied to the side. I saw search lights from a ship and hollered so loud they could have heard me back in Cherbourg. Finally, a ship came alongside and threw a line. Twice I tried to climb up but fell off. I was getting weak from the cold. Then a big wave came along; I pulled as hard as I could and two people on deck grabbed me under my arms and I was aboard.

They helped me stumble down inside the ship where there was heat. "Don't get close to that stove," someone said. "You've got hypothermia, and you must warm up slowly." Are you kidding me? As soon as they were gone, I hugged that stove. But then I vomited and passed out. When I came to the next morning, I was in an Army hospital in France. I had tea and soup and felt like nothing had happened. I was okay.

They say that war is made up of days and weeks of boredom and moments of terror. That was certainly true that Christmas Eve night on the *Leopoldville.* You lose track of time. It was probably two to three hours from the time we got torpedoed until the ship sank. I couldn't have been in the water more than 20 minutes or I would have froze to death. But it sticks in my memory as something that took forever. I relive it my mind in slow motion.[2]

God has been good to me. There were 2,200 of us on that ship that night. Over 800 drowned or were killed. I was saved. I was discharged from the Army at Fort Dix, NJ on January 6, 1946, and was home on January 7th. When I got back home, Mary Lucca, my girlfriend from over the back fence on Chandler St., was waiting for me. Mary and I got married at St. James Church on February 12th. I've been successful in business and sold a lot of TVs and furniture over the years. We've had a great family and I even learned to hit a golf ball. But none of it would have happened if God hadn't smiled on me and if those sailors hadn't spotted me with that searchlight as I bobbed like a cork in those icy waters off the coast of France on Christmas Eve, 1944.

[Joe Caprino was awarded the Purple Heart, came home from the war and owned and operated a furniture store for over forty years before retiring. He likes to play golf with his brother Pete and friend Gino (see chapter 12).]

Part Two

I was an admin-type, a paper-work guy, a yeoman first class in the U.S. Naval Reserve. The Navy was like a "fish-out-of-water" in France—the European theater was run by the Army. But somebody needed to run the harbors in Normandy after the invasion and the Navy knew how to do it. That's what my outfit was assigned to do. The only ship I had ever been on was the Queen Mary *which had taken us to Scotland early in 1944. The next ship I would be on would be an 80-foot Coast Guard patrol boat on Christmas Eve 1944, the night we went to pick up survivors and bodies from the* Leopoldville, *a Belgian ship sinking off the mouth of Cherbourg harbor.*

Wesley "Mac" McEntarfer
Yeoman 1st Class, U.S. Naval Reserve

[Little did Mac McEntarfer know that among the men he would be trying to save that night would be a soldier from his hometown—Joe Caprino.]

My Dad was a Methodist minister and I thought that someday I might be one, at least that is what I was trying to decide at Taylor University in Indiana when the war broke out. By the end of 1942, I was close to getting drafted and so I opted to enlist in the Navy. It wasn't whether I would be going into the service, but which branch of it I would be in, sort of like negotiating with a gun at your head.

I did my Basic Training at Sampson Naval Base in upstate New York and then was transferred to Norfolk for further duty. I was assigned to an outfit called DREW #1. Can't remember what it stood for but its mission was to establish advanced bases for the Navy. Probably, because of my college and typing skills, they made me a Yeoman. After training at Norfolk and Lido Beach, Long Island, we embarked in January, 1944, on the *Queen Mary* at Bayonne, NJ bound for "somewhere." That somewhere ended up being the Firth of Clyde and a small Navy base near Helensburgh, Scotland.

The trip over on the *Queen Mary* was quite an experience. The ship was unescorted and not in a convoy for protection. It was so fast that it was assumed it could outrun any German submarine. Every seven minutes we would change direction because someone had done a study that indicated that it would take at least eight minutes for a German sub to get set up for a torpedo run. We all hoped that was true, but I've always wondered what would have happened had we been "lucky" enough to turn just at the right minute into a German sub! Fortunately, it never happened.

Because we were in the Navy, we were given special treatment and were housed in the dried-out swimming pool of the *Queen Mary.* That meant we could stay inside the whole time and keep out of the cold. There were so many Army men on the ship that many of them had to spend 12 hours on the deck and then come inside for 12 hours to warm up. I never thought that sleeping in a swimming pool would be considered plush, but it was better than being outside in the bitter cold of the North Atlantic. The British crew had learned to make some money with the risks they took. We had to pay for our meals (two a day) and the food wasn't much good. One day we got soggy bread with a moldy hot dog! The best food on the crossing was a kidney soup the British served. It was a first for me but definitely a step up from the usual cuisine.

We trained in Scotland and got to like the Scottish people. Sometimes we were invited out to homes of people near the base and we always took rations with us. They were short on food because of the war and appreciated this. During our time in Scotland, we were able to visit Glasgow, Edinburgh and Loch Lomond. There were thousands of Americans in Britain at that time. As D-Day drew closer, we all began to move to the south of England to get ready for embarkation. One of my pals knew shorthand and so got to receive dictation from the brass. He found out the code name "Overlord"—the top secret name for the D-Day invasion—and we knew that somehow we would be involved.

We actually didn't get to France until late July of 1944. It had taken the infantry that much time to secure Cherbourg from the Germans. Our landing was uneventful and we were soon set up in a house near the harbor. The Allies knew that they would need the harbor at Cherbourg and so it had not been destroyed by bombing. Our job was to control the Allied shipping coming into the harbor, to insure that cargo and ammunition were unloaded as quickly as possible and sent to the front. It was hectic but not a very exciting place to be...that is, until Christmas Eve.

In the early evening of Christmas Eve someone ran into our room and yelled, "Every able-bodied man to the pier!" We really didn't know what had happened. We were told that a ship was in trouble and that men were in the water. We didn't know about the torpedoing and weren't told the name of the ship. By the end of that night we still wouldn't know. It was months later when we finally heard the whole story of the *Leopoldville.*

There were six or eight Coast Guard patrol boats in the harbor manned by Coast Guard personnel. They were used for routine patrols and for mail trips and ferrying personnel to England. We had never been on them before. But tonight, if you were "Navy," you were a sailor. We wrestled with lines in the cold and wind and got underway out of the harbor. We could see lights and activity outside the harbor and soon were there. We could see that a ship was sinking but our attention was focused on the men and bodies in the water. We grabbed at them anyway we could, with boat hooks, with our arms, with lines. After getting three or four on board we would head back in to the pier and then come back out.

It was hectic out there. Boats were given orders through bull horns. We tried to move in an organized way but it was chaotic. When you saw a man in the water or a body, you would try and get alongside. It was wet and cold and we took turns laying down on the gunwales and grabbing for those in the water. I remember one body, bare from the waist down with a big gash in the hip. That poor guy must have been located right where the explosion happened.

Soon the sinking ship was gone and the wind and current were taking the bodies southwest toward the Channel Islands. We moved in that direction but couldn't get too close to the islands because the Germans were still holed up there with artillery. After three or four runs, we called it quits for the night. I expect we had picked up twelve or fourteen men out of the water and most of them were dead, at least we thought they were. One of our screws had malfunctioned and we were only operating on half power. Because of that, our trips back and forth to the pier slowed down and we were concerned about the safety of the ship. Later, back in Cherbourg, we found the problem: the body of one of our American troops had become fouled in the propeller.

Back at the pier, some Army doctors were trying to decide who was still alive and who wasn't. There were some surprises. Hypothermia had slowed down the usual life functions and a few of those bodies in the dead pile started to move and men who had been thought dead were found to be alive. It was a night of excitement but a night of tragedy. We were exhausted, mentally and physically. What had happened? Could we have done more? What if it hadn't been at night and Christmas Eve? Could we have given a better response? As I look back on it now, I think we did the best that we could. But it was a tragic loss of human life. Over 800 infantrymen were lost that night without ever seeing Europe, without ever lifting a gun against the Germans.

I've never been back to Cherbourg, and I never again ran into any of those troops who were saved from the sinking of the *Leopoldville* that night...with one exception. Years later, back home, through happenstance, I met Joe Caprino. He was in the furniture business and I was working in a pharmacy on the corner of Fourth and Pine Streets. He was one of the lucky ones who made it. One of our patrol boats picked him up. Could it have been the boat I was on? I don't know. But we became good friends. Can you imagine it? Two guys from the same town in America ended up out on the icy waters of the Atlantic on the same Christmas Eve near this tiny harbor in France. One jumped in to save himself; the other was trying to pull people out. What are chances that could happen? But those are the kinds of things that did happen in World War II all over the world.

[Mac McEntarfer came back from the war, went to pharmacy school, and eventually opened his own pharmacy shop. When he retired, he sold the business to his son, who operated it for several years.]

Background and Commentary

[1] On December 16, 1944, the German Army made one last-ditch effort to stop the allied advance into Germany. On that day, under the cover of fog, snow and bad weather, 200,000 German troops and approximately 600 tanks attacked in the very rugged and difficult terrain of the Ardennes mountains along the German/Belgium border. Defending that area were about 80,000 American troops who were taken by surprise. Thousands died and other thousands were taken prisoner.

The Germans pushed the Americans back in a "bulge" in the lines about thirty miles deep. Finally, after General Eisenhower had sent in all of the reinforcements he could muster, the advance was stopped. (Eisenhower also ordered more reserves from England. Joe Caprino's 66th Division was one of the reserve units sent across the English Channel and one of the ships transporting the Division was the *Leopoldville.*) The German objective in the Ardennes had been to retake the port city of Antwerp, but they never made it. One of the famous stories of the Battle of the Bulge centered around the city of Bastogne. The Germans surrounded the city and sent an emissary into the town and asked the Americans to surrender. When General Anthony McAuliffe of the 101st Airborne was confronted by the demand, he replied, "Aw, Nuts!" And that is the answer that went back to the Germans. The 101st Airborne held out and Bastogne was not taken by the enemy.

By late January, 1945, the battle was over and the Americans had retaken much of the ground previously lost, but the price had been high. About

80,000 Germans and some 70,000 Americans had been killed, wounded or were missing in action. It was the last serious challenge that the Germans were able to muster in trying to stop the Allied advance into Germany. Any American visiting this area should stop and see the Ardennes American Cemetery near Liege, Belgium, where 5,328 of our war dead are buried. Many of them fell during the Battle of the Bulge.

[2] In retrospect, Joe Caprino was probably lucky that he never made it to the Battle of Bulge. His outfit had been called up in reserve, but obviously the sinking of the *Leopoldville* changed some of those plans. Of the 2,200 troops on the ship that night, 300 were killed by the blast and another 500 died in the icy water. The HMS *Brilliant*, a British destroyer escorting the *Leopoldville*, tried to go alongside and rescue the troops, but its efforts were not very successful. A secret U.S. Army report, finally released in 1958, put a lot of the blame on the Belgian crew for being negligent in performing their duties and failing to properly launch life boats. However, the Belgian steamship line that owned the ship defended the actions of the crew that night. In reality, the loss of life was probably caused by many factors, including the fact that the port facilities at Cherbourg really weren't equipped to make massive rescue efforts of this type. Men like Mac McEntarfer who were "volunteered" into service that night, had received no training in how to handle a crisis like the sinking of a troopship. There is some dispute over what actually sank the ship, a mine or a submarine, although German war records indicate that it was sunk by U-Boat #486.

9. A Young Negro Goes To War

I stand on the shore of the English Channel and gaze in the direction of France. It is June 6, 1944. The Channel seems almost deserted. Yesterday, there were ships and landing craft of every description anchored off shore. The nearby forests were filled with tanks, trucks, jeeps and battle vehicles. The narrow roads of southern England were cluttered. How could all of the manpower and so much equipment occupy such a small area? They have all gone now. The sounds of trucks, of tanks and of men cannot be heard. There is silence on the ground, but there is plenty of activity in the air. There are aircraft as far as the eye can see. Our troops have landed in France. The invasion is on. The "Big Show" has started. This is D-Day.

What am I doing here on the wrong side of the channel? I know the answer...it's because of the color of my skin. I have a strange feeling the United States Army has abandoned me. Once again, I go through that old feeling of rejection, anger, disappointment, humiliation and disgust.

Vivian A. Taylor, Jr.
Corporal, U.S. Army Reserve

[Vivian Taylor's story is a poignant reminder that it wasn't until after World War II was over that segregation in the military was abolished.]

My thoughts take me back to my hometown where I grew up, a small town in North Carolina. It was a July morning in 1943. This was the segregated, pre-civil rights south. I was 18 and was drafted out of college and ordered to report to Ft. Bragg, North Carolina. Almost everyone from the colored section of town had turned out to give their sons, husbands and relatives a hero's sendoff. The only whites there were the police, to keep law and order.

I was put in charge of the bus because I was the only one with any college education. All 5 feet 6 inches of me was put in charge of all of those older men. Some of these men were married with children. I was young, ambitious, intelligent, full of hopes and dreams and ready to serve my country. My father was a hard worker, and my mother was a schoolteacher. How proud I was that morning. Little did I know at the time that as a soldier in the United States Army, I would face all of the social indignities of a second-class citizen. Only this time I would be a second-class soldier in a segregated army.[1]

A few hours later the bus stopped in front of a restaurant for a rest stop and food. There was a "whites only" sign hanging over the front door. We were told to go to a window in the rear of the building. A man approached me and asked for our food vouchers. I gave them to him. We were told to line up at the rear window. Someone inside handed out two sandwiches, one ham and one peanut butter to each man. There was no water. We drank from a spigot. The rest rooms were for "whites only," so we had to walk to the woods behind the service station to relieve ourselves. Yet, there was one positive thing about the trip...we didn't have to move to the back of the bus (laughs)!

Basic training was no picnic. We were all thrown together in Negro units with white officers, the preacher and the pimp, the numbers runner from Harlem, and the schoolteacher from Baltimore, we were all together. There were medical students, gamblers, petty criminals, loan sharks, drug dealers, but we had one thing in common: our skin color was black. There were also a few of us who hung together who had been brought up in towns in the rural south. Our small-town, rural upbringing had not prepared us to live in a den of lions, but we made the best of it.

In the Army back then, white officers were usually in charge but blacks were the sergeants and NCOs. It would be like that all during the War. One thing I soon learned was that discrimination and general meanness were not racial characteristics. Of the two meanest officers we had, one was white and one was black. The white man's name was Ellis. I don't even remember the black man's name but we called him "Timberwolf" so that gives you some idea of what he was like. On the other hand, the two best officers we had were both white: a fellow from Virginia called Richey and a Jewish man from New York City by the name of Slinker. It was a learning experience: there were good and bad people out there and skin color didn't have much to do with it.

After basic training at Fort Bragg, we were sent by bus to Ft. Leonard Wood, MO. At Fort Leonard Wood we learned how to be field engineers in the Army. Our job was to build bridges and roads to help move the

Army along. We went out one night on a training operation right after a big rain storm. The group ahead of us had constructed a bridge over a river and now the river was raging. It was dark as we ran over that bridge and whoops! all of a sudden I was in the water, fully loaded with my rifle and packs. Somebody had forgotten to latch part of the bridge together and the pontoons had separated. I almost drowned but somehow got my pack and clothes off, fought my way to the surface and swam to shore. I almost didn't make it to Europe. That river in Missouri almost got me!

By the spring of 1944 we had been assigned to the 1317th Engineering Battalion. It was a rough group made up of a lot of misfits and ne'er-do-wells; there weren't many men who had been to college or even graduated from high school. But our training was complete and we were ready to move out for an assignment. We were sent to Camp Shanks, up the Hudson River from New York, and waited there for shipping-out orders. Those orders finally came and in March we boarded the *Queen Mary* in New York harbor and set out for Europe. The North Atlantic was rough and I was seasick the whole way across. It took us six days to cross. I had only two meals and I couldn't keep either of those down. The 1317th, being an all- black outfit, meant, of course, that we were put on the lowest deck of the ship, "E" deck. One day during the crossing, we had a submarine alert and everyone was supposed to go to the main deck. There were 15,000 men on that ship and it took those of us on "E" Deck two hours to get up to the main deck. I remember standing in a packed passageway on the ship that day as we waited our turn to get to the main deck and thinking, "What an awful way to die. After all this training and aggravation and now we go down in a lousy ship!" Fortunately, they finally called off the submarine alert. The *Queen Mary* was a fast ship and I guess it had outrun the sub.[2]

The ship landed in the Firth of Clyde in Scotland and we were eventually taken to Weymouth in the Dorset area of England. We liked England and, in general, the English treated us really well. I had learned to fly back in the States and so I hung out, when I could, at a nearby RAF base. It was great talking to the pilots and watching the planes. One of the British pilots invited me to fly but said I would need permission from my outfit. Knowing Captain Ellis and his attitudes toward such things, I decided not to ask.

One day, we received an invitation to attend a party being given for U.S. soldiers in a nearby village. Ellis said, "Only five of you can go." That made us mad, since everyone in a nearby white outfit had been invited. When we found out that Ellis was going to be away the day of the party, we waited for him to leave and then about 20 of us went to the event. We made a commitment with the white guys not to drink but you know how it goes; a few couldn't resist the temptation and walked down the street to a pub. When they came back, the words started to fly. One white guy said, "I don't like niggers dancin' with these white girls." One of our guys yelled something back and soon there were tables, chairs, bottles, and fists flying. It was a terrible scene and someone called the bobbies and MPs in to break it up. I scampered out the back door and ended up walking the whole five miles back to camp. Some of our boys really got beat up bad. Fortunately, Ellis hadn't returned by the time we got back to camp.

You soon develop buddies in the Army and I had a good group of friends who more or less saw the world they way I did—Piersall, Kilby, Johnson and Edmonds—and we always hung around together. Someone invented the slogan: "We are tired of giving our sweat. We want to give our blood!" My buddies and I were in company headquarters twice a day pleading for transfers to a fighting unit across the English Channel. I think we finally became a nuisance to our company commander, and so he assigned us to a demolition school. At the school we were given a quickie course in the use of a mine detector, the deactivation of mines and the general use of explosives. It was scary but challenging...and it would ultimately get us out of the 1317th and to the frontlines.

It was probably September or October of '44 when we got orders to move to France. Since Le Havre had been secured and the harbor could now be used by the Allies, we landed there. The five of us who had trained on ordnance demolition were detached and sent to a Minnesota National Guard outfit operating on the northern side of the front, near the Belgium border. When they would run into a minefield, we were brought up to clear it. We would find the mines with magnetic detectors, defuse them, and then stack them alongside the nearest road where someone else would come by and pick them up for final disposal. It was risky work, but we were careful and none of us got killed. Most of the time, I was wet, dirty and exhausted, but I felt like somebody. Once, as I was deactivating a mine, I heard a hissing sound. I carefully placed the mine on the ground and ran for a nearby bomb crater. Seconds later, there was a tremendous explosion. I had apparently learned enough in the short course on explosives to at least stay alive!

There were ups and downs. It was amazing for me to see how inhumane war could be and what people with a gun in their hand could do. We would stop and the CO would commandeer a house for the night or the week, just like that. "This is our house now; you move out." I could never get over the power that the military had. I recall the Russians as being especially brutal. We freed some of them from a POW Camp we came across. As soon as they had been released, they went out on the town drinking, carousing and raping women. To them, these were the spoils of war. But then, at times, my spirits would be lifted. Once, when we were in central Germany, for the first time I saw an all-black field artillery unit in action. My morale and ego soared to a new high!

The destruction in some of the towns we went through was total: there was nothing left. The bombers had leveled virtually every house and what they had left our artillery had finished off. One day something happened to me in Münster, Germany, that I will always remember. The whole town had been more or less destroyed, and as we were driving through it a girl of about sixteen flagged me down. She could speak good English and asked me to come and speak with her father who was a doctor in town. I went into the house and they asked me to help them get medical supplies from some box cars that the German Army had left behind. They said that the cars were being guarded by black troops and I suppose that to her we all looked the same (laughs). I told her that I knew nothing about it and could do nothing. And then, would you believe, that same night I got assigned to guarding those boxcars and she and several of her friends came down to the railroad yard. "Please," she said, "we need those medical supplies." What were we to do, shoot those poor, innocent people? The other guard and I decided to go in opposite directions and check on things at the far end of that railroad yard. When we did that, those folks got the supplies they needed. I guess we did the right thing, even though it may not have been according to Army regulations. It was one of those situations when you had to improvise on your own.

When the war ended we had pushed as far as the Elbe River, which was the dividing line in Germany between Russian and American troops. We had covered a lot of ground. I was now back with the 1317th and we began to help with the occupation. There were thousands of German prisoners and we had been assigned to help guard them. Then on May 8, 1945, the European war was suddenly over. It seemed like we had been in the Army a long time and now, in an instant, the fighting was over.

V-E Day was now history and we were aboard the troop transport, the *General Harry Taylor,* a week out of Marseilles′, France, approaching the Panama Canal and headed for the big battle to take Japan. Rumor had it that Negro troops would be used in the first wave in the invasion of Japan. Unbeknownst to us, two atom bombs had been dropped on Japan since we had set sail. Then one day, over the PA System, came a special message from the skipper of ship, Captain Leonard B. Jaudon: "Now hear this, watch the shadow of the ship as it turns toward New York. The war is over!" The 3,000 soldiers on board went wild! White GIs and black GIs hugged each other. It was August 14, 1945, V-J Day, victory over Japan. We arrived in New York harbor on August 18th. Fireboats were spouting water, ships were blowing their horns, and there was a welcoming band on the pier with thousands of people shouting and waving. It was a great day to be alive!

Soon, it was November 28, 1945. My army life was over. It was separation time at Camp Claiborne, Louisiana. My bags were packed for my trip home. My honorable discharge was in my pocket. I headed for the mess tent. This would be my last meal in the Army. As I approached the food tent all I saw were falling bodies and swinging arms. It was a brawl between blacks and whites. "What's going on?" I asked. Someone told me that the food tent was manned by German POWs and that the local townspeople had told them not to serve Negro soldiers. What I saw was a bunch of hungry Negro soldiers who wanted to be fed.

I picked up my bags and headed for the train station and home. I can still hear that train conductor in his southern drawl, "The only coach for you soldier boys is the first one behind the engine. If you keep arguing with me, I'm going to call the police and have you arrested." I climbed aboard the dirty, smelly, overcrowded colored passenger car and threw my bags on the floor. I used one of my bags for a pillow and slept all night. The next day I arrived back in Charlotte, NC and went to the bus station. The "Whites only" signs were still there. My bus arrived and I climbed aboard. I went to the back of the bus. I was on the last leg of my journey home. Home, sweet home.

[Vivian Taylor moved north after the war to our hometown. He worked for 35 years as a factory worker, finished his college degree, and served for 16 years as a city councilman. He is now retired.]

Background and Commentary

[1]Segregation was well-established in the U.S. military at the start of World War II: it mirrored the practice then in existence in the country as a whole. The country needed the manpower from its significant African-American population but it put those individuals into all-black outfits. Although this procedure continued throughout World War II, the experience of the war and the developments that came from it brought an end to segregation in the military when President Truman ended the practice by Executive Order in 1948.

Two black leaders stand out during the war years as major leaders who continually pressured the military and policy makers in Washington to eliminate segregation in the armed forces. They were Judge William Hastie and Brigadier General Benjamin O. Davis, Sr. Hastie, a federal district court judge and Harvard law graduate, was appointed as a civilian aide to the War Department and advised the Secretary of War on race relations. Davis had enlisted in the Army in 1899 and had worked his way up through the ranks. (Davis's son, Benjamin O. Davis, Jr., became a distinguished fighter pilot with the all-black 99th Pursuit Squadron in Europe.) Both men argued not only for the elimination of segregation in the military, but for the inclusion of the existing all-black units in combat roles. Another lawyer active in civil rights matters during this time was Thurgood Marshall, who later became a U.S. Supreme Court Justice. These individuals and many others were joined by the NAACP and other advocacy groups in attempting to dismantle segregation in the military. Eleanor Roosevelt also became a voice within the establishment in Washington seeking a change in the system.

Men like Vivian Taylor were proud to serve their country and sought out ways to get to the fighting front. Black women also responded to the call for involvement in the war and some 4,000 of them served in the Women's Army Corps. However, it was not easy to break into a system which had sys-

Vivian Taylor poses with a memento he brought home from the war, a German Army Helmet.

tematically discriminated against not only blacks but women in general. It was this kind of "pushing" and "lobbying" for greater recognition and stature in the military during the war that ultimately led to the demise of segregated units with the proclamation of President Truman's Executive Order.

[2]Many of the Negro men drafted during the war were, as was Taylor, put into engineering battalions. They contributed greatly to the war effort by building and maintaining the roads and bridges needed to get supplies to the front. John Wharton, from our hometown, was in one of these battalions which was constructing and maintaining the Burma Road. (See Charlie Price's story in Chapter 14.) Another famous project completed by all-black construction battalions was the Canol Road and oil pipeline

that ran from Norman Wells in the Northwest Territories of Canada to Dawson City in the Yukon. This 500-600 mile project was built over three harsh winters in order to guarantee a fuel supply for Alaska in the event the Japanese were able to invade and isolate Alaska.

By war's end, a lot of these African-American outfits had seen plenty of action and taken their share of casualties right along with their white brethren. The 99th Pursuit Squadron, the 92nd Infantry Division, the 333rd and 969th Field Artillery battalions, and the 761st Tank Battalion, along with many others, laid a claim to their right in the American dream by their distinguished service during the war. As Vivian Taylor indicates, many blacks felt "humiliation and disgust" after doing their best for their country and then being treated as second-class citizens. But in retrospect, the sacrifices made by the "Negro" troops, as so poignantly described by Taylor, helped set loose the forces of change that would sweep America after the war and begin breaking down the wall of racial segregation.

10. Fighting Behind The Lines

I'll never forget when the Germans surrendered to us in Norway at the end of the war. There were 20 of us and Major Bill Colby was our commander. We had been operating for three months behind enemy lines blowing bridges, tunnels and portions of a railroad that ran from the North Sea to the city of Trondheim, Norway. All of a sudden the war ended and we were ordered to accept the German surrender at Trondheim. There were 20 of us and 100,000 of them (laughs). We got ready to go and ,for a little extra flair, Major Colby had us cut white neckerchiefs from our parachutes and wear them as part of our uniform.

We walked into Trondheim and met the German general in charge. Bill Colby, who later went on to be head of the CIA, was a tough guy and we had nicknamed him "bones and guts." The German general, in a gesture of friendship, put out his hand to Colby but Colby refused to shake it. Instead, Bill saluted. Colby was junior to the general and so the German had to return the salute. The general asked if he should have his men surrender their weapons. Bill said, "No." (After all, how could 20 of us disarm a whole army?) Instead he said, "Keep your weapons but if anyone gets out of line, we'll kill 'em!" Then Colby told us, "There's a lot more of them than there is of us, but we won the war. When you walk down the sidewalk wear your sidearms and if a German wants you to step in the gutter, you make him step out in the gutter." And we did (laughs)! We were real hotdogs. About a week later, the British began to send in regular Army troops to handle the details of the surrender. That's when we knew that the war was really over.

Fred Johanson,
Sergeant, Office of Strategic Services (OSS)

[At the time, little was known about the OSS. It was a top-secret operation. Fred Johanson's story is a gripping tale of what it was like to live and fight behind enemy lines.]

My family moved here in August, 1942, just after I had graduated from high school in Providence, RI. I started working at Marlin Rockwell for 35 cents an hour but knew that the military was ahead of me. Everybody was going in. I tried to enlist in the Navy but I had punctured my eardrums as a kid and so they wouldn't take me. So I volunteered for the draft and I guess I was good enough for the Army because they took me!

I had visions of becoming a doctor at one time and so I signed up for medic school and in January of 1943 was shipped out to Camp Grand, IL, for basic training. After that, I was sent to Fitzsimmons General Hospital in Denver for extensive additional training as a medic. It was way out in the boonies but now I understand that the city has grown up around it. I've never been back. At the end of about nine months in Denver, I was called in to a private, rather mysterious meeting with a civilian from Washington, DC. During the meeting, he divulged that he was from the OSS (Office of Strategic Services) and that he wanted me to volunteer for some very top-secret duty. Heck, I was 19 years old and it sounded interesting, so I said "Yes," and off I went to Washington.

What had brought them to recruit me were two things: (1) I was a medic, and (2) my parents were Swedes and I spoke Swedish. In Washington I was assigned to what was called the "NORSO" group and it was there that I learned that our prime mission would be to parachute behind the lines into Norway. They needed a medic in the group and Swedish is enough like Norwegian so they figured I could speak the language.

In January of 1944 we were sent for further training to England where they broke our outfit up into small OGs or "operating groups" of about 20-30 men, about the size of infantry squads. There were two to four medics assigned to each group. A major was assigned as commander of each group and there were several sergeants and technical sergeants in the group. It was an elite outfit with a lot of qualified personnel.

Of course, plans are always made to be changed, and D-Day changed plans for us. Despite all of our Scandinavian expertise, we were redesignated for France and began to make plans to jump into France on D-Day, June 6, 1944. In order to get ready, we were sent to the British parachute school at Ringway Royal Air Force base, near Manchester in the Midlands. Surprisingly, we found out that the Brits use only one parachute; they don't believe in reserve chutes, so we trained with only one chute. That made it

Two hometown boys, Robert Anderson (left) and Fred Johanson with the OSS on leave in London. Anderson was killed later in a plane crash in Norway.

kind of interesting. We actually trained by jumping from barrage balloons—the balloons that were put up to discourage German fighters. They were tethered and had a basket and we would float up and then jump out of the basket. Actually, it was kind of fun, but it always seemed to be raining. They get a lot of rain in the Midlands. Also, interestingly, the British don't let a parachutist pack his own chute. A group of WAFs (Woman Air Force) packed all of the chutes and the British had tough standards. If there were any "streamers" where the chute malfunctioned, the woman who packed the chute would be court-martialed.

The purpose of our going into France was to assist the *maquis*, or French underground. We found them to be a rather unorganized bunch of rabble-rousers, many of them leftist or communist, but obviously very patriotic. We parachuted in at about one a.m. on D-Day into the Province of Hautevienne, near the City of Limoges, about halfway between Paris and Marseilles'. We were over 200 hundred miles from Normandy, way behind the lines, and our mission was only indirectly related to the activities of D-Day. Our job was to help organize the French Resistance into a better fighting force and to disrupt German supply lines by blowing (demolishing) rail-lines, bridges, and other transportation systems which were used in supplying the front lines. The *maquis* had the heart to fight, were periodically harassing the Germans, but often didn't have much impact because they were disorganized. Our job was to train them into becoming a more effective and more disciplined fighting force.[1]

One fact we quickly learned was that the Resistance was disciplined as far as secrecy was concerned. Before we went in, we had been preceded by the "Jedburghs"—a team of one American and one British officer—who had evaluated the French Resistance in this area. They had found them to be tough and competent enough to follow orders and had radioed this information back to London. This was confirmed early on the morning of June 6th, when we parachuted in. The *maquis* had lit fires in three corners of a field, just as we had been told, and we landed right in the middle of these markers. There were four of us in each of five different B-24 Liberator bombers and we jumped through a hole in the belly of the plane where the bomb bay was usually located. In addition to us, the planes carried all kinds of supplies to the Resistance—bazookas, cigarettes, C rations and ammunition. Obviously, the Frenchmen were interested in getting these supplies. The actual jump was a piece of cake. We had 15 practice jumps in training and this was just another practice jump. I landed in a potato field, in soft ground up to my ankles, and didn't even fall over.

Despite their excitability and disorganization, the French Resistance had been able to damage the German war machine. As a result, the local German SS (elite Nazi stormtroopers) had put out the word that if the underground kept it up, there would be retribution. Just before we landed, the Nazis had gone into a little town called Oradour-sur-Glane, put all the women and children in the church, set fire to the men outside of the church, then machine-gunned the women and children when they came out of the Church. After it was all over, they burnt the town. The SS wanted to teach the French a lesson and so 640 people were killed that night. We got there a week later and, poetically, there was still a crucifix standing near the church where the atrocity had taken place.[2]

During our time in France, I became friendly with an officer in the French Reserve forces serving with the *maquis* near Limoge and, before I left, we exchanged addresses. Just last year my wife and I visited his widow back in France, and after all these years, the friendship was still there. She is 93 and we still correspond at Christmastime. We talked about the tragedy at Oradour. She told me that after the war her husband and a comrade went to Germany, found the Colonel of the SS who had ordered the massacre at Oradour and executed him. This happened a lot after the war. Scores were evened and debts repaid outside the usual channels of justice. She told us that this was only one instance of over 4,000 such cases of undocumented retribution of this type which took place after the war. The underground knew who the bad guys had been and they made sure that justice was done after hostilities had ceased. They settled the score. In this country we didn't experience the brutal heel of the aggressor. They did, and after the war they got even.

After our parachute drop near Limoge, we set up tents in a woods near the field where we had landed and after that usually moved only at night. The Frenchmen were happy to see us and quickly learned to take orders. We had set-up targets to hit and they assisted us in our missions. We had only one casualty during our two months in France and that was Captain Larson, who lived near Meadville, PA. We called him "GI Larson" because he wanted us to salute for everything, even when we went to the latrine (laughs)! But Larson made a mistake. On one of our missions, we had set charges along a railroad to dynamite a German troop train. When the train got close, it slowed down. Some of the Frenchmen had been careless and had left cigarette butts along the rail line. There were German soldiers on a flat car in front of the engine with a machine gun and, when they saw the cigarette butts, they had the train stop. The Frenchmen got excited and started shooting and throwing hand grenades. A real firefight developed. Although the *maquis* had been ordered not to engage, they did anyway. In the middle of all of this confusion, Captain Larson, who was about 20 feet from me, stood up (which was the mistake), and a German 20-mm cannon blew him apart.

Unbeknownst to me, Captain Larson had also been told by our commander to disengage and retreat. We were there for demolition, not engagement. However, Larson never had a chance to tell me before he was

Photo taken by Fred Johanson of the church at Oradour-sur-Glane after it was burned and its inhabitants massacred by the SS. The crucifix of the church is still standing amid the carnage.

killed. So I was stuck and the Germans were coming. But, as I said, we were well-trained and had been told what to do in circumstances like this. I dug a hole and covered myself with dirt and brush. I stayed there for 24 hours while the Germans scoured the place and then, just before dawn the next day, I began to work my way back with a map and compass to our command center. Three days later I walked into our camp in the woods and everyone was amazed that I had made it. It was a joyful occasion. They thought that I had been killed or taken prisoner and had already reported me as Missing In Action (MIA). This episode was a good lesson for all of us. We wore uniforms, but we all knew what the outcome would be if we were ever captured...we would be dead men. Usually, no prisoners were taken when OSS personnel, working behind the lines, were captured.

Why did I survive this? I would say good training and discipline. There were four medics in that group that dropped into France and medics have a reputation in the military of being the pansies. However, the four of us decided that we wanted to carry our own weight and be as good a soldier as anyone in the outfit, so we worked and trained hard. When you think about it, it is really amazing that we went through that entire mission in France and only lost one man. I can only attribute it to the tremendous training that we had been given. I survived because I paid attention. We were young, well-trained, we knew how to fight and, as far as we were concerned, we were the best there was. We had a pride, a great pride, in our outfit—an indescribable feeling really.

We were there in France for two or three months. When we had to move long distances, the Frenchmen would commandeer some old farm trucks that burned charcoal for fuel. Boy, did they make a racket! One day when we were coming back in one of those trucks after blowing a tunnel, we got buzzed by an American plane. We thought he was going to strafe us, so we got out some American flags and began waving them until he saw that we were Americans. He then flew low over a nearby tree line. We surmised later that he was trying to tell us that there was a large concentration of German troops there because they opened fire on him. The plane got hit and started to burn. Maybe the pilot was wounded. We will never know. But what he did next was unbelievable. He turned that burning plane around and flew right into the German position killing himself and many of the enemy. The crash caused a helluva explosion and the Germans had so many of their own problems that they forgot about us. It's just another MIA story from the war. We never found out who that pilot was and probably nobody will ever know, but his heroic action that day undoubtedly saved our lives.

By August of 1944, the Allies were firmly entrenched in France, and Patton had broken out near Saint-Lô and was racing across France. On August 15th, French and American forces opened another front in southern France. The Germans were now trying to supply troops and supplies to two fronts rather than one. Our primary job was to keep blowing the railroads and disrupting the German supply and transportation lines that led to the southern front. Sometime in September the decision was made to pull us out of France. The OSS figured we had trained the *maquis* adequately and they also wanted us to get ready for our original operation in Norway, so we were sent back to England.

It was quite amazing how we got out. The French Resistance set up a landing field which they could mark with bonfires at night. We got our hands on an old steamroller and rolled a runway in the middle of a wheat field. At midnight one night, a couple of C-47s came in from England and picked us up. It went like clockwork. We hopped into the planes and flew a low-level, indirect flight back to England. One of our duties had also been to gather downed pilots who had been able to escape German detection, and so several of these fellows also flew out with us.

As I look back on it, it was quite remarkable that we were never discovered by the Germans. However, the French underground was tough, enforced secrecy, and ferreted out enemy spies. They had ways of finding out about German informers and took care of them. One day a couple of Frenchmen came up missing and we never inquired about it. We assumed that they had been removed by the *maquis* for security reasons. It may sound strange, but at the time, getting captured never really worried us. In some ways, I suppose, it was because we were just young and naive.

One interesting story developed near the end of our stay in France. We stayed for awhile at a Chateau which had been the home of Laracha Fucuot, a French philosopher. A seamstress at the Chateau had made a couple of handkerchiefs for me out of my parachute. I gave one of those handkerchiefs to one of the pilots we had rescued who was from Bergen, NJ—his name escapes me—and I asked him to deliver it to the girl I was going to marry who lived in Washington, DC. I said to him, "I would really appreciate it if you could look up Elsie Jane Gordon when you get back and give her this hanky. If you find her, tell her I'll bring the other one when I come home." Well, can you believe it—he did find Elsie, gave her the handkerchief and I gave her the other one when I got home! To this day, she still has those two handkerchiefs. We got married right after the war and have been married now for 49 years.

When we got back to England, we started right in with more training to get ready for our drop into Norway. The OSS always went first-class and most of the time in England we stayed in castles or the estates of wealthy people located away from civilization where we could do our training in secret. It was at this point that Major Bill Colby was assigned as our commander. He had been involved in a two- to three-man advanced "Jedburgh" counterintelligence unit in northern France. In November or December of 1944, our group was sent for final training to Lord Lovett's hunting lodge near Inverness, Scotland. This was tough mountain training but the accommodations were good. Major Colby was a small, skinny guy, but he was tough. Oh, was he tough! He probably weighed only 150 lbs. soaking wet and we called him "guts and bones," but he was a leader, a real leader.[3]

We knew at the time what our job was going to be, although we didn't know exactly what part of Norway we would be dropped into. We had been trained to work with the *hgemefruten* or "home-front" which was the name for the Norwegian underground or resistance. They were a small group, compared to the French *maquis,* but they were more professional and had more discipline. When we jumped in on one cold March day in 1945, we found ourselves about half way up the Atlantic coast of Norway near a town called Trondheim. Our mission was to disable the railroad that supplied northern Norway. The OSS had told us that our mission was to "Blow it up, blow it up, blow it up!..." so that's what we did to the tunnels, bridges and track of that railroad. There were about 400,000 German troops in Norway and Hitler wanted to get them back to attack the Allied Armies advancing into Germany. Because of the difficult Norwegian terrain, there was only one railroad from north to south, and if we could keep that rail line disabled, we could help keep those German troops bottled up in Norway. If they tried to

FRED JOHANSON AND HIS OSS COMRADES BURY ROBERT ANDERSON AND THE OSS CONTINGENT AND BOMBER CREW WHO WERE KILLED IN NORWAY AFTER THEIR AIRCRAFT HIT A MOUNTAIN WHILE TRYING TO EXECUTE A PARACHUTE DROP.

move those troops by sea, the British Navy would sink the troop transports so they had to come out by land via the railroad. There were only 20 of us plus the Norwegian resistance fighters, but we were credited for keeping most of those German troops bottled up in Norway.

Our camp in Norway was located on a farm along the Norway/Sweden border and most of our trips were made on skis, pulling sleds loaded with explosives. Periodically, we would be resupplied by air from Scotland. It was difficult flying. Those planes were being flown by 20-year-old kids, just like me, and sometimes they made mistakes. Several planes crashed into the mountains during training exercises or in trying to get through to us. My best friend from back home, Robert Anderson, the fellow who introduced me to my wife, was killed in one of those crashes. He was an OSS medic like me and his group was being flown in to join us in Norway. They never made it. The plane ran into a mountain. Some Laplanders came into camp and told us about the crash and so we went with them to the site. Eight men were killed—four of our OSS fellows, including Bob Anderson, and the four crew members of the plane. We buried them as best we could with rocks from the mountainside. I took Bob's ring and Zippo lighter with me and finally got them back to his mother after the war. She had hoped he was alive, but when she saw those items she came to grips with the fact that he had died.

Strange and bizarre things happened during a war like this. One of our OSS groups, through poor navigation, was mistakenly dropped in Sweden and for a while they were interred as prisoners. (Sweden was technically a neutral county.) One of my friends with a Swedish heritage from that group told me an incredible story. One day, while he was in Sweden as a prisoner, the government decided to move him someplace by taxi. The taxi stopped for a traffic light and, of all things, his sister crossed the street! She, of course, never realized he was in the cab. What are the chances of that happening? But those were the kinds of things that did happen in World War II. That group of internees was eventually involved in some kind of trade between German intelligence operations and the OSS and they joined us later in Norway.

Another guy in that same group was a Norwegian/American and after the war he went home to see his family. He found out that his brother was a Quisling, had collaborated with the Germans and then joined the

German Army as a major. With his family's consent, this man sought out his brother and killed him because of his betrayal to the Nazis. It's impossible for us to conceive of such a thing, but you must realize that the Germans were brutal oppressors in Norway. For example, when they built the submarine pens at Trondheim, they did it with slave labor and some 7,000 men are buried in the cement there. When the workers would drop from exhaustion, the Nazis would just dump their bodies into the cement. People swore that they would get even after the war, and they did.

It's hard to believe today that we could endure the physical challenges we encountered. In Norway, my leg muscles were as hard as rocks because of all the skiing. We called the skis "torture boards." We were dressed in all-white gear, and would pull those fully loaded pulkas (sleds) 50-100 miles to our objectives along the railroad. Every bone in our body would ache but somehow we got it done. We did a lot of damage to that railroad over the course of three or four months.

Then, of course, the war ended. We were still up in the mountains when Major Colby got the word that we were supposed to go to Trondheim and take the surrender of all German forces in Norway from a Nazi general. It was quite a day. He made all of us spiff up in our best uniforms. We cut up our parachutes and made scarves to spruce ourselves up, and then we went through that incredible surrender ceremony I told you about before. What an experience it was. Before we left Norway, I also cut out three panels of my parachute and brought them home. I was hoping that Elsie would use them for her wedding gown, and was thrilled when she did!

The Norwegian guys in our outfit used to rib us Swedes. "10,000 Swedes went through the weeds, chased by one Norwegian!" they would say. But it was in good jest because we were all Americans, and we got the job done. Those days in the OSS were indeed a highlight in my life. Can you imagine what the world would have been like if Hitler had won that war? It is incomprehensible.

[For his courage in action, Fred Johanson was awarded the Bronze Star and Norwegian Freedom Medal. After the war, he came back home and went into the family insurance business. He is now retired and his son, Dan, continues to operate the family business.]

Fred Johanson and his wife, Elsie, on their wedding day after the war. Her dress is made from the parachute Fred used jumping into Norway.

Background and Commentary

[1]As the blitzkrieg of German troops stormed across Europe in 1939 and 1940, organized military opposition quickly vanished. Puppet governments were set up in the occupied countries and offices of the German intelligence and the Gestapo (secret police) were established to enforce the terms of the occupation. However, local resistance forces, like the French *maquis,* began to coalesce in opposition to the German occupation and, as the war progressed, they became better organized and more effective in fighting the occupation. The underground also became involved in trying to save those being persecuted by the Nazis.

Although Fred Johanson's experiences took place in France and Norway, the Resistance was active in all of the countries that the Germans had invaded. In Holland, for example, the Resistance was very active in trying to hide Jews who were being rounded up and sent to concentration camps. An estimated 25,000 Jews went into hiding in Holland, and, although approximately half of them were discovered and sent to the death camps, the remainder survived the war, many through the help of the Resistance. One of the famous stories from the war, *The Diary of Anne Frank,* came from the pen of a 13-year-old Dutch girl who remained in hiding for two years but eventually was captured and died in one of the camps.

The Resistance forces also worked together to establish escape routes for downed pilots and refugees. These routes stretched from Belgium through France and Spain to Gibraltar; many downed flyers and others caught behind the lines made it back to England through this clandestine transportation network.

The Allies, of course, did everything they could to encourage the Resistance and assist it in harassing the Germans from the rear. Supplies, weapons and ammunition were air-dropped to the underground. Political leaders like General Charles de Gaulle would go on BBC (British Broadcasting Corporation) radio urging active opposition to the occupation. The BBC kept the underground advised of progress in the war and would often put code words in its broadcasts which had special meaning for the underground. To lead this effort, in the summer of 1940, Prime Minister Winston Churchill created the top-secret Special Operations Executive (SOE) in England, whose purpose was to gather intelligence and also assist the resistance forces in Europe. Later, after the United States entered the war, the Americans formed a similar agency called the Office of Strategic Services (OSS). To lead this agency, President Roosevelt tapped a prominent attorney from Buffalo, NY, known as "Wild Bill" Donovan. A Medal of Honor recipient from World War I, Donovan was a strong leader, widely respected in the country; through his efforts, the OSS became a formidable force in the war effort.

[2]Fred Johanson was right about the brutality of the German occupation as well as the retribution inflicted by the Resistance. In the massacre at Oradour-sur-Glane, of the 653 people who lived there, 642 died: 245 women, 207 children and 190 men. Only 11 people survived. In France as a whole, it is estimated that some 25,000 French citizens were executed during the war and another 200,000 sent to concentration camps by the Nazis. In retaliation, after liberation, it is estimated that the *maquis* summarily executed some 11,000 German collaborators. This was in addition to the acts of retribution that took place in Germany after the war as described by Fred Johanson. Other French citizens, who were considered too friendly with the Germans during the war, were subjected to various forms of public humilation. (See Bob Kerr's account in Chapter 5.)

[3]The SOE and OSS worked closely together during the war and established a system of small, multinational teams, code named "Jedburgh Teams," which were dropped behind the lines to link up with and evaluate the resistance forces. Bill Colby, Fred Johanson's commander in Norway, was in such a team and, with a British and a French counterpart, parachuted into France after D-Day. The Nazis made a practice of attempting to infiltrate the Resistance and on this mission, Colby was nearly captured when a double agent informed the Germans of the mission. Later, Colby was flown back to Scotland where he trained and then led Johanson's team into Norway. After the war, Colby became part of the newly formed Central Intelligence Agency (CIA), America's first attempt at centralizing and coordinating the intelligence activities of the nation under one organization controlled by the President. He served with the CIA in Italy, Sweden and Vietnam. From 1968 -'71 he was granted the rank of Ambassador and served as Deputy to the Commander, Military Assistance Command Vietnam. Colby's government service culminated in 1973-'76 when he served as Director of the CIA in Washington.

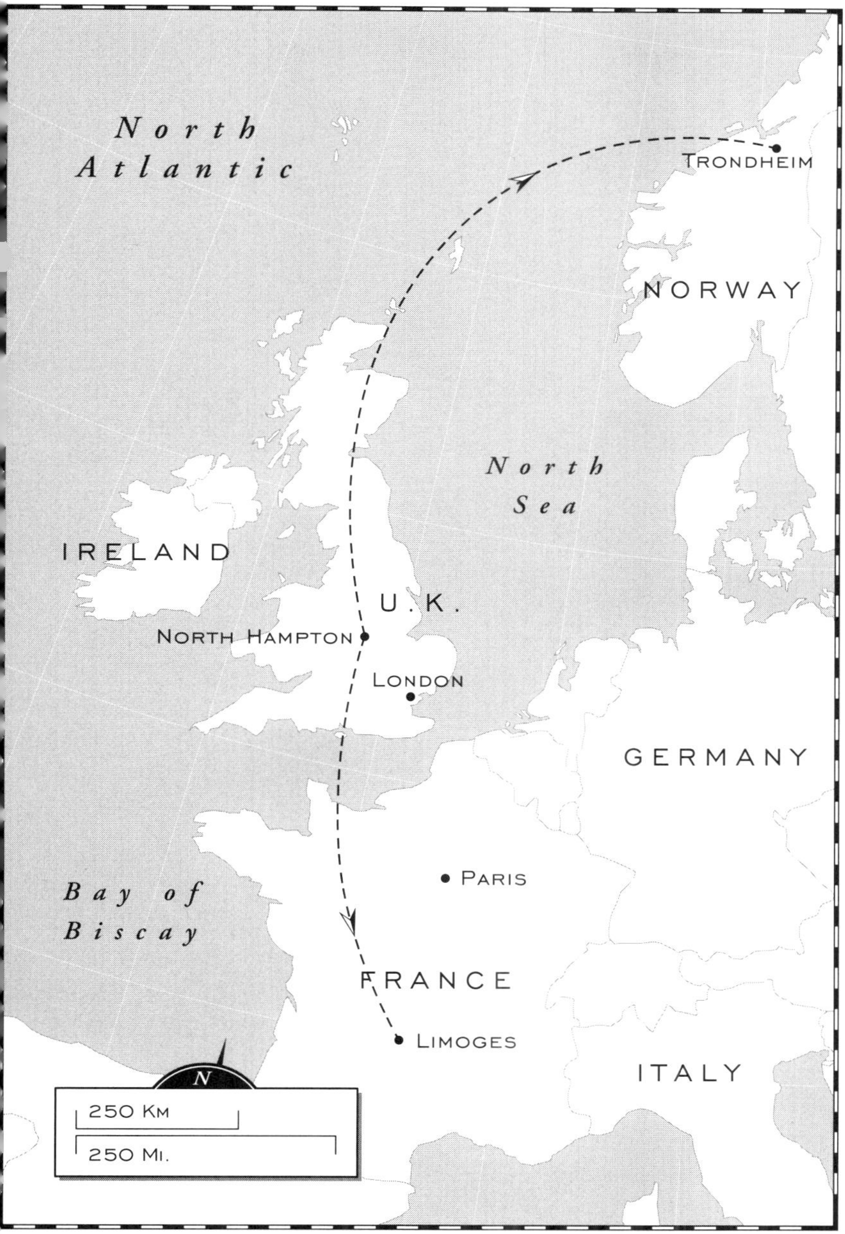

Travels of Fred Johanson

11. The Italian Campaign

My two brothers were in, too. They both had it tough. One of them was in a jeep with four other guys and hit a land mine. He was the only one that lived. He had a plate in his head and always had back problems. The other one was in the Mountain Division and saw a lot of action. He had mostly mental problems from the war and was always in and out of the VA Hospitals. I guess I was one of the lucky ones. I still carry one of my dog tags on my key chain which has my old serial number. I often forget my social security number, but never my serial number. It brought me good luck, it brought me home from the war. I am #12,054,994. I'm a lucky man!

A. Robert Putney
Tech Sergeant, U.S. Army Reserve

[Bob Putney was an infantryman in the 45th Division and served in North Africa and Italy. His story focuses on the experiences he had fighting the Germans on the Italian Peninsula.]

I was on a hot date in Buffalo on Pearl Harbor day. I guess it wasn't too hot a date because I can't remember the girl's name. It was after dinner and we had the car radio on. We heard that the Japanese had bombed Pearl Harbor. It didn't really hit me then that anything would happen to me because of it. But, of course, a few days later it became clear that if you were male and my age, you would probably be going into the military.

I was two years out of high school, just drifting around, doing a little work for my Dad at the Chevy dealership. He thought it might be a good idea for me to get a job at a tool and die shop. "They'll need those jobs at home and maybe you won't get drafted," he said. To me that didn't have any appeal. My friends were going in and guys my age were gung-ho about volunteering. I didn't know what I wanted to do anyway, and so I went to the Marine recruiter. Lucky for me, I was colorblind and couldn't get in the Marines. So I enlisted in the Army and off I went to Fort Niagara to be mustered in. After a week there, they sent us to Camp Croft in Spartansburg, SC, for basic training.

After basic, I was assigned to the 45th Division at Pine Camp (Fort Drum) in upstate New York. The 45th was a National Guard outfit from Oklahoma so most of the guys were farmers. We had a lot of Indians and Mexicans too. Fellows like me were there to fill in the ranks. We drilled and trained as infantrymen through that hot, dusty summer, then moved to Fort Devens, MA and finally to Blackstone, VA to await a troopship. In October, we shipped out to Norfolk and got aboard the USS *Culvert* bound for somewhere. It wasn't until we got off the coast of North Africa that we knew where we were.

Oran, Algeria, is a fairly big town but we were bivouacked outside of town. It was dry and dusty—lots of Arabs around trying to sell things. We slept in tents. It was hot in the daytime and cold at night. For something to do, we'd go down to the water and "go fishing" with grenades and then go back and have a seafood dinner (laughs). But we didn't stay in that camp very long, maybe four days. Things were heating up to the east and so they put us in 6-by-6s (Army trucks) and we headed out for the front.

I'll never forget the first night at Kasserine Pass. Rommel had knocked a hole in our defenses and we were sent in to back up troops on the front line. You could hear the rumble of artillery and the sky was lit up with tracers. The 180th infantry regiment, 1st Battalion, Company B (my outfit), dug in and none too soon. We didn't see the Germans but they saw us and it was my first experience at being shelled by 88s. They were terrifying when they came in. We were scared shitless and stayed in our foxholes for the night. No one in our outfit, as I remember, was killed or wounded. One thing we found out that night was that our equipment was inferior to the Germans'. Our old tanks and the O-3 rifles were no match for what the Germans had. That would soon change with the Sherman tanks and the M-1s we were to receive, but in North Africa our weapons put us at a disadvantage.

The next day the Germans pulled back. We Americans had taken a helluva beating and we were lucky when Rommel pulled out. [See Tony Costanzo's account of Kasserine Pass in Chapter 4.] The 45th Division had just been a backup force so we were okay. However, we had been baptized in combat. After Kasserine Pass, we withdrew to Oran again where we spent a lot of time getting ready for our next battle, wherever that might be. We practiced on embarking on landing craft, using nets strung over the sides of ships, and made amphibious landings along the North African coast. We knew that there was more to come.

On the front line we had eaten K Rations: a waterproof bag with biscuits and a can of food. We always had water but had to add a chemical called "abadan" to it to insure we didn't get sick. Mail call was sporadic on the front but sometimes it came with the supplies being brought up. What you missed most was not getting a shower. We never saw showers until we moved back into a reserve position.

You didn't think much about patriotism. What kept you going was thinking about survival. We were just a little piece of action in a big war and often you didn't even have a good handle on the situation in your own area. For example, it wasn't until after Kasserine Pass that I realized just how badly we had been beaten. One thing that did help morale was General Patton being assigned as our Commanding Officer after Kasserine Pass. He got us together in groups of several hundred back in Oran. Every other word was "fuck" and "shit" but he got his point across. Later, he would often drive by us as we walked, heading for the front. He would always encourage us and we knew he would be with us on the front lines where the action was. He seemed to be unafraid and was not asking us to go somewhere he was unwilling to go. Most of us liked Patton; he was a pretty sharp cookie.[1]

When we shipped out of Oran, we didn't know where we were going but assumed it was for an invasion. We were on the USS *Culvert* again, packed in like sardines in a can, and ran into one helluva storm. The waves were so big that periodically a nearby destroyer would dip below the waves, be gone from view and then pop up again. Thank God I didn't get seasick, but many of the guys did.

It was June now and into summer and on the morning of July 10, 1943, we found that we were going into Sicily. We were in the first group landing at Gela on the southwest coast. The 36th Division was on our right and the British with Montgomery were going in on the southeast side of the island. It was amazing at first since there was no resistance from the Germans. But then it happened. Our platoon had landed and was 300-400 yards from the beach when we came over a rise and were surprised by (and also surprised) five German soldiers. I was lucky. It happened so quickly that we just went at each other. He didn't have time to fire and neither did I, but I had my bayonet in and he didn't. I just went for him in the upper body. I'll never forget it since I had a hard time pulling the bayonet out, it was stuck on a bone. (In training, they had taught us to always twist the bayonet going in so that it wouldn't get stuck in a bone...but in the heat of battle, I forgot.) A little traumatic but things were happening so fast that you just did what you had to do. We killed three of them and two more surrendered. We stripped the two prisoners of weapons, sent them back toward the beach, and kept moving.

We were seasoned soldiers now, this was the real thing. My buddy Mike Oriel from Rochester was killed that day. I didn't see it happen but it puts a big hole in the bottom of your stomach when you find out. Mike was a big 6'2" guy who I drank a lot of beer with in Watertown at Fort Drum. In addition to that, our Regimental Commander, Lt.Col. Schaeffer, was captured that day. He liked being out in front of the troops and I guess in this case he got a little too far out front.

Other outfits took more of a beating on Sicily than we did. After the first day, we didn't see much action. We moved northeast toward Palermo, but we were really backups in that action. We saw a lot of bodies and burned-out German vehicles around Palermo but kept on moving toward Messina and along the north coast. It was a pretty country and someplace I'd like to go back to. The Germans had occupied some small towns and every once in a while we would get hit with 88s. But Patton was smart. We would just move inland, go over some hills and avoid the pockets of resistance. It was obvious the Germans weren't going to stand and fight on Sicily and so our object was to get to Messina as soon as possible, join up with the British and capture as many of the Germans as we could.

The whole Sicily campaign took only a month, and the first day was the worst one for Company B. Probably the most disappointing thing I witnessed was the decimation of our paratroopers by friendly fire when they parachuted in to Gela on the first night. The ships and artillery never stopped shooting and many of them were killed by our own guns. [See Sam Price's story of this same event in Chapter 2.]

We rested up at Messina, replenished the Division and got ready for the next move. It came in less than a month with the invasion of Italy at Salerno. On September 9th we stepped off the landing craft again, just south of Salerno. Although some outfits got hit, we moved ashore without resistance. It seemed like Sicily all over again. It was flat terrain and you could see the mountains of the Amalfi coast off to the left. We were to head toward the hills behind the beach and try and nail down the high ground. I will never forget a scene as we moved through a small village. A German soldier was sitting with his blond hair blowing in the breeze, but he was dead. You couldn't see any wounds on him at all. I stopped and took the cigars out of his pocket and kept moving. I will never forget that as long as I live.

About noon we stopped to regroup and then headed for a small hill to dig in for the night. We broke camp early the next day and just in time. Just as we got off that hill, the Germans zeroed it in. They unloaded on it with a tremendous artillery barrage. We moved inland again toward the northeast and were attacked by German planes and more artillery but no one got hurt. We built slit trenches for foxholes and dug in for the night. I remember that foxhole because I left a new Kaywoodie pipe in it that had been sent to me from back home by my buddy, Don Elfin. (Brother of the future federal court judge in Buffalo.) I bet some Italian guy is still smoking it (laughs).

The next day, I was sent out on patrol and we came across a German patrol of 14-15 people. All hell broke loose. My gun was tied up with an antitank grenade mechanism. I stuck the stock in the ground and fired the grenade, but like a damned fool, in the intensity of the moment, I forgot to pull the pin, so it did no good. My buddy Steve Semanski from Long Island was hit and dying, so I grabbed his BAR (Browning Automatic Rifle) and opened up. I remember killing a couple of Germans. They were running. It was all over quickly. Most of us survived, and shortly thereafter, they pulled our outfit back toward the beach for rest and replenishment. We were somewhere near Naples by then, and it was there that I made Tech Sergeant, a new title but not much more pay.

I found out that my good friend, Bud Lundquist, whose family ran Lundquist Hardware back home, was now stationed in Foggia on the east coast of Italy. He had gone into the Air Corps early and had shot down several German planes in the wrap-up of the Tunisian campaign. I believe he flew P-40s or maybe P-47 pursuit planes. At any rate, I got leave to go see him and met an officer/pilot of a C-47 who said, "Come with me, I'm going to Foggia." He treated me like a king, got me a good meal in the officer's mess at Foggia, and then gave me his jeep to go find Bud.

Talk about living right! The Air Corps had a trailer with beds, linen and a small kitchen that they towed behind them. I was envious. For two days Bud and I wined and dined our way around Foggia. It was in the British sector. One day I saw a long line of guys and commented to Bud that it must be the "chow line." "No way," he said, "that's the ass line!" I always felt that the British took better care of their troops from a personal standpoint than the Americans did.

When I got back to Naples, the Army had already begun its move toward Cassino. We headed through the mountains walking. We had to take a mountain near a town called Venafro which was located somewhere south of Cassino. On the other side of the town was a valley we called "Purple Heart Valley." But getting up the mountain to even look at the valley was tough. We bivouacked in a church with no roof and the next day we started up. It was rocky and there were a lot of olive trees in the area. I got hit with a mortar on the way up, but it was a superficial wound. The aid station treated it and I got back to workin'. I think it took four or five days to get to the top of that mountain because we were in continual firefights. It was a rocky, tough place to climb. You couldn't dig in because of the rocks, so the only thing you could do was stack rocks around your position. Nobody wanted to take prisoners because it was risky and took too damn long to take them down and then climb the hill again.

On the top, we got mortared, and two guys no more that 10 feet away were hit. One fellow was killed instantly. The other had a leg blown off and the medic couldn't get the blood flow totally stopped. There was too much action and we couldn't medivac him down. We gave him all the morphine we had, but he was delirious and finally died after a couple of days. Luck plays a game with you, you know. Earlier, east of Salerno, I got hit and was knocked ass over tea kettle. I could feel the warm blood running down my leg. But when I brought my hand up there was nothing there. The shrapnel had hit my canteen! I was wet with water and all it did was leave one helluva big bruise spot. One time I saw a helmet where a bullet had gone in, traveled around between the liner and the helmet and then come back out again. Why do these things happen? They just do. And you know, after the war, I felt that I had fought in the safest part of the war. In the Southwest Pacific it was much tougher.

Once we got to the top of that hill overlooking Purple Heart Valley, we could see, in the distance, Cassino, with the monastery perched on top of the mountain where the Germans were holed up. I remember seeing our bombers, I think they were B-17s, hitting the mountain with tons of explosives. During lulls in the fighting I did a lot of target-shooting with my .45 (.45-caliber pistol). I came to the conclusion that the .45 was the most inaccurate gun every manufactured. [See Gino Micciche's experience at Cassino in Chapter 12.][2]

All of that time on the Venafro front, it rained; there must be something about a war that creates rain. It wasn't bad on the mountain; it was solid rock. But down in the valley it was a mudhole. Your feet were always wet. The roads weren't paved and everything got bogged down. It was a good thing we had mules.

It must have been in early January when they pulled us back to Naples, and there we got ready for another landing. We didn't know it at the time, but we were headed for Anzio. The actual landing at Anzio on January 22, 1944, was quiet. There was virtually no opposition and we walked two to three miles inland and dug in. Then, the people in charge made a big mistake. We just sat there for three or four days; and, of course, that gave the Germans time to move in troops. When we did try to break out, they had us hemmed in. We lost a lot of troops there. We heard through the grapevine that Darby's rangers had really got shellacked on one operation, but I never got the whole scoop on it until after the war.[3]

We were dug in along this railroad that ran straight toward the hills near Aprilia. We called it the factory because there was an old factory in the area. The railroad was the only high ground and so for protection we dug caves into the side of the railroad embankment. You know, in a situation like this, your war is just a little thing. The whole Anzio front seemed to be only about ten square miles and our little area probably wasn't bigger than a large field most of the time. You thought about survival, not about the big picture. One time the fighting got so tough that we even had to arm the cooks and support personnel.

The Germans had good weapons. They had this huge railroad gun we called "Anzio Annie." They would roll it out at night and bombard us. The German Schnauzer was also a good gun, but probably sounded worse than it really was. We called it the "burp gun." The Germans were good at having their weapons make a lot of noise. It helped with the fear factor. As far

"Now that ya mention it, Joe, it does sound like th' patter of rain on a hot tin roof."

DRAWINGS ABOUT THE CAMPAIGN IN ITALY FROM ONE OF THE GI'S FAVORITE CARTOONISTS, BILL MAULDIN. MAULDIN WAS AN INFANTRYMAN IN BOB PUTNEY'S 45TH DIVISION. HE CREATED THE CARTOONS, FOUND A PRINT SHOP, SOLD BOOKS OF THE CARTOONS TO GIS FOR 25¢ AND USED THE PROCEEDS TO PUBLISH THE DIVISION NEWSPAPER. THESE CARTOONS CAME FROM A PAMPHLET CALLED *Mud, Mules and Mountains*, PRINTED IN 1944 IN PALERMO, ITALY. WHEN INTERVIEWED, MAULDIN SAID: "IT PROBABLY SAVED MY LIFE. WHEN I WAS PUBLISHING THE CARTOONS, I COULDN'T BE IN THE FRONT LINES TO GET SHOT AT!"4

as our weapons were concerned, I liked the M-1 carbine the best because it never failed. Our Thompson submachine gun could be unreliable. It often jammed if you used a belt, so we always used a clip when we could. We were there six weeks or so and exchanged positions several times back and forth with the Germans. They were good soldiers. We respected them. There was no hand-to-hand combat for us at Anzio, but we did see a lot of Germans at close distances and I shot a few.

Of course, you always do some crazy things in a situation like that. I

"Why the hell couldn't you have been born a beautiful woman?"

remember someone defusing a grenade and then throwing it into a group of guys. He was laughing but were we pissed! Another night, I was sitting near a big hole in the ground where we threw extra mortar increment bags and where the artillery guys would dispose of unneeded powder. I wondered what would happen if I threw a match in there, so I lobbed one in (laughs)! What a show!! Smoke, fire, explosions! Nobody knew what had happened but I came "clean" with the CO and told him that I had accidentally thrown my cigar in there. I could have got my ass in a real sling over that one!

Then one night I got hit. It was one of those multiple mortar barrages the Germans had...one right after the other. I got hit by shrapnel in the leg and it severed my Achilles tendon. My buddy Nick Malanek was also hit. He got it in the back. We weren't bleeding too badly so we walked back to the aid station. My leg was okay but my foot just flopped around because the tendon was gone and so the walking went pretty slow. At the aid station they put us on a litter and an ambulance got us back to the Army Field Hospital on the beachhead. It was a huge tent or series of tents and there were litters all over with wounded men and they got me right in and reattached the Achilles tendon. I don't think they had done many operations like that but it worked out. I really haven't had much trouble from it. I met Jim Scarpino at that field hospital. He was a friend from back home and was working as a medic in the hospital. After the war, he became a surgeon.

What I remember most about the field hospital was the hot food. We hadn't had hot food for six weeks on the front. When I saw it, I took two plates and put one under my cot. But I wasn't used to eating a lot and couldn't even finish the first plate (laughs)! I got a complication, though. It was cold and damp and I wasn't moving, so I came down with pneumonia. When that happened, the Army flew me back to Naples on a C-47, to the 36th Division Hospital. I thought that the medical care was good under the circumstances. The 36th Division Hospital in Naples was run by a medical group from Buffalo. There I ran into Ted Jacobs, a half-assed relative of mine from Buffalo, who was a major and a surgeon with the group. Needless to say, I got good treatment. The hospital was really a gymnasium that had been made into a hospital. I remember a lot of screaming at night. Some guys would hallucinate in the night and think they were still out on the front.

After a couple of months, they sent me back to my outfit. I got a ride on an ammo ship to Anzio and then hitchhiked north. By that time, we had broken out and had pushed the Germans back toward Rome. When I finally linked up with my Company, the only guy I recognized was the First Sergeant. Everyone else had either been killed, wounded or sent home. When he saw me he said, "Putney, what in the hell are you doing back here?!" I told him that I was better and that the Army said I was ready for combat. "Bullshit!" he said. "You've fought your war and deserve to go home." So they cut me some orders and sent me back to Naples. In a week or so I was on a troopship home.

The ship landed at Norfolk, VA, and we were put in a nearby army camp before transitioning out. By that time I had five stripes and was an old salt. One day, I forgot to salute a Lieutenant and he jumped me about it. "What the hell's wrong with you Sergeant!...etc." Just then a Major came by, looked at me, looked at the Lieutenant and then said to the Lieutenant, "Listen, you son-of-a-bitch. While you've been sitting over here on your fat ass, he's been off fighting in Europe. You should be saluting him!" And then he kindly suggested that the Lieutenant move on along. That made me feel good.

The Army asked me where I wanted to be discharged, and I said, "California." I thought it would be nice to see some of the country and have the Army pay for it. But they sent me back to Pine Camp (Fort Drum) in Watertown, NY. It was in the summer of '44, and I took a bus to Syracuse, the train to Westfield and then hitchhiked back home. I didn't tell my folks I was coming— I don't know why. They were really surprised and happy because just the day before they had received word that my brother was missing in action.

I came home right to this house on Beechview Ave. There were times when I didn't think I would ever make it back. A couple of years later, I married a girl from around the corner. She had been a Navy nurse stationed in Long Island during the war. We've been married for 48 years, have three boys, a daughter and ten grandchildren. I live today in the same house I grew up in and have had a great life. I have no regrets about the war. We were fighting for a good cause, but it made you grow up real fast. I guess I was one of the lucky ones, and I was lucky to be born an American.

[Bob Putney came home from the war with three Purple Hearts and a Combat Infantryman's Badge. He initially went into the family business of running a Chevrolet dealership, and after that business was sold, he went to work for a local bank where he was employed for many years. Today, he is retired and spends most of his free time at a hunting camp that his father built years ago, located just a few minutes drive from town.]

Background and Commentary

[1]The first direct conflict between American and German forces was in North Africa. At the beginning of the war, it was the only place where the Allies had a reasonable chance of inflicting any losses on the German war machine. Algeria and Morocco were being held by French Vichy forces (the

collaborationist French regime that had capitulated to the Germans). It was felt that French resistance would be minimal and that eventually they would come to the Allied cause. Some of the initial battles were tough, but the French finally did turn their forces over to the Allies. In the meantime, British forces under the leadership of the British General, Bernard L. Montgomery, had defeated German General Rommel's forces on the outskirts of Egypt, in the brilliant battle of El Alamein. "Monty," as he was called, then moved toward the west while General Dwight Eisenhower with his American and British forces pushed toward the East. The Germans were caught in a squeeze as they retreated back toward Tunisia.

Bob Putney arrived in North Africa just in time for the infamous battle of Kasserine Pass. The Allies had already taken Morocco and part of Algeria and were now pushing toward Tunisia when the Germans counter-attacked and punished them at Kasserine Pass. A lot of lessons were learned there by the Allies. Some of the guns and tanks had proven to be inadequate against stronger German weapons, and better equipment was soon coming from the States. Eisenhower also discovered who some of his better and less capable commanders were. One that he liked very much was Major General George S. Patton, Jr. Patton was a swashbuckling, outspoken commander who believed primarily in one thing...attack, attack, attack! Eisenhower would later bring Patton back to England and ultimately to France where he led the 3rd Army in its breakout from Normandy and subsequent sweep through central France.

[2]The fighting for Bob Putney and the Allied forces in Italy was very tough. It may have been, at times, tougher than the fighting in the Pacific. Especially during the winter, this mountainous, hilly country became an ideal defensive battleground for the Germans. Trucks and mechanized vehicles couldn't move in the mud, so men and mules carried the supplies to the front so that the battle could be joined. It was for this reason, among others, that Generals Eisenhower and Marshall had opposed an all-out push in southern Europe. Had Prime Minister Churchill had his way, the primary attack on Germany would have come in the "soft underbelly" of Europe, from the south. Bob Putney and the men of the U.S. Army found out that there was nothing "soft" about fighting the German Army in this terrain. Eisenhower and Marshall obviously won the day with policy makers in Washington and London, and so plans continued for the invasion of western

France and for the all-out push across central Europe from that direction.

The waters on either side of Italy, combined with the incredibly rugged mountains in the country, made it easy for the Germans to establish strong and well-fortified defensive positions. One of these defensive positions, called the "Gustav line," ran across the Italian peninsula just north of Naples. The center of the line was anchored by a high mountain at Cassino, atop which was a 6th century Benedictine monastery. From this mountain, with their artillery, the Germans could control all of the access roads north to Rome. Here, for five months, during the winter of 1943-'44, the Germans stopped the Allied advance. Thousands of Allied soldiers were killed or wounded trying to take Monte Cassino. In desperation, the Allied forces dropped tons of bombs, leveling the old monastery, an act the Benedictines have never forgiven, despite the fact that their monastery was rebuilt by the Allies after the war. A Polish Division, fighting with the Allied forces, finally took the mountain top in the late spring of 1944.

Today you can drive a beautiful, winding road to the top of the mountain, and it is worth the trip. As you near the top, you can see on an adjoining mountainside the stark, white cemetery crosses that mark the graves of several hundred Polish soldiers who died in the assault on Monte Cassino.

[3]With their armies bogged down along the Gustav line, the Allies gambled and decided to make an amphibious landing behind the German lines at Anzio, southwest of Rome. In retrospect, the landing probably should never have been attempted. The buildup was already going on for the invasion of western France and supplies in Europe were tight. The number of fighting divisions that could be committed to the Anzio operation was limited. In essence, the Allies at this point were just too strung out to attempt an operation of this magnitude. Nevertheless, plans went ahead and Bob Putney and his comrades were thrust into this endeavor. The British went ashore at Anzio and the Americans landed just south of them, at the town of Nettuno.

In addition to the logistical problems, the commanding officer of the operation, Major General John P. Lucas, was a cautious man. After moving several miles inland without significant opposition, he halted the advance, consolidated his position, and had the men dig in. Instead of driving Patton-style for the high ground, the Alban hills on the road to Rome, he hunkered down and waited. This gave the Germans time to send rein-

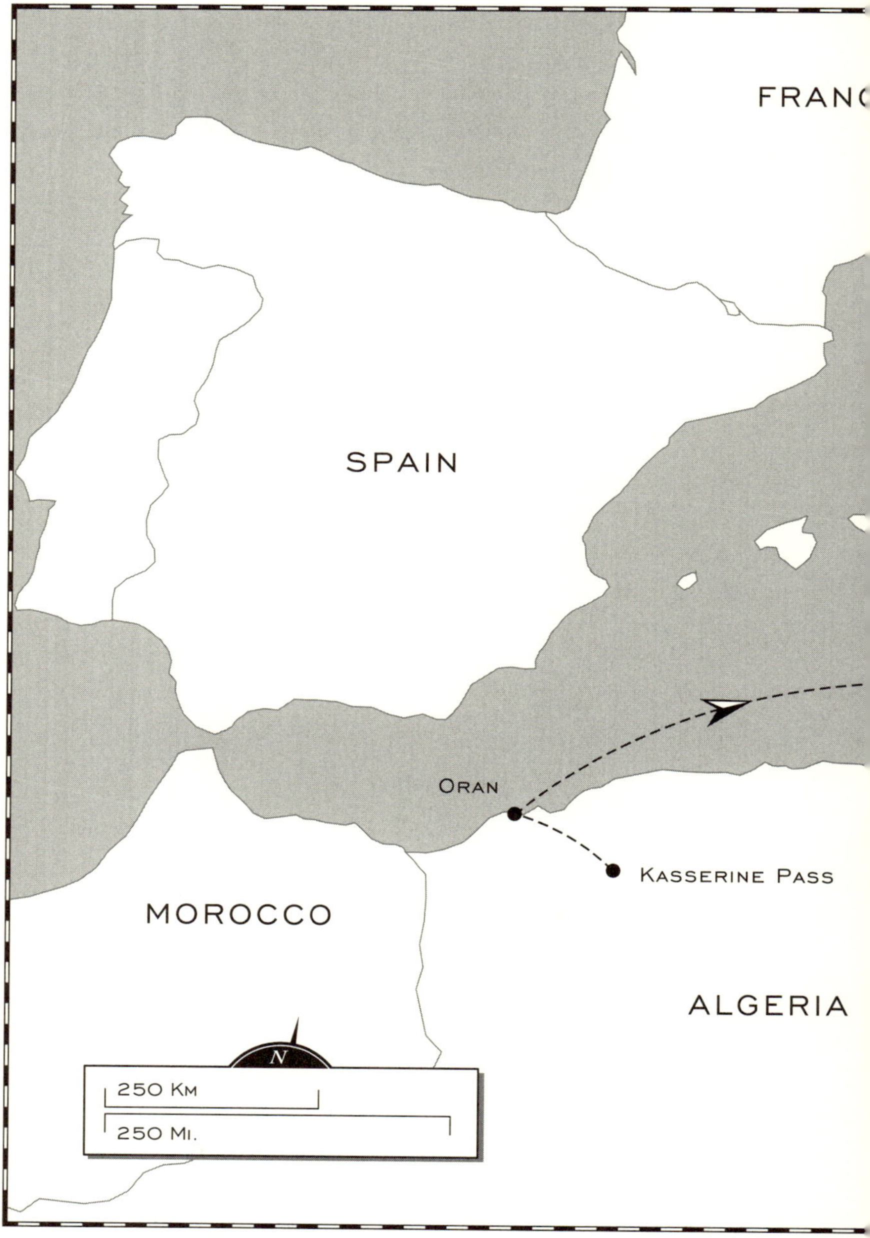

TRAVELS OF BOB PUTNEY

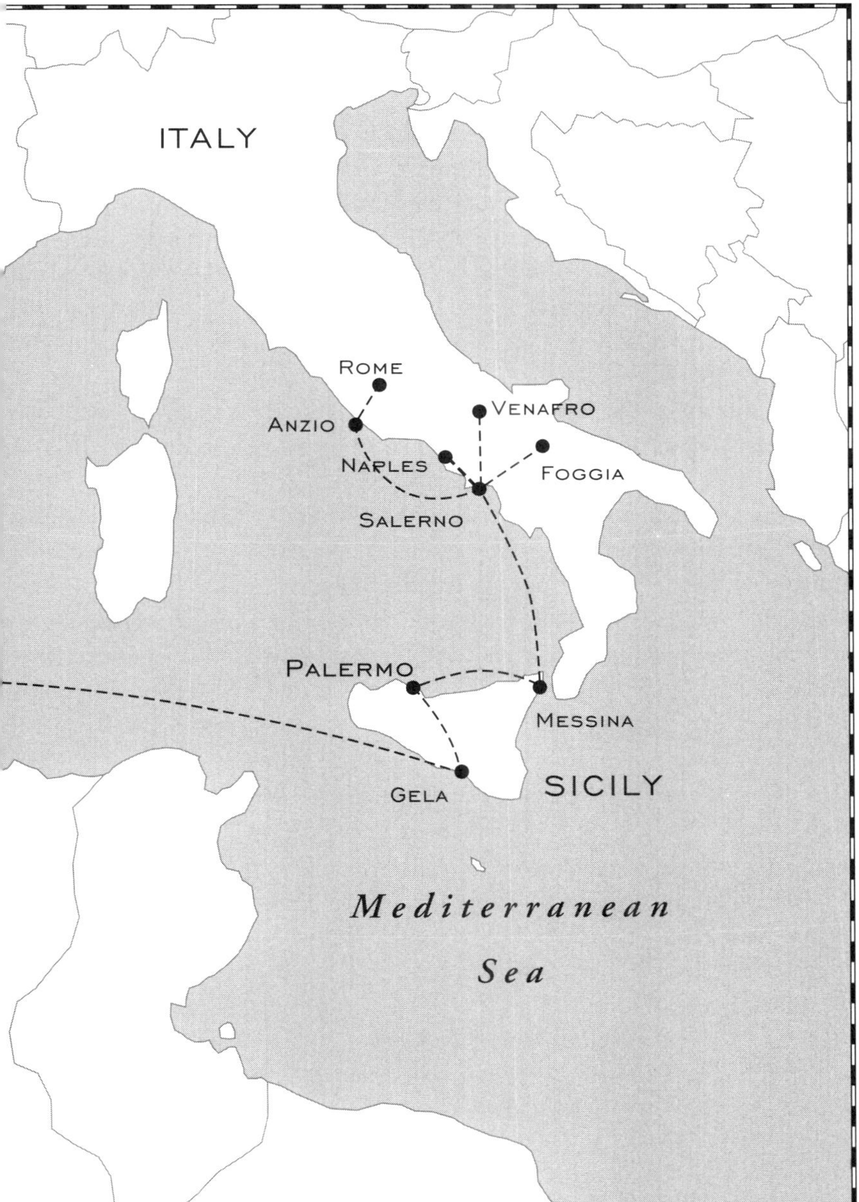
ITALY
ROME
ANZIO
VENAFRO
NAPLES
FOGGIA
SALERNO
PALERMO
MESSINA
GELA
SICILY
Mediterranean
Sea

forcements; they were able to contain the British and American forces in a small area, all of which was in range of German artillery and mortar fire. It was a brutal battle and was only broken when Monte Cassino finally fell in May of 1944, and the Germans began to retreat to the north.

Bob Putney referred to the disaster that overtook the Ranger Battalion commanded by Col. William O. Darby. On the night of January 29th and 30th, Darby's Rangers attempted to get behind German forces under the cover of darkness by sneaking up the Pantano Canal which led from the beachhead into the German lines. After the troops were committed and too far from friendly lines to receive assistance, they were ambushed by the Germans. Of the 767 men in the Ranger Battalion who went out that night, only six returned; the rest were either killed or taken prisoner. The ill-fated mission of Darby's Rangers was typical of the heartbreak and human waste that characterized the operation at Anzio.

Over the years, the men who fought in Italy and at Anzio have felt, and probably rightfully so, that their efforts in World War II went relatively unnoticed. They gave it their all, fought their best, and left a lot of their comrades on the battlefield. However, the attention of the world swiftly shifted to the west after the invasion at Normandy, and the war ended with everyone's focus being toward Japan and the Pacific. The reality, though, is that the Italian front was critical to the outcome of the war. Since Germany had to continue to maintain and supply several divisions of troops in Italy, these were troops that couldn't be committed to other fronts. In essence, the battle for Italy kept the German army tied up in southern Europe so that it couldn't fight more effectively elsewhere.

If anyone unfamiliar with the war wants to feel the impact of the fighting in Italy, they should visit the Sicily-Rome American Cemetery at Nettuno Beach. Here, shrouded by beautiful, large umbrella pines right in the midst of the old battleground of Anzio, are the graves of 7,862 soldiers, sailors and airmen who died in the war in southern Italy. Right after the war and before many of the next-of-kin opted to have the remains of their loved ones brought back to the United States, there were approximately 22,500 Americans buried here. In the entire Vietnam war, approximately 57,000 Americans died. By comparison, in World War II, in just one theater of the war—the area in Italy south of Rome—22,500 Americans gave their lives.

12. Fighting On The Other Side

The Italian Navy

In early 1943, our destroyer was shuttling convoys to Yugoslavia primarily to provide food to starving people. I was Assistant Commissary Officer and I told the sailors to save all of their food, even leftovers, because the people were hungry. When we got to the port serving the city of Zagreb, people were lined up waiting for food and I went down on the pier to help with the distribution. A German officer came up and told me to stop giving out the food or he would shoot me. I told him, "If you shoota me, they (men on ship) will shoota you!" He didn't shoot and I kept distributing the food.

That night three or four of us went up on the mountain outside of town for dinner. It was off-limits, but we heard that there was a good restaurant there. While we were eating, a big guy with guns and bandoliers of ammunition hanging on him came in and sat down. He was a partisan fighting against the Germans. He could have killed us all. But word travels fast and he had heard of our confrontation with the German on the pier and of our bringing food to the city. After dinner, for security, he walked with us down the mountain, said goodbye, and we returned safely to the ship.

Gino Micciche
Lieutenant Junior Grade,
Italian Republican Navy

[Gino Micciche had a unique experience during the war. Initially, he served in the Italian Navy when Mussolini was in control. Later, after the Allies invaded Italy, he fought with them against the Germans.]

I was born in Milano (Milan), in northern Italy and was 16 when the war began. My love was soccer and I was a good player. (After the war, I was a substitute on an Italian soccer team and we came to America. That's how I met my wife, Nancy Lucca, who lived on Franklin St.)

After graduating from high school in Italy, I was recruited into a Navy school where my main duty was to play soccer. But in 1941 the war was heating up, and instead of being commissioned in two years, we were commissioned in 13 months. School and soccer were over and I was sent out to the fleet.

Back in those days people liked Mussolini. They didn't like the *fascisti,* the quasi-military political groups that surrounded him, but people in general liked Mussolini for what he had done to improve the economy and the Italian standard of living. Most of us weren't into politics and stayed away from it. I went into the Italian military because it was my duty. Most of us felt that Mussolini didn't have much choice but to enter into an alliance with Germany. If he hadn't, Hitler would have probably invaded Italy just as he had France.

I volunteered for my first assignment and was sent to a torpedo boat base at La Spezia, on the northwest coast. They were called "MAS" boats, fast patrol boats with three-man crews and two torpedoes. It looked pretty much like a suicide operation to me and after two or three months I "unvolunteered" myself and was sent to submarines.

The submarine, *Colombo,* was based in Pula, far to the east on the other side of the Adriatic Sea. I was only there about six months, and during that time we made two deployments into the Mediterranean. Our job was not to attack shipping but to spy on British convoy activity around Malta. Malta was the last British outpost in that part of the Mediterranean. We would radio back to Rome the movements of allied shipping and then presumably these ships would be attacked by other submarines or aircraft.

After that initial submarine experience, I volunteered for destroyers and was transferred to the *Missori,* a destroyer homeported in Bari on Italy's southeast coast. It was an old "three-stacker" destroyer and was assigned the duty of accompanying convoys enroute to Yugoslavia, Albania and Greece. It was good duty. There were about 100 men on board, the Captain was a fine individual, and our mission didn't involve a lot of risk. I was assistant commissary officer and was on the *Missori* until early spring of 1943. As I look back on it, the highlight of that experience was my confrontation with the German officer at the pier near Zagreb. That may have been the closest I came to being killed in the whole war.

On June 30, 1943, our ship went into the port at Napoli (Naples) for repairs and I was able to get home to Milano on leave. While I was there, the fascist government fell. The night that happened, many fascists were killed in the streets. Many of them were innocent but the mob didn't spare anyone, and some friends of my father were killed. When my furlough was over, I left for Napoli to return to my ship, but by that time, Italy had surrendered to the Allies and Germany was now in control of the country. The train was stopped several times by the Germans and when I finally arrived at Napoli, my ship had already left for Bari.[1]

I took a train to Bari, caught up with the ship, and we were soon underway for Greece. But a few days out, we had an accident on the ship. A boiler or steam line ruptured in the boiler room. I was close by and rushed to help the men caught in the blast. They were screaming and trying to get out. I helped them get out but in the process got burned myself. The ship turned around and limped back into Bari for repairs. The injured, including myself, were put in a hospital near Bari.

What happened next just shows you how the "luck-of-the-draw" can determine your fate. While I was in the hospital, the *Missori* got underway on another supply mission to Greece. When the ship came into Patras, Greece, the Germans, who had been told of the Italian surrender, were waiting and told the Captain to give up the ship. He refused. So they killed him along with all of the crew members and sank the ship. If I hadn't been in that hospital in Bari, I wouldn't be here today.

Those of us who were in the Italian military were in a quandary after Italy surrendered to the Allies. What were we supposed to do? We had been fighting the Americans and British and were now supposedly on their side. The Allies didn't know what to do with us either. What happened from a practical standpoint was that if you were in the Allied sector, you became a prisoner of the Americans or British. If you were in the German sector, like Pete Caprino was, the opposite occurred. Since I was in the south and in the British sector near Foggia, I ended up in a British POW camp.[2]

The British kept a group of Italian soldiers and sailors, including myself, in a holding area or camp near Bari. There wasn't much to do and I remember a lot of complaints about the food. We weren't used to British food or maybe they were just giving us their leftovers. One day, somebody in the British Army said, "You wanta good food? Go fighta with us!" It seemed like a good idea, and within a week I was training in an Italian Marine Battalion that was to be sent to the front to fight against the

Germans. It was really an elite group and for five months we were put through intense combat training. In March of '44, Prince Umberto of Italy and General Bagoglia came to Gallipoli to congratulate us and they named us the "San Marco Battalion."

Soon after that, we moved out toward the front lines to the north. It was the spring of 1944 and the Allies were bottled up along the Gustav line that ran through Monte Cassino. I was a platoon commander and they put us with the American 5th Army but attached us as support to a Polish division which had been charged with moving up the right flank of Monte Cassino. Monte Cassino was a 2,000-foot steep mountain with terraced vineyards and olive groves on its sides. At the top was an ancient Benedictine Abbey, and from the top, the Germans had secured the high ground and had stopped the Allied advance throughout the winter. Our outfit patrolled an area around Valvori, just south of the Rapido River. Our mission was to protect the left flank of the Polish troops. We lost a few men to gunfire on patrols and one day I got boxed in by German mortar fire in an old house. But most of the German fire was targeted at the artillery and supply buildup behind us and so the shells usually went over our heads.

The Polish fighters were tough and seasoned. They showed no mercy as far as the Germans were concerned. They lost hundreds of men on their first unsuccessful attack on Monte Cassino. After that attack, I remember one Polish soldier marching back into camp at the base of the mountain with a German head under his arm. I doubt that many prisoners were taken in that battle. Before the second assault in May, the Americans unloaded on the Abbey at the top with a ferocious artillery and bomber attack. The next time the Poles moved out and up the right flank, they took the top of Monte Cassino and the Germans began to fall back. They had won the battle, but the price of that battle can be seen today in nearly a thousand crosses marking Polish graves at that top of that miserable mountain.

After Monte Cassino, we were pulled back in reserve and the rest of my war memories are good ones. I was assigned as Harbor Control Officer at a little port called Molfetta, north of Bari. It was a quiet, lazy little Italian town and I was like a king—I controlled the fishing permits! Soccer, vino, girls, sun, being the boss...it doesn't get any better than that (laughs)!

Today, when I'm out with Pete, Joe and my other pals, we talk more about these things than we used to. I guess it's a part of getting old. We all love golf and you can get a lot of war stories told over 18 holes. What really upsets my buddies, though, is my Italian Navy pension. "Hey," they say "we wonna the war, and you getta the pension!" "Yeah," I say, "and I getta a bigger than usual pension because I also fought for the Americans with the San Marco Battalion at Monte Cassino!" I don't tell them that because of my work with the San Marco Battalion, I was also awarded the Medaglia D'Ozo, the equivalent of the Medal of Honor in this country. That's the truth. My name is listed with all of the others who received the award in the Honor Roll of Combat in Roma (Rome).

[After the war, Gino Micciche received the Medaglia D'Ozo for his work with the San Marco Battalion. He moved to America and married Nancy Lucca, the sister of Joe Caprino's wife and the girl that he had met when he came to America on a soccer trip after the war. He owned a wood-working business for many years and is still active as a consultant in the furniture business.]

The Italian Army

When I was 14, I became a barber. I'm still a barber and have had this little shop on Lafayette St. for over 40 years. When Mussolini drafted me into the Italian Army in 1941, I decided,"Why not be a barber?" Then, when I surrendered to the Germans in 1944, they needed a barber. I cut a lot of German hair...until the day the American bombs started falling from the sky like rain!

Pete Caprino
Private First Class,
Italian Republican Army

[Pete Caprino is now a barber in town, but during the war he cut hair for the AXIS powers: first the Italians and then the Germans. At the same time, his brother Joe was a U.S. citizen serving in the U.S. Army.]

When we were kids in Tortorici, Sicily, my Mama taught us to always have a vocation. There weren't a lot of choices at the time and so me and my three brothers were taught how to be both a tailor and a barber. I had been born in Sicily in 1922. My brother Joe had been born in America in 1919 before my parents moved back to the old country. My younger brother Al was also born in Sicily and we all figured that between barbering and tailoring somehow we would be able to make a living.

Those early years in Sicily were exciting ones. Mussolini was popular and did a lot of good things...at least that is what we were taught. In Sicily, he challenged the Mafia and people liked that. For years the Mafia had been an oppressive force in Sicily and Mussolini was the first leader to stand up to them. It sounds crazy now, but as a young boy I got caught up in it and joined the young fascisti. We went to meetings and parades. To me, at that time, it was like being in the boy scouts or something.

In 1941, when I was 19, I was drafted into the Italian Army. My brother Joe also got a draft notice but he laughed it off. He was in America. [Pete's brother, Joe Caprino, was in the U.S. Army. See his story in Chapter 8.] I reported to the Army and for the next year and a half, I worked at an Army base near Padua in northern Italy. I was now in uniform but nothing much had changed. I was still cutting hair.

In July, 1943, came a big surprise. We had been told all along that Mussolini was still strong, that the Axis was winning the war, and that Germany was our ally. Then one day, out of nowhere, the newspapers announced that Italy was surrendering to the Allies. None of us knew what to do. A friend of mine, and I can't remember his name, said, "We'd better get out of here before the Germans come." And so we took off for his home which was in a little town not far away called Resana. For the next six months or so I lived there with him and his family. They gave me room and board and in turn I helped out and became one of the town barbers. They were wonderful people and treated me like a son. I never saw them again after I went home from the war.

The Germans in that area were the tough SS troops of Hitler. One day they put up a sign that said: "All Italian soldiers who have deserted report to us. If you do not, you will be killed!" My friend and I talked it over. One day we had been to a town near Monte Grappa and had seen several Italian young men who had been hung by the Germans. After several days their bodies were still hanging from the trees that lined the road. The Germans said that they had been Italian Army soldiers who had not turned themselves in. After seeing that, we decided to take our chances with the Germans and so turned ourselves into the SS unit in our area.[2]

Actually, the Germans did not treat us badly. They were fine as long you didn't double-cross them. I started cutting hair for the Germans, and every night went back to my friend's house to sleep. Most of the other Italian soldiers were assigned to putting up concrete posts, bunkers and other obstructions to try and stop the inevitable march of the Americans and British coming up from the south. We ate at a central mess with the German soldiers every noon. The food wasn't bad but I never did get used to that dark German bread.

There was a large villa near the house where I lived in Resana and the German brass were housed there. American intelligence had found out about it, and almost every night it would get bombed. First, planes would come and drop flares and illuminate the countryside. You could see for miles and sometimes could almost see Venice in the distance. Then other planes would come strafing and bombing the villa. The sirens would all go off, and we would have to get up in the middle of the night and head for the woods. It was the only safe place to be.

There must have been spies around reporting to the Americans because they also found out about the central German mess and our tradition of always eating lunch around noon. One day when I was having lunch, I heard planes and looked up. Here came this thing that looked like a little egg. All of sudden, whoom!, the bombs hit...everything was blowing up. Tents, timber, arms, heads and legs...were all flying through the air. I got thrown about 100 yards and was knocked out. When I came to, there was a lot of screaming and crying. The Germans still alive said, "Let's get out of here!" Those of us who could, left the area.

The next day we were sent back to the site of the bombing. It was a terrible mess. Bodies and body parts were all over the place and for three or four days we worked to clean them up. The Germans built a mass grave for burial. There must have been 500-600 men who died in that attack. I was just lucky. When I went back to where I had been standing, there were two bombs there that hadn't detonated. If they had gone off, I wouldn't be here today. This bomb attack killed mostly soldiers, but often during a bombing raid children and old people would get killed too. The American fliers didn't intend to kill the innocent, but often the innocent got killed.

We kept hearing over the radio that the Americans were coming. Florence was taken and then Bologna. They were heading our way. Sometime in March or April of 1945 the Germans split. The Americans were getting close and apparently they had decided not to fight. About two days later, the American troops marched into town. It was a happy day with lots of celebration. We had been liberated! For us, the war was over.

A month or two later, the war with Germany was over. Yet, there was no way to get home. All of the trains and transport were under the control of the American military and civilians could not travel. I had not heard from my family for two years. Sometime in July or August of 1945, I was finally able to get a train back to southern Italy and took a ferry to Sicily.

Tortorici is a small town and I got there by bus. Mama lived up on a hill outside of town and the word traveled fast that I was home. What a homecoming! I'll never forget it. Then a month later, my brother Joe came. Here I was an ex-soldier of the Italian Army, and here came my brother with his Sergeant stripes and fancy American uniform. I hadn't even known that he had been in the American Army. We had a great homecoming! Here we were, two brothers who had been on opposite sides in the war standing on my mama's porch in Sicily. I will always remember my brother standing on that porch and throwing out Lucky Strike cigarettes to the neighbors. They were good cigarettes, the wine was delicious, it was a wonderful day...we had a lot to celebrate!

[Pete Caprino came to America after the war and became a citizen. His brother Joe was already a citizen and fought with the US Army during the war (see Chapter 8). Pete has been a barber his whole life and still cuts hair at his small shop here in town.]

Background and Commentary

[1] Mussolini had been popular in Italy, but the Allied victories in North Africa and the bombing of Italy that resulted began to turn Italians against the fascist dictator. The final straw that brought down his government was the successful Allied invasion of Sicily. On July 25, 1943, the fascist gov-

Joe and Pete Caprino with their mother and brother, reunited in Sicily after the war.

ernment fell and Mussolini was arrested and put in prison. The Nazis were successful in rescuing the deposed dictator, who established a German-dominated Republic in the northern part of the country called the Republic of Salo. However, Mussolini's future was now tied directly to the success of the German Army. His luck finally ran out on April 28, 1945.

With German forces collapsing all around him, he tried to escape to Switzerland. He was discovered and, along with his mistress, was executed by Italian partisans fighting for the Allied cause.

[2] By the end of 1943, the Allies had invaded the mainland of Italy. The British came ashore at Taranto and soon dominated the southern "boot" of Italy and quickly pushed up the east coast heading for Foggia. Their goal was to take control of the airfields around Foggia and secure the east coast. The Americans had landed at Salerno on the southwest coast and controlled that area of the country. It was a difficult time for people serving in the Italian military. Technically, the country was now allied with the United States and Britain. Yet, for obvious reasons, the Allies wondered how deep the commitment of the former enemy was to this new status. As a result, at least on temporary basis, men like Gino Micciche were put into POW camps. Men in the north, like Pete Caprino, had to surrender to the German army or face execution. Micciche was given a way out by volunteering to fight for the Allied cause. The Italian Marine unit, the San Marco Battalion, of which Gino Micciche was part, went into action on the Venafro front near Cassino on April 9, 1945. Later, after Micciche had been transferred to new duties, the battalion was transferred to the Abruzzi and Macerata areas of northern Italy where it assisted the British 8th Army in the fighting in that region.

13. Americans In The Persian Gulf

Most people don't realize it, but at one time, during the war, we had 40,000 troops in Iran. We were a part of it. We didn't realize it until after the war, but for awhile we were even stationed in the same city, Khorramshahr, which means "City of Delight." There wasn't much to be delighted about. It was a place in the desert along the Persian Gulf. The British and the Americans had transformed the place into a major receiving port for supplies headed for the Soviet Union to help the Russians in their fight against the Germans. A large pier had been constructed that could serve seven ships at a time. Thousands of tons and millions of dollars of supplies came in through that port. A huge railroad siding had been built alongside the pier to handle the rail traffic heading north with supplies for the fight against Hitler on the eastern front.

The U.S. Army also built two truck assembly plants in southern Iran where American GMC and Dodge trucks were assembled and made ready for the 1,000-mile trip up the narrow dirt roads of Iran to the Russian border. From there, the Russians would drive these trucks loaded with American war supplies another 1000 miles to the front lines where they would be used in the fight against the Germans. It was a big operation but not many people know that it happened. What's even more strange is that at least four of us from this little town ended up being sent to Iran. Jack Rowe and Gordon Nelson also served there. Not only did we come from the same town, but, by sheer coincidence, three of us live on the same street over on the west side of town![1]

Allen Findlay
Private First Class,
U.S. Army Reserve

Norman VanVlack
Lieutenant,
U.S. Army Reserve

[This is an intriguing story of two men from the same street in town who ended up serving in Iran during the war. Not many were aware, but millions of tons of military supplies were sent to the Russians through Iran.]

The Piers at Khorramshahr, Iran–1944.

Norm: I ended up in Iran sort of by accident. My dad was a medical officer in the Army and had been sent to Teheran before the war. When war broke out, I was just an 18-year-old kid living there with my parents. My first involvement in the war effort was as a construction worker. An American company, Foley Brothers Construction, was in the country reconstructing and double-tracking the railroad that led north from the Persian Gulf, and so I went to work for them. However, in April of 1942, I joined the Army. The Army needed men and so I just went down and signed up. Never went to boot camp or anything. They just gave me a uniform, made me a PFC (Private First Class), and I started working in the motor pool. Later, in 1943, the Army would send me back to the States to Officer Candidate School, but, at the beginning, I was working as an enlisted man.

Al: I got to Iran, I suppose, through regular channels. I was drafted and went into the Army on June 13, 1942. We were sent for basic training to Fort Bragg, NC, and from there went to Indiantown Gap, PA, where we learned how to unload ships on a mock-up of a ship the Army had constructed in a field. We called it the "Go-Nowhere Ship" (laughs). [Bob Olson was trained at the same place. See Chapter 17.] From there, we were taken by train to New York and put on the USS *West Point,* which before the war had been the oceanliner SS *America.* We were told that the name of the ship had been changed because the Germans thought that they had sunk the *America,* and our government wanted them to continue to believe it. We left New York for Rio De Janiero, Brazil, where we picked up supplies. We were there for three or four days but they wouldn't let us off the ship. From there we went to Bombay, India, where we did get a chance for leave and finally got off the ship. From Bombay, we were put on a smaller British ship and that took us to Khorramshahr in the Persian Gulf.

Norm: I was assigned to the motor pool in Bushire, a town up the coast from Khorramshahr. We had an assembly plant there where the Army would assemble the trucks being brought over for transport to the Russian front. Sometimes the engines would have to be installed, tires were put on, the chassis would be attached to the body of the truck and the trucks would be test-driven. One of my jobs was to train the Iranians to drive the trucks. That was probably the most dangerous part of my duty during the war! Many of them had never even seen a truck and sometimes they did crazy things—like taking a loaded truck out of gear and letting it roll going down a mountain road. From time to time, drivers would be killed just because of their own carelessness. The roads, of course, were terrible, two-lane, sometimes one-lane, dirt roads. On a few occasions, I remember seeing drivers come back from those trips all black and blue from the rough and bumpy riding they had to endure.

After 50-100 trucks were assembled, we would take them in a convoy over the mountains to Shiraz and then other troops would supervise them on their journey to Teheran and finally to the Russian zone. We were never allowed to go into the Russian zone. When those trucks reached the Russian zone, no Americans could go beyond. The Russians did use some Iranian drivers, however, and so we had to keep training drivers to replace those who didn't come back. The one thing I didn't like about those trips to Shiraz was that sometimes I would have to stand guard duty with a gun because we would periodically be raided by bandits along the way. If we kept moving we were okay, but if the column of trucks stopped, these renegade tribesmen, who lived in the mountains, would climb into the trucks and start looting the supplies.[2]

Al: The work was hard. I usually worked the 3 to 11 shift (3 p.m. to 11 p.m.). However, in the summer, because of the heat, we had to shut down operations during the afternoon. When that happened, I would usually go to the 7 p.m. to 3 a.m. shift. I was in the 378th Port Battalion at Khorramshahr and the Americans operated the cranes and were responsible for getting the supplies and equipment off the ship. Once we had unloaded supplies onto the pier, the Iranian coolies, or "wogs" as we called them, would carry the stuff to the trucks or railroad cars for reloading. Some of these guys were incredibly strong. Many of them had a wooden pack that was strapped on their back. Another fellow would load them up with 150-200 lbs. of stuff and they would walk it away from the piers. It was something to see! We didn't know how to speak their language but it was never a problem. When I said "Bia!" that meant "come." "Boro" meant "go." That's about all you needed to know to get along.

It's hard to describe how hot it was over there. Some days, in the summer, it would get up to 130 -140 degrees. You just couldn't work under those conditions. We didn't have air conditioning. You just had to get out of the sun and hope there was some breeze. You've probably heard about frying eggs without a fire...well, we did it in the desert in Iran. On one of those hot days, I took the pan from my mess kit, dropped an egg in it, and, in about five minutes, I had a fried egg (laughs)! We often had guys who got second- and third-degree burns from leaning up against a truck or laying their hand on the hood of a vehicle when the sun was out. It was godawful hot over there. One time Jack Benny and Jane Russell came to Khorramshahr for a USO show. It was so hot that Jane Russell passed out! Needless to say, the troops were distraught about that (laughs). Although she didn't sing or dance, thankfully, she was able to make a short appearance.

Probably one of the toughest things about being where we were is that there was nothing to do. We lived in a barren wasteland, a desert. There was no town to go into for liberty. It was work, eat and sleep. In the winter, it rained and got muddy. In the summer, it was hot and dusty. We all looked forward to the few times when we could get out of Khorramshahr. The only place to really get away from things was in Teheran, about 500

Al Findlay, on the docks at Khorramshahr.

miles away. Twice I got to Teheran. It was a beautiful city and the Army had a recreation center where we could hang out. We went out to see the ruins of an old city called Ray. It had been built by Alexander the Great and then later destroyed by Genghis Khan. The place I enjoyed most though, was going to see the Peacock Throne at the Palace where the Shah lived. It was a beautiful thing to see, all covered with gold, silver and jewels.[3]

The train ride to Teheran was something in itself. We usually had to sit on hard wooden seats and it was a pretty rough ride. We could sleep three on either side of a compartment by one guy curling up on the seat, another lying on the seat back which folded down, and the smallest guy would crawl up in the luggage rack (laughs). It was quite a scene. The toilet was a hole in the floor with two foot marks but it wasn't easy to hit the hole with that train bouncing all over the place (more laughs).

The rail line itself was an engineering marvel. It had been constructed in the 1930s by the Germans and it went through extremely mountainous

A sign on a locomotive headed for Russsia indicating hundreds of thousands of tons of delivered war supplies. Exact number was marked "censored."

terrain. Sometimes, the tracks would wind up the side of a mountain, going in and out of tunnels in switchbacks, almost like a mountain road. We used to describe the railroad this way: it was built by the Germans, owned by the Iranians, controlled by the British and operated by the Americans! That was really true.

Norm: Living in Iran in those years took some adjustment for an American. Iran was really an alien culture to us. Their food habits were something I never did adjust to. I recall once taking a trip to Teheran on the train. A waiter came by with a dish of steaming rice with some delicious smelling mutton on it. I thought of buying a portion but decided to go to the dining car first and see the kitchen. What I saw turned me right off. The kitchen was a mess. It probably hadn't been cleaned in months. You walked on grease and dirt that had been ground into the floor boards of the dining car. No thanks. I decided to stay hungry. Another time, near a market in Teheran, I heard a loud buzzing sound. I turned a corner and here was a meat market and the flies were so thick they could be heard! When someone would buy meat, the butcher would slice off a hunk, cut a

Railroad tressel on the train to Teheran.

hole in it, put a piece of string through the hole, and the customer would walk away with it. They didn't believe in wrapping meat. After seeing that, I always stayed away from the local cuisine.

The Russians were interesting. We would see them at work but they were ordered by their government to fraternize with the Americans only when necessary. They had their own barracks and camps and our contact with them was strictly business. They were there to get trucks, equipment and supplies and that was it   One time, a Russian officer drove into the motor pool in an American jeep. They had taken out anything written in English, had put Russian names on things, and had even put the gear shift instructions in Russian. This fellow could speak good English and asked me how I liked his "Russian Jeep." He knew it was an American jeep but I guess Stalin had told him to spread the lie. At the time, I really wondered why we were giving the Russians all of those supplies. It didn't seem to me to be the right thing to do. In retrospect though, I can see now how it helped in our winning the war. The Soviet Union was a major force in the final destruction of the Nazis.

Al is right, the heat was terrible in the desert. It was also a lonely place to be as an American. When Marco Polo went through this area of Persia on his way to China, he described it as being covered with olive trees and vegetation. It must have changed a lot in a thousand years, because now nothing grew in that part of Iran. It was a barren landscape. There were a lot of Americans there, but we still felt isolated. The most difficult thing for me, though, were the dust storms. One summer we had 65 consecutive days of dust storms. You couldn't keep the sand out of your bed, your clothes, or anything. There was always a film of dust on everything...you lived, worked and slept in it. I made a poem trying to describe it. When you start writing poetry about things like that, I guess it means that it must be an important factor in your life (laughs). The first verse went something like this:

Another summer sunset,
In August's early days.
And old Phaeton's eye gleams evilly,
In the murky, yellow haze...

Al: Norm's right you know. When I got off the ship in New York after the war, a guy who helped me with my duffel bag almost fell over from the weight. He yelled, "Hey, what do you have in here, half of Europe?!" "No," I said, "I wasn't in Europe. What's in that bag, is half the desert from Iran!" My Mom couldn't believe it when she washed those clothes after I got home. She said they weighed half as much, after she finally got all of the sand and dirt out of them!

[Al Findlay returned home after the war and made a career working for over 20 years in a toolmaking shop in town. He is now retired. When Norm VanVlack returned from the war, he decided to start his own business in town. He operated a sport and camera shop for many years on Main Street, and sold it to his partners when he retired.]

Background and Commentary

[1]Before America's entry into the war, the battle against Hitler had been waged primarily by the British and the Russians. In retrospect, in one of the

great miscalculations of the war, Hitler decided to invade the Soviet Union. This was actually a blessing for the British because now hundreds of thousands of troops, which could have been used to invade Britain, had been moved to the east to attack Stalin and the Soviet Union. For almost two years, the Germans pushed the Russians back and it looked like the Russian front might collapse. Winston Churchill, Britain's Prime Minister, knew that somehow the Allies had to get military supplies to Stalin so that the Russians could hold on. There were only two choices for that flow of war supplies, the northern run over the top of Norway to Murmansk (see notes in Chapter 15), and a southern route through the Middle East, the Persian Gulf and thence north to the southern extremities of the Soviet Union.

There were initial political problems at first. The Shah of Iran was friendly to Germany and couldn't be trusted. Thus, the British engineered a coup d'état against the Shah and put his 22-year-old son in control of the country. The Russians simultaneously invaded from the north and the British from the south, and that ended Germany's influence in Iran. The Russian "zone of influence" started about 60 miles north of Teheran and the British controlled the rest of the country. But again, the Americans were needed. A port had to built, the railroad upgraded and most of all the military goods needed to be delivered. In December 1942, American forces began to land at Khorramshahr on the Persian Gulf. By April 1943, there were 18,000 Americans working around the clock to speed up the supply line to Russia. By August, there were 30,000 GIs in Iran moving jeeps, tanks, trunks, guns and ammunition to the Soviet Union to be used in the offensive against Hitler's armies. Norman VanVlack and Allen Findlay were in this group of American troops, far from home, in a backwater area of the war, supplying the fighting forces of another country.

[2]The American effort in Iran, called the Persian Gulf Command, was another marvel of supply and logistics that occurred in World War II. In 1942, Khorramshahr was a small desert town in southern Iran. By 1944, it was one of the busiest ports in the world. The U.S. Army sent 57 diesel powered locomotives and 1,650 freight cars to Iran in order to upgrade the ability of the allies to supply the Russian front. The Americans trained 7,500 Iranian truck drivers and assembled some 10,000 trucks, loaded them with supplies and sent them north toward the Caspian Sea. By the end of the war, over 5,700,000 tons of war material had reached the Soviet

Union through the Persian Corridor, slightly more than was sent through the northern route to Murmansk. The supply route to Russia also offered an escape route for refugees trying to flee Nazi oppression. Approximately 120,000 Polish soldiers and civilians were brought back to the Persian Gulf on the empty railroad cars that delivered supplies to Russian cities near the border with Iran.

[3]Teheran also became famous during the war as the location of one of the major meetings between the allied powers. Americans were blessed by having a strong political leader during World War II. Franklin Roosevelt, though despised by many conservatives for his domestic social programs, was respected by virtually every American for his invaluable leadership in leading the war effort. Both Roosevelt and Britain's Winston Churchill met on several occasions during the war to map out allied strategy. It became important to also involve Stalin, Russia's leader, so that a unified strategy

Persian rugs being sold on the dirt streets of Teheran.

Travels of Al Findlay and Norm Van Vlack

could be developed in defeating the Axis powers. The first meeting between Stalin, Roosevelt and Churchill took place in November, 1943, in Teheran. Stalin was always suspicious of British and American intentions and never trusted his partners in the war. He had probably already mapped out his post-war plans to spread international communism and dominate the politics of eastern Europe. But he had to defeat Hitler first, and for that he needed help from Britain and the United States.

The Teheran Conference was significant. Churchill continued to push his hopes for an invasion of southern Europe, the "soft underbelly" of Europe. Stalin demurred. He sided with the Americans and insisted on the invasion of France. He wanted a strong push from the west to take pressure off his troops on the eastern front. Roosevelt talked about his vision for establishing the United Nations after the war. Stalin listened but didn't commit himself. Roosevelt wanted Stalin to declare war on Japan and attack Japanese forces in Manchuria, but the Russian leader said that he didn't have the manpower to do it. Stalin did agree, however, that he would attack Japan once the war with Germany was over.

The chemistry at the meeting, especially between Roosevelt and Stalin, was good; and one night, at dinner, Stalin proposed a toast to the Americans in gratitude for the war supplies that had been sent to Russia. In his toast, he acknowledged that without American supplies and equipment, the troops of the Soviet Union would not have been able to finally turn the tide against the Germans. It was a historic meeting and had to be an overpowering experience for anyone who witnessed it. Here were the three leaders of the Allied nations making the military and political decisions that would decide the war and determine the shape of the post-war world.

There is one other interesting historical footnote to come out of America's Persian Gulf Command and its incredible effort to supply the Russian front through Iran. A little-known American adviser to the Iranian government, a Colonel by the name of H. Norman Schwarzkopf, became a leader in persuading the new, young, Shah of Iran to make needed changes in improving the professionalism of his military and police forces. Little did Schwarzkopf know that one day his son, General H. Norman Schwarzkopf, Jr., would command another major operation in the Persian Gulf—the 1991 operation called "Desert Storm."

14. Two Friends Meet On The Burma Road

It was during the monsoon season of 1944, so it must have been in October or November. It had been raining like hell and the Burma Road was down to one lane. I was driving this six-by-six going up a mountain on my way to Myitkyina with a load of mortar ammunition. All of sudden, around the bend comes a weapons carrier going the other direction, and we almost hit each other. We stop in the middle of that dirt/mud road and neither of us can move because now we're stuck.

I jump out of the truck and so does the other driver to see what can be done, and I'll be goddamned, the other driver is John Wharton from back home. We'd gone to high school together and worked together on the County Highway Department during the summers. John was a black guy and his Dad was steward at the Country Club. Talk about shock! Here we were on this godforsaken road in the middle of Burma and we literally run into each other (laughs).

Well, somehow we got unstuck. I had a winch on the front of my truck and we winched John out and then I hooked onto a tree and winched myself out. John was with a black engineering outfit that had been assigned to keep the Burma Road open. They had heavy equipment and bulldozers and every time there was a washout, they'd go out and rebuild the road. He asked me to come back to his camp, which I did, and he gave me some canned chicken, GI soy sausage and a can of hard candy. He took care of me real good. I'd been eating rice twice a day with the Chinese, and so it was a real treat to get that food! He asked me where I was going, and I told him. He said, "Jesus, Charlie, you don't wanna go down there, the jungle is full of Japs. They'll get you!'" Well, he knew the area better than I did, but I told him that I had to get that ammo through, so after a few minutes I left.

For a while after the war, John worked as a security guard at the bank but I don't know where he finally ended up. At one point, I tried to help him get into the Hotel School at Cornell. That didn't work out and I always felt bad about it. We had been friends before the war, but that chance meeting on the Burma Road had brought us closer together. That experience—the sur-

prise of it, the chance meeting, the conversation, the hospitality shown me on the Burma Road by John Wharton—is one of my most cherished memories of the war.[1]

Charles Price
Lieutenant, U.S. Army Reserve

[Charlie Price ended up spending his war years in the China-Burma-India area of the war. It was here that British and American forces, working together, accomplished the difficult mission of supplying and training the Chinese army so that China could fight effectively against the Japanese.]

I went to Williams College in 1936 and graduated in 1940. My Dad was a lawyer in town and so I suppose I was almost predestined to become a lawyer and go back to the firm. Therefore, in the fall of '40, I entered Cornell Law School and started down the road of becoming an attorney. Of course, the war changed everything. In March of '42 I was drafted and that ended, for the time being, my plans of becoming a lawyer. I was sent to Edgewood Arsenal in Maryland for my basic training. Edgewood was designated a "chemical warfare" school, but its primary purpose was to train soldiers in the use of white phosphorous ("willie peter") mortar shelling. White phosphorous had been found effective against jungle defenses because the explosives would pierce through the trees and get down to where the enemy was. We were trained in how to do this, our primary weapon being the large 4.2-inch diameter mortar.

From Edgewood, the Army sent me to Camp Gordon, near Augusta, GA, for more advanced training in infantry and mortar tactics. It was there that I got recruited for Officer Candidate School (OCS). With college under my belt, the Army wanted me to do it, so back I went to Edgewood for OCS. After I got my commission, I went to work as an instructor at Edgewood. After six weeks of that, I was so bored and disgusted with it that I asked for overseas duty. The Army willingly obliged, and started sending me to classes in Chinese. That was the first inkling I had of where I would end up.

In February of '43, I got orders to New York and boarded the SS *America* for my trip overseas. It was a fast ship, could outrun the German submarines, and so we steamed by ourselves without a convoy. The ship

2nd Lieutenant Charlie Price, 1942.

stopped in Buenos Aires for food and fuel, and they brought goat carcasses on board for our meat rations. Our food hadn't been the best and now I knew why! There were colored troops on board with us and I expect that some of them ended up with me later on the Burma Road. They were stacked like cordwood on the lower decks of that ship and, obviously, a lot of them had come right off the farm someplace with virtually no education. I remember being stopped by a fellow one day. "Lieutenant," he asked, "how do we know where we is? There ain't no trees." I gave him a little lesson in navigation as I knew it and I think it calmed him down.

We stopped at Capetown, South Africa, for replenishment and then headed across the Indian Ocean to Karachi. From there we were taken to a staging area or camp in the Sind Desert and remained there about three weeks awaiting further orders. What a place that was! We lived in wooden barracks which had been so dried out in the heat and sun that they were like tinder. The termites had gotten into the wood and every morning you would have to shake the sawdust from the termites off your bed roll and clothes. The days were hot and the nights were cold. There was very little water and no refrigeration. In order to keep enough fluids in our body, we had to drink warm grapefruit juice from those #10 tin cans. I was glad when we left.

I had a very interesting assignment in India. General Stilwell had convinced the Chinese to bring troops to India for training. Most of them were just 16-year-old, uneducated peasants. They had never been exposed to modern life at all. There were three Americans (an officer, a sergeant and a corporal) assigned to each Company, and through interpreters we undertook to train these men (or boys) in infantry and mortar tactics. We also had to teach some of them to drive, because they would need to use trucks on the Burma Road. You really took your life in your hands when it came to driver training because many of these kids had never even seen a truck! A lot of them couldn't swim either, and so we took them to a nearby river for swimming practice. There were a lot of rivers in Burma and they would need to swim to get across some of them. It would take us about eight months to get our training done and then we would escort these Chinese troops back into Burma and into the war against Japan.

Our training command was set up in Rangar, India, about 80 miles north of Calcutta. One of my ancillary duties was to act as PX officer in charge of supplies for the Officer's Club. The Army gave me a Harley Davidson motorcycle to run around on and, periodically, I would have to go to Calcutta for supplies. Talk about poverty...you've never seen anything until you've seen Calcutta. Cows all over the place, people peeing in the street, beggars on the sidewalks, the smell of sewage—I'd never seen anything like it. On the other hand, there was also tremendous wealth in India. I was introduced to it because I was a tennis player. India in those days was run by the British. They liked tennis and, because I could play, it enabled me to meet a few new friends. One day I was invited to play tennis at the home of a Maharajah. Talk about money! This guy had his own servants, tennis courts, elephants, zoo and even a Rolls Royce. He had heard that I also played squash, and asked me about it. I recommended the game and suggested he build a squash court. I'll be damned if, a couple months later, he didn't have a new squash court (laughs)! He invited me back to play, but

I couldn't make it because I was on one of my trips up the Burma Road.

One day when I was working on my PX duties in Rangar, General Stilwell came into the Officer's Club. He was checking the place out because he was hosting Madame Chiang Kai-shek there that night. She had come to India to take at look at our training operations for the Chinese. As was his custom, Stilwell wasn't wearing any rank insignia, but I recognized him. I was doing something at the O-Club that day and when he saw me, he asked, "Lieutenant, are you in charge of the arrangements for tonight?" And I said, "No, Sir, I'm sort of co-in-charge." (I thought maybe he was upset about something and I didn't want to take all of the blame if he were.) Apparently he had heard that I was part of the U.S. Cadre training the Chinese and thanked me for my help on that, and we chit-chatted for awhile. Then he asked what I thought was really on his mind, "Lieutenant, what do I have to do to buy a drink in this place?" I said, "General, you've got to have more rank than you've got right now. You can't buy anything in this place. It's free!" Well, he laughed when he heard that, and I went behind the bar and mixed him a drink.[2]

While at Rangar I also met Major Frank Merrill of the famed Merrill's Marauders. They were an all-volunteer American force that went behind the lines in Burma and really raised hell with the Japanese. A part of his force were also natives from the Naga Hills. We called them the Naga Headhunters. They carried only knives and they would sneak out at night through the Japanese lines and attack the enemy. I believe they were paid by the number of men they killed because they would often bring back heads to prove it. I never saw them do it, but after looking at these guys, you could believe they were capable of it. There wasn't much that would strike fear into the heart of the Japs, but I'm sure these guys did.

It must have been November of '43 when I took my first group of Chinese troops up the Burma Road. We were on trucks and went south toward Calcutta, crossed the Ganges River on a ferry, drove miles through tea plantations, and then went on to Chumbiang on the Burma border. There I turned the troops over to a Chinese commander. From there he would move them toward the Japanese lines. On another trip, I took one of our Chinese Companies into Burma by horse and mule. It was quite an experience. The first horse I got on was so small that both my feet touched the ground! That obviously wouldn't work, so we had to get some bigger horses out of Calcutta that had come over from Australia. Once we had the bigger horses, we headed out by train and stopped at the Ganges River for the ferry. The Indian guy running the ferry said, "Sorry, we don't have any room for you." Needless to say, I wasn't pleased with his attitude and said, "Fellow, I have two hundred armed men here and I am armed myself. I think you'd better find a way to get us over the river." All of a sudden, he became very cooperative. In the process, he commandeered a river cruise ship and invited us for a midnight cruise on the Ganges. I had brought along about six beers for a special occasion, and figured this was the time to use it. So we sat on the back of the cruise ship, drank beer and had one helluva nice cruise that night on the Ganges River!

Later in the war, as we began to push the Japs back, we took our troops further up the Burma Road to Myitkyina. After I had delivered the troops, I decided to catch a plane ride on a C-47 to get back to India. There had been some fighting in the area so they sent a fighter up first to strafe some suspected Japanese positions near the airport. I don't believe we took any fire when we took off, but it wasn't very reassuring to have a fighter clearing the decks for you before you got airborne. All in all, I probably made four or five trips up the Burma Road to either Chumbiang or Myitkyina. It was on one of those trips that I met John Wharton in that very surprising, almost head-on collision experience between our trucks.

In late '44, I was transferred to Kunming, China. By this time, the Japanese were more or less on the run and the Army wanted the teaching cadres, of which I was one, to help train the Chinese Army in China. It was evident to me then that China was not unified as a country in any real sense. We would go on long hikes and marches with government soldiers out into the provinces and countryside around Kunming. What we found was that each province was controlled by its own warlord with very little allegiance to the central government. I guess it should have been no surprise when right after the war the country fell apart into civil war. Because of those field marches and constantly having wet feet, I developed jungle rot on my feet and ended up in an Army hospital in Kunming. And guess who walked into the hospital ward to say hello? Charlie Ulrich, an old buddy from back home. He was an X-ray Technician in the medical corps and had been sent to Kunming. Small world. On New Year's Eve, Charlie somehow got me out of the hospital and we got drunk on canned grapefruit juice and

Chinese vodka! What a time (laughs)! The care at the hospital was good, but the food was lousy. I ended up complaining to the base commander about it and the food improved. I could eat crummy food when I had to, but had no tolerance for it when people could be doing better.

China-Burma-India (CBI) was sort of a backwater during the war. We were keeping the Japanese busy so they couldn't go elsewhere, but we weren't on the front page as far as the fighting was concerned. The same attitude prevailed when the war ended. Japan capitulated in August of 1945, but it wasn't until November 6th that I finally got a plane back to India. I thought I was heading for home but a new, hotshot Colonel thought that because of my legal training I should stay for a few extra months to help iron out some of the legal claims that had been made by Indians against the U.S. Army. He had been there for ten days and I had been there for three years. I wasn't interested in staying any longer. Fortunately, back in the days when I had been supply officer at the PX in Rangar, I had become good friends with a Colonel Fuller. On my trips to Calcutta, he would often ask me to help him out with a "booze requisition." I had made sure he was well-stocked with scotch and gin. When I told Colonel Fuller about my problems with the new Colonel, he took care of it and I was promptly on my way home.

When I had gone to India, much of the Mediterranean had been controlled by the Germans. With the war over, we could now use the Suez Canal. We were on a converted transport ship that had been modified for use as an aircraft carrier. The Army must have put just enough food on board for the minimum expected time for getting home and they misjudged it. We hit a helluva storm out of Gibraltar which slowed us down. It got so rough that the water peeled back part of the flight deck on that ship. The ship ran out of food, even though two thirds of the men hadn't been eating because of seasickness. They ended up feeding us powdered eggs and ketchup for the last three days before we got to New York. I'd had lousy food in Burma, lousy food in China, and now the Army was nailing me one last time with lousy food on this ship. I was hell-bent now on getting home for a good Christmas dinner! I made it and so did my brother Sam who had been in the Army. [See Chapter 2 for Sam Price's story.] Needless to say, Christmas 1945 was one happy day at the Price household on Crossman St!

[After the war, Charlie Price went back to Cornell Law School and finished his training to become a lawyer. He joined a law firm in town that had been started by his father, and he still practices law today.]

Background and Commentary

[1]Charlie Price spent his war years in the China-Burma-India (CBI) theater of the war, an area of the world that was considered by many to be a "backwater," or secondary theater of action. However, during the early years of the war, it was this battleground that kept the Axis powers from totally encircling the globe. After Pearl Harbor, the Japanese quickly moved into Southeast Asia and captured the important oil fields of the Dutch East Indies. They quickly conquered Hong Kong, Java and Sumatra; and, after a two-month siege, the largest British outpost in Asia, Singapore, fell to the Japanese. They also invaded Burma with the ultimate goal of sweeping through India and linking up with the Germans in the Middle East. The British and Americans were forced to make a stand in Burma in order to try to stop the Japanese. They also needed to maintain a supply link to Chiang Kai-shek's forces in western China which were fighting the Japanese.

In 1942, CBI was one of the few areas of the world where the Allies had any good news. For most of that year, the Germans and Japanese were winning battle after battle. One of the few bright spots came from a group of American volunteer pilots known as the "Flying Tigers," under the leadership of Colonel Claire Chennault; they flew many successful fighter missions against the Japanese in western China.

[2] The Commander of American ground forces in Burma was General Joseph Stilwell. However, Stilwell didn't have the men and supplies to stop the Japanese, and in 1942 was forced to withdraw to India. He was known as a leader who stayed with his troops, and in keeping with that tradition, he walked with his troops out of Burma on a very difficult and humiliating 140-mile trek. When he arrived in India, he was given responsibility for coordinating Allied military activities in the CBI Theater.

With Burma in their hands, the Japanese were able to cut off the Burma Road, the only surface transportation link with China. Thus, it became Stilwell's priority to retake the Burma road and to rebuild it in places where it could avoid the Japanese. Stilwell, a very able officer, always felt that he had been forgotten in Burma and India, and that his troops were not adequately supported by either the British or the Americans. He was a rather dour, serious man and, based upon that reputation, earned the name "Vinegar Joe." He also had continuing conflicts with Chiang Kai-shek and Chennault over the conduct of the war. He tried to use Chinese troops in fighting the Japanese in Burma, but would often be overridden by the orders of Chiang. Chennault also made continuing and extraordinary demands by insisting that most of the supplies coming from India be in the form of more planes, avgas and ammunition to wage the air war. Stilwell felt that more of the Allied resources should be reserved for supporting forces on the ground. Because of these conflicts, President Roosevelt finally relieved Stilwell of his command in 1944. However, as far as those who served in the Army were concerned,Charlie Price, that afternoon in the Rangar Officer's Club, met one of the most beloved General officers of the war. Stilwell had done his best, under almost impossible conditions, to train, supply and organize a joint British, American, Chinese effort against the Japanese.

Ultimately, Allied forces did push the Japanese out of Burma and reopened the Burma Road. The Chinese troops that Charlie Price helped train were moved up to the front and went into action. One of the most significant stories in CBI was the successful effort at keeping China in the war by supplying it through the air. With the Burma Road cut, all supplies had to be flown in. It was a 500-600-mile, one-way trip over the high passes of the Himalayas, and American pilots in C-47s, C-54s and converted bombers, flew thousands of trips from India into China, over "the Hump," as it was called, to supply the Chinese. (See Chapter 2 for pilot Tony Mangine's story.)

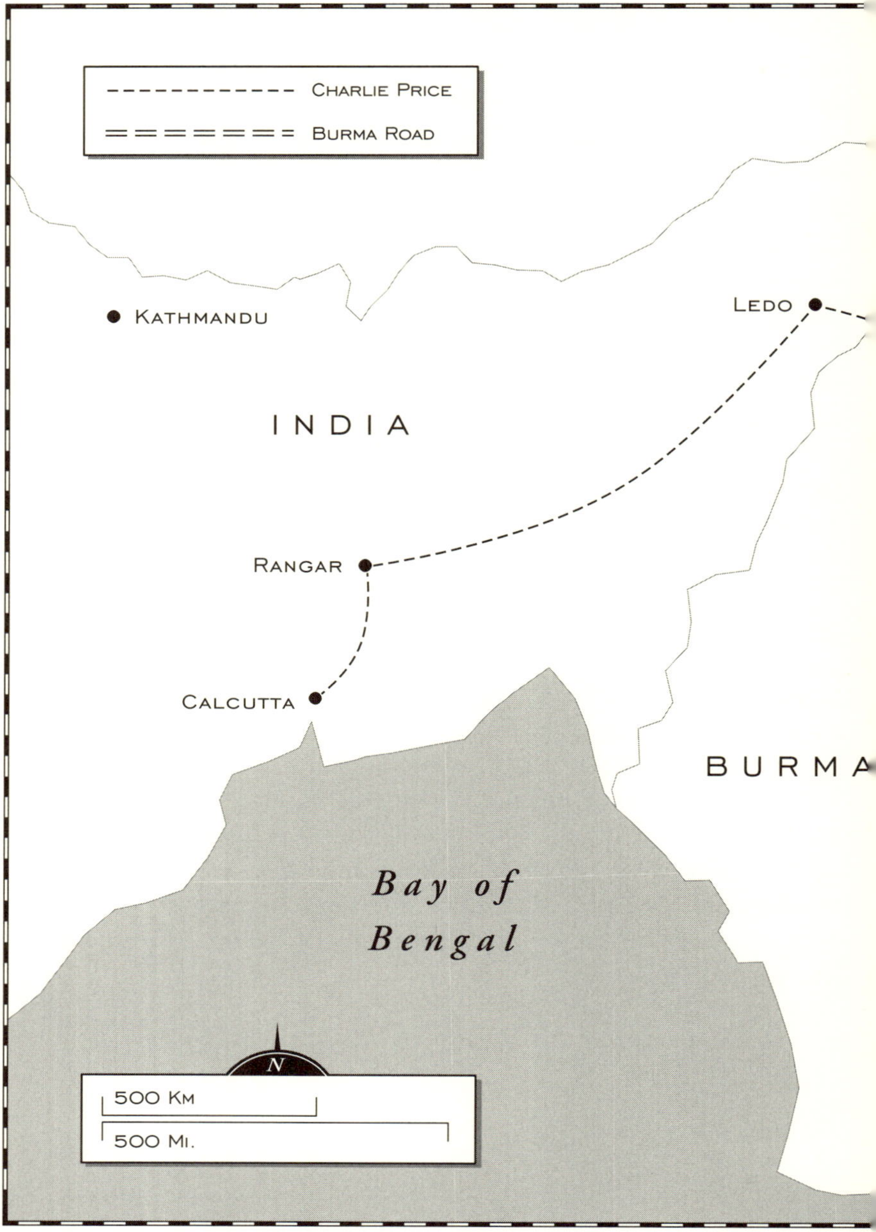

TRAVELS OF CHARLIE PRICE

CHUNGKING
CHINA
KUNMING
1YITKYINA
LASHIO
HANOI
INDO-CHINA
SIAM
(THAILAND)

15. Identical Twins Go To War

Newly commissioned ensigns: Bob and Sam Robbins.

We'd always done everything together. We were born together as identical twins in 1920. We grew up together, went to high school and college together, married our wives within three months of each other in the same church, were in business with each other. The only thing that ever separated us for very long was World War II.

We graduated from William and Mary College in 1942 and received direct commissions in the U.S. Naval Reserve and reported for duty at Norfolk, VA. The war had started and we knew that we had to go in, so going into the Navy in the Supply Corps seemed to be a pretty good option. We stayed together through a two-month officer training school at Harvard Graduate School in Boston, and in November of '42 we reported back to the Navy in Norfolk for our assignments. One of us would go to Europe, the other to the South Pacific. It was the last we would see each other for over three years.[1]

Bob and Sam Robbins
Lieutenants, U.S. Naval Reserve

[Innumerable times during World War II, brothers were sent off to the war together. In this case, they were identical twins and both were naval officers. Sam would report to a ship in the South Pacific. Bob would go to Europe first, and then his ship eventually took him to the Pacific as well.]

Sam: We had some good times in the Navy and some unforgettable experiences. Bob probably had some closer calls than I did because he was on six different invasions during the war. But I've always thought that we probably came closer to getting killed in Boston than in any other place. One night in the fall of '42, while we were in school at Harvard, we went downtown for some partying. The hot place to be was the Coconut Grove, a big dance hall and cabaret in Boston. Hildegarde was singing there and Buck Jones, the actor, was there that night. The place was jammed and we could barely get to the bar, so we decided to leave and go down the street to another place. Later that night the Coconut Grove caught fire and 400 people were killed, including Buck Jones. It was a terrible tragedy and Bob and I came within a hair's breadth of being there.

We got back to Norfolk late in November and our orders were awaiting us. My orders were to report to the 12th Naval District in San Francisco and from there I would ship out for the South Pacific. Bob had other orders. There was a ship in Norfolk, the USS *Thurston* (APA-77), an attack transport ship, and he was going aboard as an Unloading and Supply Officer. The Navy was splitting us up but it was probably for the best. For the first time in our lives, we said good-bye to each other and who knew, with the war going on, if and when we would ever see each other again.

Bob: The *Thurston* was built to carry troops and supplies for amphibious landings. We could carry 800-900 Army troops and also had space for 2 large LSMs (Landing Ship Medium) and 16 LCVPs (Landing Craft Vehicle/Personnel). During landing operations, we would hoist these boats over the side and then load the troops, trucks, guns, supplies, etc. down into them.[2] My job was to be a loading officer, out on the deck insuring that all of this got done. Our first excitement came in November 1943 when we picked up our first troops in Weymouth, England. We were anchored out off the beach and were scheduled to get underway for North Africa. One night at about dusk, we were attacked by some German

The Robbins boys with their mother before going off to war.

bombers. The bombs didn't hit the ship but came so close that the shaft that drove the propeller bent. Most of us were ecstatic, "Now, we won't have to go to North Africa!" we thought. But the Navy needed us and a repair ship pulled alongside. Within a few days we were ready to leave England for our destination.

At the beginning of the war, I don't think any of us realized how busy we would be. Without harbors to use, virtually all of the Allied landings would be done from invasion beaches, and throughout the war, we would be involved in amphibious landings all over the world. The exception would be our first landing in North Africa. In December, by the time we reached Oran, Algeria, the Army had secured the area and we were able to land at piers in the harbor without opposition. Soon after we arrived, we moved to a place called Mers-el-Kebir where we conducted continual landing exercises on the big, sandy beaches in the area. The U.S. Army was in North Africa to open up another front against the German forces of General Rommel. The plan was that we would squeeze them from the west and the British would push them back from the east across the desert from Egypt. Between the two, hopefully, we could push them out of Africa. By the time we got to Africa, the British and American forces had nearly accomplished this and so we began to train for the next invasion, though at the time we did not know where it would be.

We got liberty at Mers-el-Kebir and most us went into the city of Oran. It wasn't much of a town and you didn't dare eat the local food for fear of getting sick. It was a place to go to, but not much was going on. However, it didn't take our sailors long to figure out a way to make money. They would leave the ship with a bedsheet tied around each leg under their pants. They could buy them for $1 a piece on the ship and sell them for $20 on the beach in Algeria. What a deal! Lots of cash for liberty (laughs). But liberty soon ended. In May of '43 the Allies finally kicked Rommel out of Africa and shortly thereafter we got our orders to get underway for the invasion of Sicily.

Sam: I guess it was late November of '42 by the time I got to San Francisco, and I was soon on a ship headed for the South Pacific. We were on a converted Dutch cruise ship called the *Sommeldyke* and there were probably 4,000-5,000 of us jammed on that thing, all going to Australia. We landed in Brisbane, which was MacArthur's headquarters. I was supposed to pick up my ship there, the USS *Celeno* (AKA 76), but it wasn't in port. So the Navy sent me to Milne Bay, New Guinea, because someone thought the ship would be there. It wasn't. Milne Bay was a real armpit—mud, mosquitoes, hot and muggy—not a nice place to vacation. I waited for a couple of weeks and the ship still didn't come in, so finally I conned the captain of a seagoing tug headed for Guadalcanal into taking me on board. That's where I finally caught up with my ship.[3]

It was at Guadalcanal that I also ran into two fellows from back home—Stan Weeks and Dr. H. Wolcott Ingham. They were there in some kind of support capacity for the campaign going on in the Solomon Islands. (The fighting had pretty much subsided at the "Canal" but was still going on at Bougainville and some islands to the north.) Here we all were from the same little backwater town in America, and we had ended up on a little island in the South Pacific that, until a few months earlier, no one had ever even heard of. That was the story of the war and I'm sure it happened to others from towns all over the country.

Our ship was essentially a supply ship which hauled cargo of all types to the troops. However, we usually followed up the initial landings, bringing in replacement and support troops after an area had been taken from the enemy.[4] Around April or May of '43, the ship was sent to New Zealand for drydock and repairs. Talk about good liberty. I met a girl who was quite a fast mover by the name of Pamela Talbot, a real babe and very British. She made the time go quickly. Women would almost die for nylon stockings back then because they were hard to come by. When I told my mother about Pamela, she actually sent her a pair of nylons (laughs)! I was never around to reap the benefits of that because we were soon underway again heading back north. I never saw that girl again and I've never been back to New Zealand, but they were a few weeks that I'll never forget!

The New Zealanders loved Americans, probably because we had stopped the Japanese at the Battle of the Coral Sea; but for whatever reason, we really hit it off with them. I met a guy in Auckland named Tiki Whye who had an old Chrysler and who used to take us to the horseraces. In typical British fashion, the horses ran in the wrong direction, counterclockwise around the track. You could bet on the ponies but they didn't actually have betting windows; you would buy betting tickets in town before the race started. We also spent a lot of time at the Peter Pan Nightclub, which was the place to be and where the action was. It didn't hurt that I was a supply officer and, of course, we had to reprovision the ship. A lot of the meat we got from that area of the world was lamb and mutton and whew, did some of that smell (laughs)! In the process of buying supplies, I had to work with the USJPB—the United States Joint Purchasing Board. They were responsible for supplying all the U.S. ships that came in, and they usually got me a cab whenever I needed it. It's hard to beat those days that I spent in New Zealand.

Bob: All in all, I was on six amphibious invasions, four in Europe and two in the Pacific. In Europe we landed troops in Sicily, Salerno, Normandy on D-Day, and Saint-Tropez in southern France. Then the Navy sent us around the world, through the Panama Canal, so that we could make the landings at Iwo Jima and Okinawa. But, I guess the closest I came to getting hit was the first time, at the invasion of Sicily. We were loading boats and getting ready for the landing when some German bombers came at us. It looked like one of them was making a suicide run. He'd probably been hit and was going down and was thinking he could take out our troop ship. I saw him coming in and hit the deck trying to get some protection behind a hatch cover. Some bombs hit and shrapnel was flying. A few of our guys, including the captain, were hit and injured, but I was okay. I went back to loading boats and we finally got our men and supplies ashore.

Sometime after the landing at Sicily, we went back to North Africa for replenishment. Things were more relaxed back there and during this time I somehow found out that my good buddy from back home had been operating with the invasion fleet on the command ship, the USS *Ancon.* I knew one of the signalmen on our ship and he signaled the *Ancon* on the flashing light for me. The message said: "Lt. Robbins sends his regards to Sgt. Samuel Penfield Price." A message came back indicating that Sam Price was indeed on that ship, but despite our efforts and the fact that we were on several landings together, we never did get to actually see each other during the war. [See Chapter 2 for the story of Sam Price.]

After the Salerno landings we got orders to leave for England and prepare for the invasion of France. We actually went to Greenock, Scotland, on the Firth of Clyde and arrived there sometime in January of '44. We practiced landings, almost from the day we arrived, on some sandy beaches on the Firth of Clyde, just south of Loch Lomond. Those were good times with a lot of liberty. I met a girl there too, Mary MacMillon. She was English and in later years, married an Englishman who had a pretty good job in the meatpacking business. Sometime in the 1950s, after the war, they decided to visit the U.S. with their three kids and we invited them to stay at our house. I think they stayed for two weeks. My wife wondered if they would ever leave (laughs)!

Everybody talks about D-Day at Normandy, and, of course, it was an incredible event. What I remember most is the number of ships. There were thousands and it was a hectic day. We got our troops ashore and were able to get all of our supplies in that first day before nightfall. When you think about it, getting 175,000 men ashore in one day was really quite a feat and took a lot of planning and coordination. Just four years earlier, in 1940, before the war started, there were only 175,000 people in the whole army. On June 6, 1944, we put that many ashore in France in one day! It's truly amazing what this country can do when it decides something has to be done. Aside from the hard work and long hours of D-Day, I also remember the wounded coming back to the ship. When we pulled out that night, we probably had forty wounded men on board and the doctors on board were busy trying to patch them up and save lives. I remember one guy with his arm mostly blown off pleading with the doctors not to remove it. But I heard later that they had to take it off to save his life.

Following Normandy, on August 15, 1944, we participated in the landings in southern France at Saint-Tropez. After that, we received orders to go to the Pacific, and we arrived there in time for the invasion of Iwo Jima on February 19, 1945. This small, black, volcanic island was only 700 miles from the home islands of Japan and it was to be a difficult battle for our Marines. From our standpoint, the landing ships were not greatly threatened because by this time the Japanese air threat in this part of the Pacific had been virtually wiped out. What made the Iwo Jima landing tough for us was the fact that we couldn't anchor. It was a volcanic island and the water depth dropped off to 90 fathoms almost at the water's edge. We couldn't drop anchor and had to stay underway when we were launching boats. We also lost some of our boats on the beach because of the deep water. Usually the boats would drop a stern anchor when they landed so that they could winch themselves off the beach after the troops were off. Because of the deep water at Iwo Jima, they couldn't do that. Their only hope to keep from broaching was to keep their screws turning and force their bows into the sand. It was a tough day for the boat captains. After leaving Iwo Jima, we started getting ready for the invasion of Okinawa.

Sam: Bob and I were probably off the beaches at Okinawa at the same time, but we never saw each other. The fighting here was very tough and it was here that the Japanese started using their kamikaze suicide attacks. Airplanes loaded with explosives would try to fly right into ships rather than drop bombs or torpedoes. A hospital ship right next to us, the USS *Henderson* was hit, and although the ship didn't sink, a lot of people were killed and wounded. Of course, it was hard for the Japanese planes to make out what type of ships they were diving on. We had smoke-makers and smudge pots going on our bow and stern along with every other ship, so the whole harbor at Okinawa was loaded with this fog and smoke haze. It did help to hide us from the kamikazes but it also made it hard to see.

It was just a few weeks after Okinawa that I saw Bob's ship. I believe we were in the harbor at Tinian and I looked out and saw APA-77 anchored nearby. My brother's ship! I hopped in a motor whale boat and went over to his ship. I didn't even know that he had come to the Pacific. I scrambled up the accommodation ladder and the petty officer of the watch saluted me and said, "Mr. Robbins. You just left. What brings you back?" The poor guy couldn't tell I was an identical twin (laughs). He thought I was Bob. What he did tell me though is that my brother had just left about an hour before I got there for the States. He had put in his time, had earned his "points," and had been sent to shore duty in Brooklyn. I hadn't seen him in three years, and here I had just missed seeing him by an hour!

It wasn't long before the war was over. I recall stopping in Guam for provisions and meeting another guy from back home. I was in a jeep and a guy yelled at me, "Hey, Robbins!" I stopped and there was John Price. The poor guy was living in a tent with no cot, had just received a "Dear John" letter from Betty Chilson, and was generally feeling lower than whale shit at the bottom of the ocean. I perked him up. Got a cot from the ship and brought him some International Harvester Cigars. We all thought the cigars were lousy but I guess they helped John. He told me, after we got home, that he smoked every one of them.

I imagine that I was fortunate to be on that supply ship. I saw everything there was to see in the Far East and, being a Navy officer, the food and living were good as long as your ship didn't go down. I even lucked out when I got stateside. The ship docked in Mare Island, near San Francisco, and I went into San Francisco to see the sights. Bob had told me about an old girlfriend he had met there when he was going home. She found me or I found her, I can't remember. (There are advantages in having an identical twin brother.) Billie Jo Crocker was her name...but that's another story. The war was over. It was November of '45 and the last time I'd seen Bob was November of '42. It was time to go home. I got on a train and headed east.

[Sam and Bob Robbins inherited their father's entrepreneurial spirit. They came home and bought a very successful box and packaging company. They also invested wisely in real estate. They and their wives remain best friends and still do many things together. These identical twins still look so much alike that many folks in town have difficulty telling them apart.]

Background and Commentary

[1]When the war came along, virtually any eligible male over the age of 18 was either drafted or, because of the draft, encouraged to enlist in the military. It didn't matter if your brothers were already in, the Army wanted you, too! Sam and Bob Robbins were not only brothers but were identical twins. Their father had died while they were very young and they had been raised by their mother. Surely, although proud to see her sons in Naval officer uniforms, she must have been very sad to send them off to war. At least, though, they were not on the same ship. In order to minimize the loss of brothers from the same family, the Navy had passed regulations prohibiting siblings from serving on the same ship.

Early in the war, there had been some very tragic events which had claimed the lives of brothers living and working together on the same vessel. For example, there had been tremendous personal and family loss when the USS *Arizona* had been sunk at Pearl Harbor. There had been 34 sets of brothers serving on the ship. Approximately 80% of them were killed during the attack and are buried in the underwater wreck. A father and son, serving in the Navy together, also perished on the ship that day. However, perhaps the greatest family tragedy of the war would occur the following year, on November 8, 1942. The USS *Juneau*, a light cruiser involved in the battle for Guadalcanal, had already been damaged that day by Japanese attacks when it was hit amidships by a torpedo from a Japanese submarine. The ship broke in two and sank in twenty seconds with great loss of life. There were only ten survivors. Five brothers from Waterloo, IA, by the name of Sullivan, were serving on that ship, and they were all killed. It was shortly after this incredible tragedy that the Navy changed its regulations, forbidding brothers from serving on the same ship.

To commemorate this great loss, on April 4, 1943, the Navy commissioned a new destroyer called the USS *Sullivans*. It was unusual to name a ship in the plural, with an "s" at the end of the name, but this ship was being named after five sons. Mr. and Mrs. Thomas F. Sullivan of Waterloo, IA, were at the ceremony the day of the commissioning, and it was Mrs. Sullivan, the mother of these five boys, who christened the ship. This ship, bearing the name of her sons, would head back across the Pacific and take up the fight again against the Japanese. Before the war finally ended, the *Sullivans* would be involved in nine combat engagements against the enemy. The USS *Sullivans* today is located at the port of Buffalo, NY, where it is part of the city's Naval Museum.

2 The Robbins boys were given assignments on support ships. Bob ended up as a deck officer on a troop transport whereas Sam was sent to a supply ship. Throughout the war, Bob's ship was assigned to the amphibious landing forces. Every initial landing, both in Europe and the Pacific, had to be made from landing craft hitting the beaches. Once a battle had been won, it was often possible to use existing port facilities, or in the alternative, military construction crews would build new port facilities to handle the supplies of war. But, initially, it was up to the boat coxswains from ships like the *Thurston* to maneuver their small boats through gunfire and obstructions and get the troops to the beach. Never in history had amphibious landings of this size and magnitude been made.

Bob Robbins' ship was of conventional construction and therefore landing craft had to be winched over the side and men would climb down nets to get into the boats. However, in World War II, many new types of vessels were developed to handle the tasks of the amphibious landing forces. Ships called LSTs (Landing Ship Tank) with flat bottoms and fronts that would open, would actually push right up to the beach and unload tanks and heavy cargo. Landing craft boats with doors that acted as ramps would drive into shallow water and discharge troops, jeeps and smaller cargo. Tracked vehicles, called "amtracks" or LVTs (Landing Vehicle Tracked) were built which were half tank and half boat. They could churn their way through shallow waters and crawl up onto the beaches, firing as they went. Amphibious landing operations required tremendous coordination between air, sea and land forces and good weather was important to the success of the whole operation. The men of the USS *Thurston*, having conducted six amphibious landings, could have been one of the most experienced amphibious warfare crews of the whole war.

3 The area in the Pacific in which the U.S. Navy operated was immense. It is difficult to describe just how big it was, the miles that had to be traveled to get there, and then the distances that had to be covered to supply our troops in various locations. There were battles as far north as the Aleutians in the Arctic and as far south as the Coral Sea, which was below the equator and adjacent to Australia. From Hawaii in the east to the Philippines in the west, you had to operate in over ten time zones. If you compared the area to

the western hemisphere, it would have covered an expanse of territory stretching from Labrador to Argentina and from London to San Francisco. In supplying this area, America was on its own. Whereas we received substantial help from the British in taking supplies to Europe, the United States, virtually alone, had the burden of supplying the Pacific theater of war.

4 The task of supplying the millions of fighting men and women around the world is one of the great stories of World War II. Not only did America support its own troops, but under "lend-lease," it sent over $48 billion worth of equipment and supplies to its allies. In total, between July 1, 1940, and July 31, 1945, the factories of the United States produced 296,601 aircraft, 71,060 ships and 86,388 tanks. All of this equipment had to be transported overseas and Sam Robbins' supply ship, the USS *Celeno*, was just one of hundreds of ships involved in making these deliveries. Not only were U.S. Navy ships involved, but hundreds of merchant ships called "liberty" ships were built to carry the supplies of war to Europe and the Pacific. This was very dangerous duty, especially early in the war when convoys were attacked by German submarines.

Perhaps the most dangerous supply route was the one that went through Arctic waters, from Iceland over the top of Norway and down into Russia. It was called the "Murmansk Run." One of the great tragedies in getting supplies to the fighting front occurred in June 1942 when a convoy named PQ-17 set out on this ice-laden Arctic route. There were 35 merchant ships in the convoy carrying $700 million worth of planes, tanks, and war supplies to the Soviet Union. They were escorted by some 47 British and American combatant ships. Nevertheless, in July, they were attacked off the coast of Norway by German U-boats and the Luftwaffe. Twenty-two ships were sunk, most of the equipment and supplies were lost and 153 men died in the icy water. Despite losses like this, the convoys continued and ultimately enough supplies got through both in Europe and the Pacific to win the war. However, men like Sam Robbins, who carried the material of war to the fighting front, often went to sea at great peril.

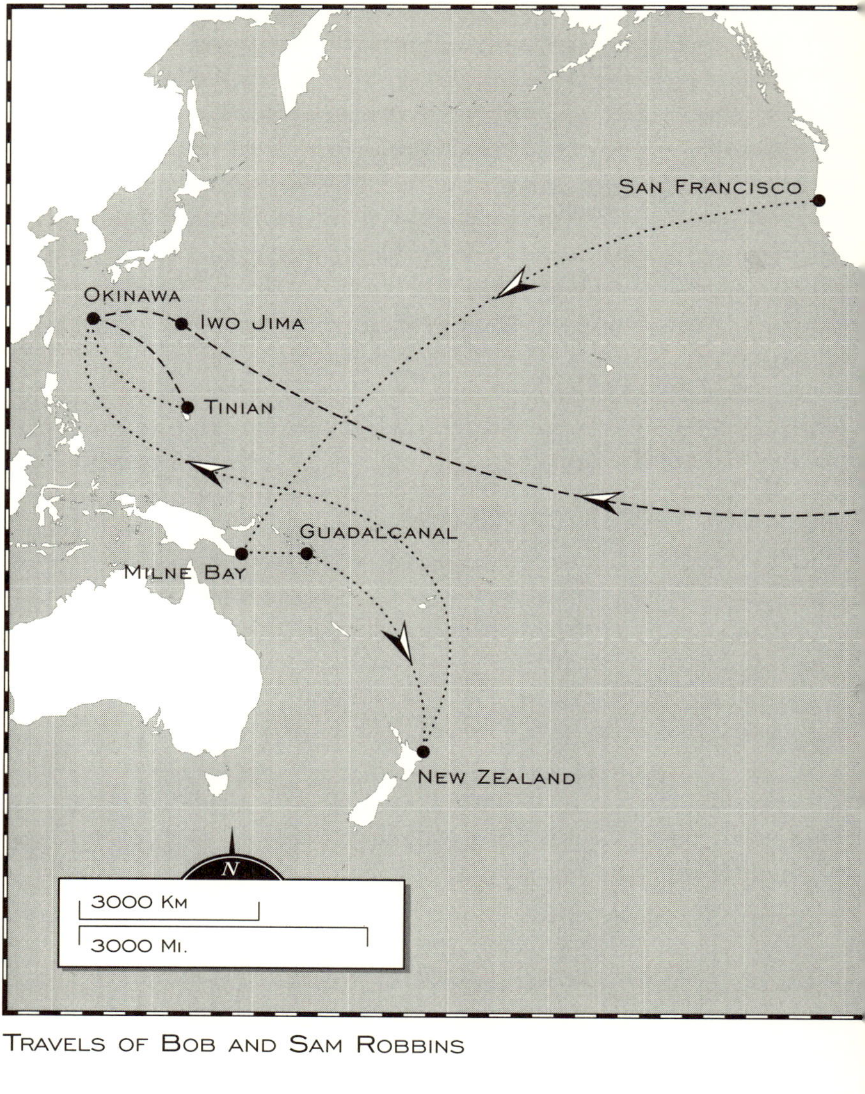

Travels of Bob and Sam Robbins

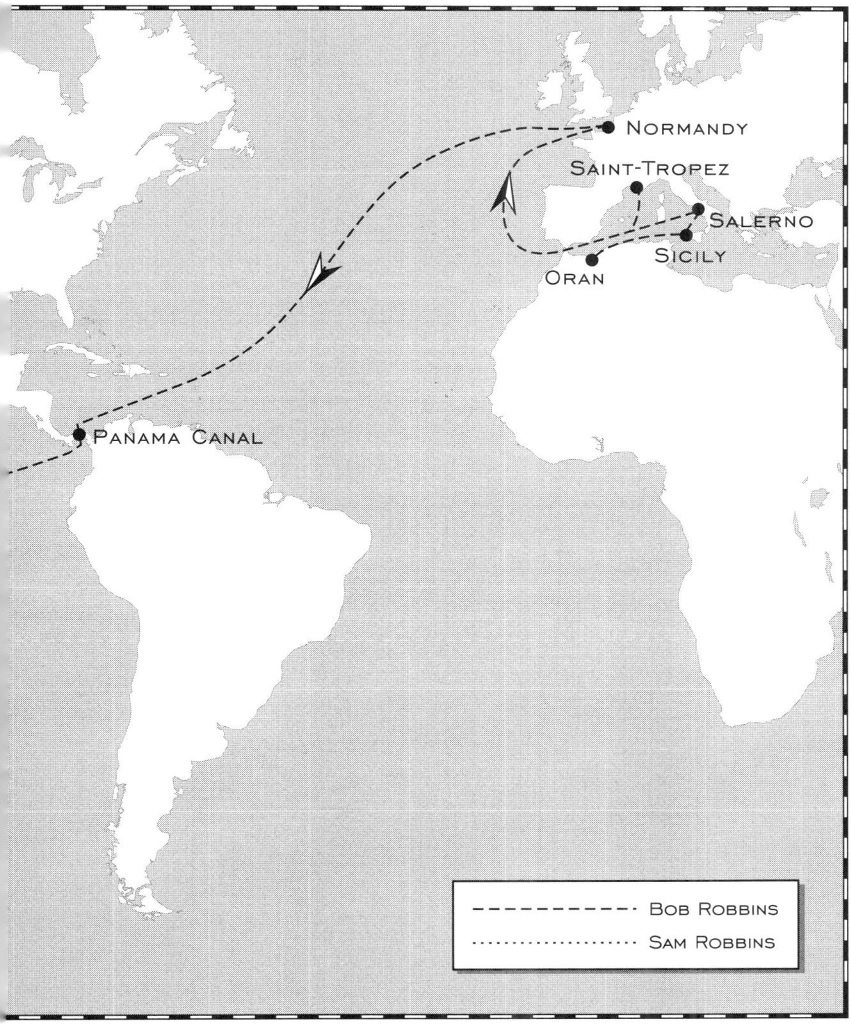
Normandy
Saint-Tropez
Salerno
Sicily
Oran
Panama Canal
Bob Robbins
Sam Robbins

NORMANDY INVASION

Mr. Robbins

AP77/A4-3
Serial: 002

Western Naval Task Force
Assault Force "O"
Assault Group O-3, T.G. 124.5
U.S.S. Anne Arundel (XAP76)(F)
U.S.S. Thurston XAP77
Portland Dorset,
2 June 1944.

TOP SECRET - NEPTUNE

TASK ORGANIZATION

(a) Ship based landing craft.

24 LCVP's	(P77-1 to P77-24)
2 LCM(3)'s	(P77-A and P77-B)

(b) Landing craft furnished from other sources

4 LCI(L)	from Assault Group O-3
LCI(L)	93, 487, 495, 497.
3 LCT(A)	from Assault Group O-1
LCT	2037, 2287, 293.
1 LCM(3)	from U.S.S. Chase
1 LCM(3)	from U.S.S. Anne Arundel
16 LCVP	from U.S.S. Jefferson
9 LCVP	from U.S.S. Anne Arundel
7 LCA	from Prince Boudouin
6 LCA	from Amsterdam

1. General Situation: NEPTUNE is a combined British - American operation with the immediate purpose of establishing a beach head in the Bay of the Seine Area of the north coast of France. Assault Group O-3 will land troops on beaches in the "OMAHA" area in support of the initial assault made by Groups O-1 and O-2.

Enemy Forces: (a) Detailed information as to enemy forces is given in the Intelligence Plan, Annex Able, of CTF 124 Operation Order No. BB-44.

Own Forces: (a) The landing will be made by the U.S. 1st Army and the British 21st Army supported by the combined U.S. 9th Air Force and R.A.F. and the Western and Eastern Naval Task Forces.

Force "O" will land the 1st Infantry Division of the VII Corps of the 1st U.S. Army. Elements of this force embarked in this vessel are:

18th Inf. 5th FA. 413th AAA
348th Eng. 5th E.S.B. 249th Sig.
745th Trk, 6th NBB, 453 rd Trk.
210th LMP, Hq & Serv. Co. 5th
FA Bn, 453rd Trk Co. 294th
Sig, 6th Naval BB, 97th 619th
413th, 4141 st. QM, 61st Med.
336th, 348th Eng. 5th E.S.B.

- 1 -

First page of the Operation Order given to Bob Robbins' ship for the D-Day landing at Omaha Beach.

16. Flying Hellcats In The Pacific

November 5, 1943: *Our fighter squadron lifted off the* Saratoga *(the* "Sara"*) at 7:30 a.m., rendezvoused with the dive bombers and torpedo planes, and together 109 aircraft headed for Rabaul. Rabaul, a port in New Britain, was the center of Japanese activity in the South Pacific and we had received word that they were about to launch a naval strike against our troops landing at Bougainville. We expected a rough reception since this was the first time U.S. forces had attacked this strategic stronghold of the enemy.*

As we arrived over Rabaul, the Japanese ships were trying to scramble out to open sea to avoid the attack. The sky was full of smoke from the antiaircraft fire, but the dive bombers and torpedo planes went down through it heading for the ships. We held at 12,000 feet to provide protection from the Japanese fighters. I saw my first Zero about 1,000 feet above me, pulled up into a sharp climb and fired. My tracers went in front of him and he was gone. I pushed over looking for Dixie, my wingman, and all of sudden heard a terrible racket behind me. I looked back and saw a Zero on my tail. He was firing and the bullets were dinging as they ripped through the plane. I was hit, but okay; the armor plating behind the seat had saved my ass. I went into a dive to outrun him, and guess I did. He couldn't keep up. It was my first brush with death. It was the most frightening moment I had ever had. I felt like my heart was in my mouth. My tongue was drier than the Sahara desert. When we got back to the Sara, *the ground crew counted 49 bullet holes that the Zero had put into me. That F6F Hellcat had taken one helluva beating and still brought me home...what an airplane!*[1]

Warren (Bud) Fisher
Lt. Commander, U. S. Naval Reserve

[Bud Fisher became a Navy fighter pilot flying the famous Grumman F6F Hellcat. From college student to one of the hottest fighters of the war—it was quite a transition and an unforgettable journey.]

I was about to graduate from Miami University in Oxford, Ohio, when I got accepted into the Navy flying program. It was the spring of 1941 and

GETTING READY FOR TAKEOFF ON THE SARATOGA.

the draft board back home was after me. "Better the Navy than the Army," I thought, and so I took and passed the entrance exam for the Navy flight program. The war in Europe was in full swing but most of us still hoped that America could stay out of it. No one realized how soon it would consume us all.

My orders required me to report to Floyd Bennett Field in Brooklyn in December and so I spent the summer at home. It was a time to relax and enjoy. I don't think the lake was ever any more beautiful than it was that summer. It just so happened that my orders required me to arrive at Floyd Bennett on December 4th, which I did. I planned a big weekend with my brother, who lived in the New York area. We capped it off with tickets to a professional football game on Sunday—the New York Giants vs. the

Brooklyn Dodgers. (There was a professional football team in Brooklyn in those days.) We thought it was sort of odd when the loudspeaker announced that a certain General attending the game had to report to the security office, but we didn't think much about it. Then, when we got back to the car and turned on the radio, we got the news. The Japanese had bombed our fleet in Pearl Harbor. My brother drove me back to the base immediately. We both knew that the war had begun.

[Editor's note: Bud Fisher went on to become a naval aviator flying F4U Corsair and F6F Hellcat fighters. He was assigned to VF-12, a fighter squadron which flew from the USS *Saratoga.* He kept a flight log and diary of his war experiences in the Pacific. The following are selections from those writings.]

November 1, 1943: This morning the *"Sara"* launched her group of torpedo planes (TBFs), divebombers (SBDs) and fighters (F6Fs) before dawn. No wind made it difficult, but the ship made 31.5 knots on her own, enough to launch planes. Even then, it was not enough for everyone as four planes went into the drink on takeoff. All pilots were recovered safely. An attack was made on the Japanese bases at Buka and Bonis, Japanese installations in the northern Solomon Islands. Three planes from VF-12 did not return, but two pilots were recovered at sea. (The third pilot, Wells, was captured by the Japanese, held as a prisoner of war and returned to the U.S. at the end of the war.) I did not fly on this mission.

November 2, 1943: We launched at dawn and I was part of the attack group to again attack the Japanese in the Buka Passage area. I was on Dixie Martin's wing and we escorted the torpedo planes and dive bombers to the target. There were no enemy fighters in the area and so we preceded the other planes with a strafing attack on the piers on Buka Island. It was my first experience with antiaircraft fire (AA), not real heavy but not a good feeling to be shot at. We started our run from 12,000 feet and put it up to 350 mph and went for the piers. I doubt if I hit anything. My windshield fogged up as we went from the cold air above to the hot, tropical air on the deck. We were lucky. I had started on Dixie's left but when we got to 50-100 feet off the water, I was on his right. How we ever did that without colliding with each other, I'll never know!

A wounded gunner being pulled out of a divebomber after the Rabaul raid.

We got back to the carrier at 0900, refueled, got more ammo and went back. This time I was ready when we made the dive. The windshield still steamed up, but I was ready for it and held my position. AA was not as bad and this time I hit more of the piers and did more damage. On completing the run, we swung down the west shore of Bougainville Island strafing several ships and AA positions. It was rugged going through the AA even though we were at 50 feet and doing 270 mph. Although there were a lot of holes in the planes, we only lost one pilot. Fewer casualties than we thought. At the debriefing, we were told that our attacks on the shipping and airfields around Buka passage had prevented their use by the Japs in attacking the Marine landings at Bougainville.

November 5, 1943: Flight quarters were sounded at 0400. All the pilots tried to eat a big breakfast, but I was happy with just a piece of toast and coffee. The first group was launched at 0630—all the SBDs, TBFs and

20 fighters. At 0730 the rest of us were launched and we flew hard and fast and caught up with the first group in sight of New Britain. All in all there were 109 planes, including 56 fighters from the *Saratoga* and the *Princeton,* ready for the attack on Rabaul.

There were countless ships in the harbor as we swung around north for our attack. (By coming in from the north, we could retire toward home and head south after we made our runs.) As soon as they saw us, they threw up an incredible barrage of antiaircraft fire. It seemed so thick that you could walk on it. As we held above the fray, the torpedo planes and dive bombers started down through it. One of our fighters, Tom Atwell, was hit by the flak and started to smoke. He gave us the "thumbs up" and peeled off toward the south. That was the last we saw of him.

We swung out over the island looking for Zeros and we found them...about 70 of them. Soon the air was full of dogfighting fighters. I saw my first one about 1,000 feet above me, pulled up and fired. My tracers whipped in front of him. Don't know if I got him. I pushed over trying to catch up with my wingman, Dixie. It was then that I saw the smoke, heard the racket and felt the Jap bullets hitting my F6F. I pushed it over, gave it all I had and headed for the deck. Down I went, and I guess outran him. Then I saw Dixie, going into a turn and waiting for me to catch up. Just then a Zero came from the other direction. Dixie took a shot and then the Jap turned in my direction. I unloaded as many rounds as I could and my tracers went into him. He headed down and looked in trouble, but it wasn't a confirmed kill—we didn't see him hit the water. We claimed a probable kill.

It was all over in ten minutes, and our bombers were retiring from the attack. As we flew over the harbor, several of the cruisers were burning. One had rolled over on its side. There were ships burning; you could see the flames. We had hit Rabaul, the heart of the Japanese Empire in the South Pacific and had survived. The wardroom was full of stories. Johnny Magda was credited with shooting down three Zeros. Dose got one as did Torchie and Moto. Doc Gould racked up one or two and so did "Red Dog" Gray. It was our first real baptism in fighter-to-fighter combat.

We didn't get back unscathed. I had over 40 bullet holes and some of my hydraulic lines had been hit. I had to manually lower the landing gear but made it in okay. There were four hits on the armor plate right behind my back...thank God for that armor plate. The Japs didn't have it in their

ADMIRAL "BULL" HALSEY CONGRATULATES OUR SKIPPER AND VF-12 AFTER THE RAID ON RABAUL.

planes. "Jumpin' Joe" Clifton, our group commander, could only get one wheel down and crash landed on the carrier deck. Two tail gunners in the SBDs and one of the photographers in another plane were killed by AA fire. In addition to Tom Atwell, we lost Art Teall, who crashed into the harbor after dropping his bomb. Carl Roberts got jumped by some Zeros and after a hefty fight got separated from the rest of us. He ended up flying to Munda and then on Espiritu Santo where we later picked him up.[2]

November 11, 1943: Back again to Rabaul. This time we felt more ready for combat. I guess once is enough to make you feel like a veteran. It was the same approach— come in from the north and retire to the south. Only this time we weren't attacked by fighters. Simpson Harbor at Rabaul came into view, not as brimming with ships as before but still a large number of them around. We were at 15,000 feet and saw our quarry—two

"Jumpin' Joe" Clifton, our skipper, offering all of us cigars after the successful strike on Rabaul.

heavy cruisers and several destroyers, heading out to sea at full speed, trying to get in the protection of a storm and weather front moving in. We held overhead and the bombers went down, through the clouds, to drop their eggs. They scored well:

1 Jap cruiser sunk
1 Jap cruiser badly damaged
2-4 Jap destroyers sunk or damaged

Our losses were less than the attack on the 5th. Nyrodie went down in his TBF over the harbor. Culver got shot up by a Zero and limped back to the ship. He had to parachute out and ditch the plane, but was picked up by one of our destroyers.

November 19, 1943: *Sara* aircraft made three attacks today on the Island of Nauru. The primary objective was to destroy a Japanese airfield on the island. For the first two attacks my group held over the carrier as a CAP (Combat Air Patrol) but no bogies (hostile aircraft) threatened the fleet. The third and last raid of the day was launched about 1400. We escorted the bombers and torpedo planes to the target, meeting no opposition. However, just as the TBFs pushed into their run, I saw three Zeros flying about 1,500 feet above me on an opposite course. They made no attempt to stop us, but soon ran into a number of our fighters. (John Hughes got one by shooting him off his wingman's tail.) We followed the TBFs down and strafed gun emplacements that had been shooting at us. They stopped shooting either because we had hit them or because of the terrible racket of the F6Fs and our .50-caliber machine guns. (It sometimes scares me when I hear those guns!) No losses of our own; it felt good to get back to the *Sara* with all of our buddies intact.

November 29, 1943: Tarawa: The Marines had recently taken this island in one of the bloodiest battles of the South Pacific. There had been rumors for sometime that we would be going to the island, to be land-based for awhile. I guess the fighting was going on longer than expected. In late afternoon, we were flying CAP (Combat Air Patrol) over the ship and received orders by radio to immediately fly to Tarawa and land. We left without the chance to pick up any of our gear. At about 1700 we broke up and landed on the little island of Betio, a godforsaken piece of blown-to-hell real estate.[3]

It was our first experience at going through a mess line and eating field rations. It was quite a time-consuming experience. You passed through a line, dipping your mess gear in various drums of water to sterilize it, went through another line to get chow, and yet another line to clean up. There were no tables or chairs. We sat on boards that had been nailed up between bullet-spattered trees. The biggest problem was getting your food down fast enough in order to beat the flies which came in swarms to devour your food. They gave us tents to sleep in but we used them as mattresses to take the bumps out of the coral. Most of us slept under the wings of the planes.

We toured the island and saw the incredible defenses and concrete bunkers that the Japanese had built. It had been a tough battle for the

Marines. The Japanese would not surrender and the Marines had to use flamethrowers to finally knock out some of the defenses. The stench was indescribable. As soon as the sun came up and until late in the afternoon, the smell of rotting flesh permeated the place. It wasn't until evening that the ocean breezes would blow the smell away. When you saw the burned and bloated bodies of the dead Japs, you knew what kind of a hell the Marines had gone through in taking this place.

We left on December 3rd, and just in time. That night the Japs bombed Betio and several planes were destroyed. The *Sara* had left for the States and so we stopped on another carrier, the USS *Independence,* to gas up and change clothes. Then it was on to Nukifetau, Funafuti, Canton Island, and eventually Hawaii. We were on our way back to the States for a rest and were we ready for it!

[Editor's Note: The USS *Saratoga* returned to San Francisco at the end of November 1943 for replenishment and repairs. VF-12 and the rest of the air group caught up with her in San Francisco for two to three weeks of needed rest and liberty. But the war was far from over, and the *Sara* and her air group got underway again on January 3, 1944, and headed back to the Central Pacific. The fighting had now shifted to the Marshall Islands. Lt.(jg)Bud Fisher and his colleagues would first support operations in the Central Pacific, and then would leave on a special mission to the Indian Ocean to support British naval forces in attacking Japanese positions in Java and Sumatra.]

January 27, 1944: Flight quarters at 0400 and launched planes at 0600. Practiced attacks all day, getting ready for operations in the Marshall Islands. Captain Cassidy came on the speaker at 1800 and told us what was to happen. We will drop about 90 tons of bombs each day in the operation. The fleet has come a long way since the grim days of 1942. There will be 22 aircraft carriers in this operation and 1,080 planes will be in the air. It will be trouble for the Japs!

January 29, 1944: Up at 0330, took off at 0530 for Wotje. Bad launch, damned near went in the water on the port side. Attacked Wotje at 0715. Dixie and I lost track of the group but joined up with TBFs for the trip home. Lots of AA but no enemy fighters. Took off for second strike at 0945, bad weather all the way to the target. Dixie and I torched a gasoline barge and hit several other targets. Weather still lousy: ceiling 300 - 400 ft. Back to the *Sara.* Took off at 1345 for a third attack, this time with a 500-lb. bomb. Weather really bad. Had a helluva hard time finding the target, but made the attack and got back okay.

Cruisers were shelling Wotje Island when we arrived. No AA at all...we came in from the west. They've fitted our F6Fs with bombs; we can carry one 1,000-lb. bomb or two 500-pounders. I went for a pier with my bombs but missed the target and hit a beach close by. Went back and strafed. Strafed and bombed for seven and a half hours in three separate sorties.

January 30 and 31, 1944: Attacked Taroa for two days. Strafed planes in revetments and strafed a radio station on a small island. Carried a 1,000 lb. bomb for the radio station target...missed but put it right in the middle of the runway. Acted as spotter for a cruiser and helped them score hits on a fuel dump, hangars and the runway. No planes lost.

[Editor's note: from February 2 - February 28, 1944, Lt.(jg) Fisher and VF-12 strafed and bombed Engebi and Eniwetok Islands in preparation for and in support of American troops landing on those islands. On March 1st, the USS *Saratoga* refueled and rearmed at Majuro Island, and then headed for the Indian Ocean via Australia.]

March 13, 1944: We are somewhere southeast of Australia and in one helluva Antarctic-type storm. The ship has been pitching and rolling badly all day. Swells must be about 400-500 feet across and 50 feet high. Many times, our bow has been underwater and spray has risen as high as the Admiral's bridge which is 150-200 feet above the water. Gun directors on both sides are loose and will probably be knocked off tonight. I heard that one man was washed overboard. Water is all over the main deck forward of the wardroom. Ship has reduced speed to eight knots to ride it out.

April 7, 1944: China Bay, Ceylon: Have had two or three meetings with the British getting prepared for operations. Up today at 0830, not much happening. Squadron party in evening on the beach. About six nurses and ten other women were there with beer, gin, etc. Red Gray had his record-player there for dancing. I had a nurse, quite nice, but she had to leave at 2300. So I proceeded to get plastered to celebrate my birthday. (I'm 26.) Was very drunk and probably worst I've ever been. Dixie and Miller put me to bed about 0130 after a lot of persuasion on their part. Next day, up about 1030 with a terrific hangover. Was quite sick and tossed everything, including my lunch, which was no loss. Returned to the ship and stayed in the sack most of the rest of the day.

April 19, 1944: At general quarters. Fifty-four planes off for a raid with the British against Jap installations, Sabang, Sumatra. I had CAP over the carrier and at about 1,000 got vectored toward two kates (Japanese bombers). I got one and Moto got the other. Sabang raid was a success. Oil tanks, planes, ships, radio station, electric plants, AA, coal bins, barracks...all blasted. One jap destroyer strafed and set afire. Klondike was hit

Lt.(jg) Bud Fisher (far left) having a final cigarette with some of his fellow pilots after the *Saratoga* returned from its last deployment.

Win-The-War Certificate

Issued In Honor Of

Warren Fisher

Jamestown, N. Y.

For Services Rendered To THE UNITED STATES In Time of War

This WIN-THE-WAR CERTIFICATE is made possible by the efforts of the VICTORY WORKER and the loyalty of the persons named on the reverse side, who in the aggregate have purchased WAR BONDS of the total value at maturity of

★ ★ ★ $500.00 ★ ★ ★

These persons desire to show by their purchase their sincere appreciation of the services of the person to whom this certificate is issued.

In Witness Whereof, THIS CERTIFICATE is issued this 12 day of August, 1944 by the authority of the WAR FINANCE COMMITTEE, CHAUTAUQUA COUNTY, STATE OF NEW YORK.

WAR FINANCE COMMITTEE

Frank Garratt

Earl O. Hultquist

Co-Chairmen

In World War II, citizens purchased war bonds to help finance the war. They could also dedicate the purchase of that bond to a veteran fighting on the front lines by making that designation on a "Win-The-War Certificate." A group of factory workers in Bud Fisher's hometown dedicated their $500 war bond purchase to the hometown boy flying his Hellcat fighter against the Japanese in the Pacific.

by AA, had to crash at sea but was picked up by one of our subs. Gavan got hit and had his tail almost blown off but made it back okay. One plane hit a turret during landing and overturned. Pilot had several cuts but okay... plane totaled and pushed over the side.[4]

May 17, 1944: Launched at 0630 for an attack on Soerabaja, Java. Arrived over target with no interception, complete surprise. The SBDs hit the Wonokromo Oil Refinery which went up in flame, smoke and complete destruction. No AA but Robotham, the TBF skipper, got too low and was hit by debris from the explosions. He crash-landed at sea, about three miles from shore. We hope that one of our subs was able to pick him up. On the way back, we strafed Malang Airfield and caught about 20 Jap planes on the ground, propellers turning and starting to get airborne. We blasted all of them and left for home. "Mission accomplished, job well done!" the Skipper said.

June 17, 1944: We're home. Up early. Launched from *Sara* in the Straits of Vancouver and flew to Sand Point near Seattle. Bad weather most of the way. My wheels didn't come down and I had to pump them down by hand. In the process, I got a little out of formation and almost hit Dixie. It was almost like Buka Island all over again. Wouldn't that have been a terrible way to end the war...hitting my wingman. But landed okay for the final flight of VF-12. A great welcome for us. Many wives of squadron members were there. A big party in the evening at the "O" Club. Boy, was it great to be home!

I got back home for about 30 days leave and found that I was quite a celebrity. There had been some pictures in the paper of me and some write-ups on the activities of VF-12. One local factory had even raised some war bond money in my name...they did that in those days. I spent 'till the end of the war at a Naval Air Station in Wildwood, NJ, a training station for new pilots heading for the Pacific. Some of the guys from the squadron would periodically come through Wildwood and we would talk about the good old days. VF-12 really did make a difference in that Pacific war and I will always cherish those days. But my flying days were over...I had done enough of it. I had always been a fairly good artist and had a yen for photography. I spent the rest of my life in industrial advertising and photography until I retired in 1983. You always see people again that you meet along the way in life; but when it comes to reunions, the one I look forward to most is that of VF-12. If I'm still around in two years, I'll be at the reunion in Minnesota talking about those unforgettable days in the Pacific.

[For service to his country, Bud Fisher was awarded the Distinguished Flying Cross. He returned to his hometown after the war and spent 37 years as an advertising executive in local industry. He is now retired.]

Background and Commentary

1 Bud Fisher flew probably the most widely used Navy carrier fighter in World War II, the Grumman F6F "Hellcat." The single engine Hellcat was an all-around workhorse airplane for the Navy. It had a range of over 1500 miles, could carry up to two 500-lb. bombs, and had both .50-cal. machine guns and .20-mm cannon for armament. It could attain a maxi-

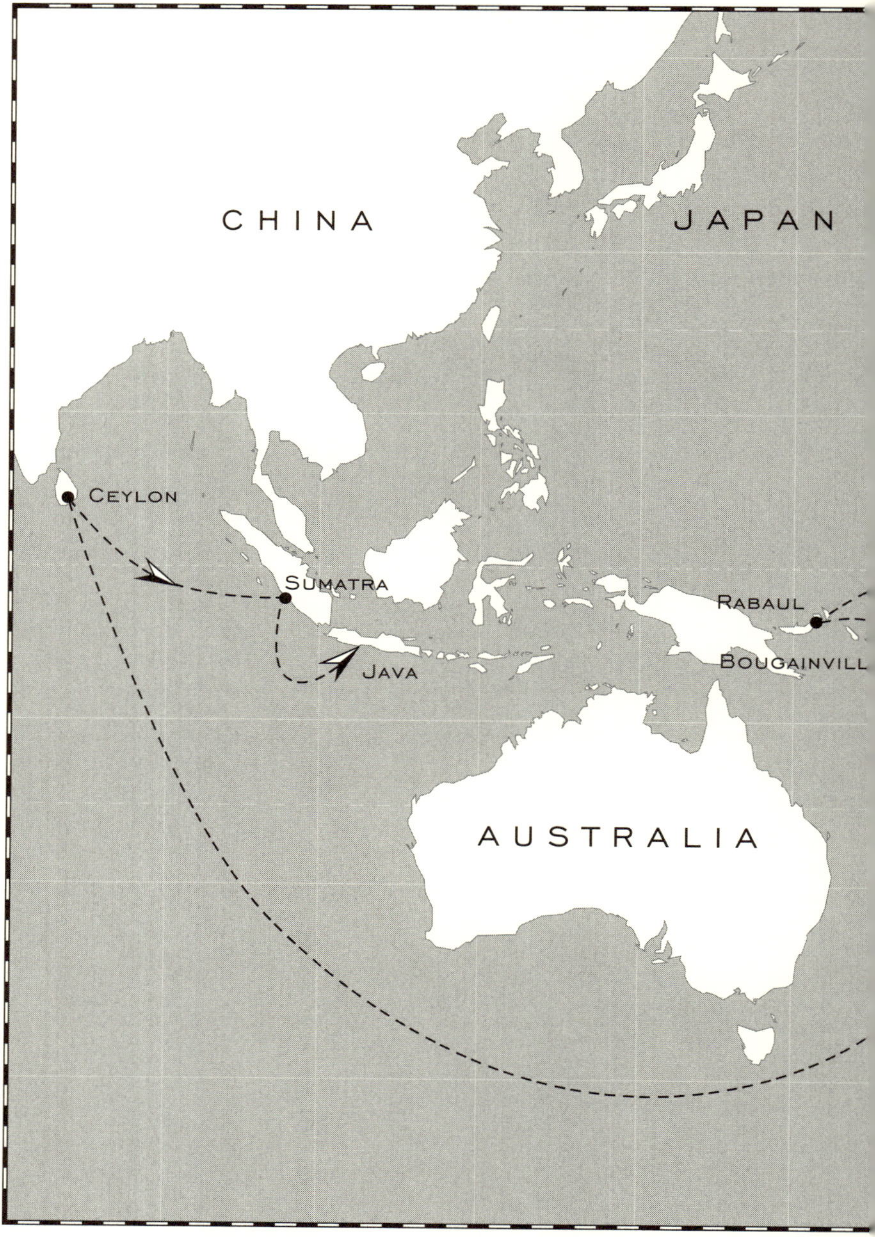

TRAVELS OF BUD FISHER

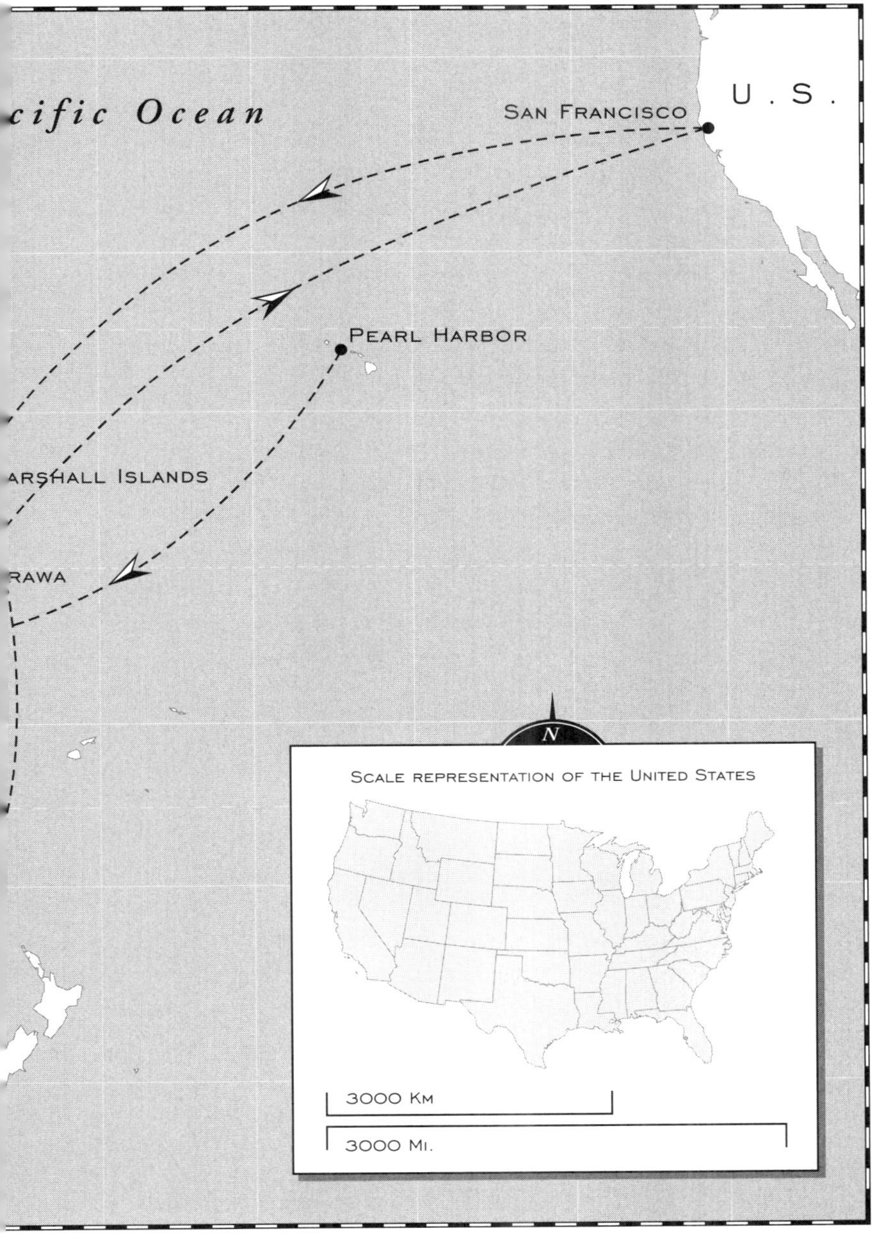
cific Ocean
U.S.
San Francisco
Pearl Harbor
arshall Islands
rawa
N
Scale representation of the United States
3000 Km
3000 Mi.

mum level speed of 371 mph, and could exceed that when diving on a target. It was a reliable aircraft and well-liked by Navy pilots. Again, it is a story of the productive ability of America's industrial machine. The F6F flew for the first time on June 26, 1942, and went into production at the end of that year. Between then and the end of the war, the Grumman Corporation delivered 12,275 Hellcat fighters to the U.S. Navy for use against the Japanese.

American pilots came to have great respect for the primary Japanese fighter plane of the war, the Mitsubishi A6M, known as the "Zeke" or "Zero." The Japanese, in the 1940s, were as skilled as they are today in building first-rate, state of the art equipment. The Zero was a flying, killing machine. It was extremely quick and maneuverable and it carried machine guns as well as cannon for armament. At the beginning of the war, it was definitely superior to anything that the United States had in the air, as was witnessed by those who saw it do its work at Pearl Harbor.

In 1942, a Zero crash-landed after being hit by ground fire while on a strafing run in the Aleutian Islands off Alaska. The pilot was killed in the crash but American forces were able to find and salvage the plane. It was taken back to Washington State, put into flying condition and test-flown by American pilots. It was a fantastic plane to fly but the tests also showed its vulnerabilities. It was light and extremely maneuverable up to 300 mph, but after that, it became sluggish. It had particular difficulty rolling to the right at high speeds. It also could not perform as well as the Hellcat and some of the other American fighters at altitudes greater than 20,000 feet. However, its biggest liability was its lack of armor. American fighters had protected fuel tanks and steel armor plate beneath and behind the pilot's seat. The U.S. aircraft could take a real beating and still return to the aircraft carrier...witness Bud Fisher's experience over Rabaul. On the other hand, if one of our pilots could get a slug into a Zero, there was a good chance he could "flame" it and kill or wound the pilot. After the 1942 analysis of the captured Zero, it became standard operating procedure for American fighter pilots to speed up and try to outrun the Zero. If they did get into trouble, rather than dogfight, they would often dive, go faster than the Zero's optimum maneuvering speed, roll right and then climb back to altitude to get into the fray again.

[2] Rabaul, a town situated on the northeast end of the 500-mile-long

island called New Britain, was the major harbor and staging center for Japanese operations in the southwest Pacific. It was from here that planes were sent to bomb Guadalcanal and troops were sent in an attempt to defeat the Australians and Americans in New Guinea. Although the port was periodically attacked from the air, it was never invaded by American forces. It was by-passed in the "island-hopping" strategy adopted by General Douglas MacArthur and Admiral Chester Nimitz as they moved toward Japan. In so doing, they eventually isolated some 100,000 Japanese troops at Rabaul. These soldiers were effectively cut off from any further participation in the war and could neither be supplied nor evacuated by the Japanese. They were eventually repatriated to Japan by the Allies after the war.

3 Within a month after attacking Rabaul, Bud Fisher and his squadron of VF-12 Hellcats had traveled on the USS *Saratoga* 2,500 miles northeast to support the U.S. Marines as they landed at Tarawa in the Gilbert Islands. The fighting at Tarawa was especially bloody. It was Marine against Marine, with U.S. troops facing 4,500 specially trained Imperial Marines. During the landings, American landing craft got hung up on the shallow coral reefs covering the approach to the island and were sitting ducks for the heavily entrenched Japanese forces. The enemy was dug in on a small, two-mile-long spit of sand with all of their tanks and artillery embedded in concrete bunkers. The operation that military planners thought would be easy took the lives of 1,300 marines—half the number of Americans that would die in all of D-Day on June 6, 1944, in France. After 75 hours of what many believe was the most bitter fighting ever experienced by the U.S. Marine Corps, the battle was over. Only 17 Japanese soldiers and 129 Korean laborers were captured alive.

As in all military actions in World War II, the news from Tarawa was censored. However, for the first time in the Pacific, photographs were cleared for print showing dead marines lying in the water on the beach at Tarawa. The result was predictable: President Roosevelt was flooded by angry letters and phone calls from the mothers of America who had sent their sons off to war. After that experience, Washington policy-makers became much more circumspect about what kinds of photographs and stories were allowed in the newspapers. Censorship was tightened and the news stories more carefully screened. War is a dirty business and, when seen in all its gory detail, is not something that most people are inclined to support, especially if their sons are involved. That was found to be all too true years later, during the Vietnam War, when night after night the bloody results of war were flashed on TV screens across America during the evening news.

4 One of Japan's vulnerabilities during World War II was the same as one of its continuing difficulties today—it did not have significant petroleum reserves. Within three months after its attack on Pearl Harbor, Japan attacked the Dutch East Indies (now Indonesia) in order to insure that it would have fuel to run its war machine from the oil fields located there. The Japanese quickly defeated British and Dutch forces in the area. Nevertheless, the Dutch were able to destroy or disable most of the oil refineries before the Japanese took control, and that insured that adequate refined oil products and gasoline supplies would remain a problem for Japan throughout the course of the war. Bud Fisher's attack with other units from the *Saratoga* was an attempt by the Allies to destroy any productive capability that the Japanese might have been able to restore to these petroleum facilities.

17. Supply And Construction In The Pacific

The Seabees

Probably my most vivid memory of the war was the day I noticed the white cross in the Los Negros cemetery that had Van Dyke Underwood's name on it. We'd grown up on the same street back home and were good buddies. I hadn't heard that he'd been killed. He'd lied about his age to get in the Army. He was only sixteen when he went in and wanted to go and fight in the war. He'd been on MacArthur's invasion force on this godforsaken island in the South Pacific, a part of the First Cavalry Division. Now here he was, far from home, buried in the sand.

At least the Americans had been buried. It was three or four weeks since the main battle and there were still Japanese bodies lying around. The stench was unbelievable. It's difficult to believe now that I was there. Not only that, but that I was alive and VanDyke Underwood was dead. Just a couple of kids from a small town who'd never been anywhere, and here I ended up being the lucky one on an island no one had ever heard of..."Los Negros." I bet there's not ten people in town today who've ever even heard of the place.

Roland A. Swanson
Ship Fitter 3rd Class
Seabees, U. S. Naval Reserve

[Wherever the U.S. military went, ports, buildings and airfields had to be built. Roland Swanson traveled throughout the Pacific helping to construct this important infrastructure for the war effort.]

Let me say first of all that I'm proud to be a Seabee, and the longer I am a Seabee the more proud I become. There were 250,000 of us in World War II and a lot of us went to the Pacific. "We build, we fight!" was our motto. Everyone in the Seabees, even today, has the "can do" spirit. Most of us have stayed a part of it. I'm New York State Chaplain of the Seabee Veterans of America. We have local chapters and I'm in "Island X-5 New York." (We used to receive orders during the war that said "go to Island

X"...so we use that terminology to describe the dispersed Seabee veterans groups around the country today.)

Many people think that the name "Seabee" came directly from our designation as Navy CBs or "construction battalions," but that's not the case. Frank Infrata, a civilian working for the CBs in Davisville, RI, came up with the Seabee name and insignia. He did it as a volunteer and originally drafted the logo as a beaver because of its good reputation as a builder.

The Seabees Insignia.

However, someone pointed out to him that a beaver usually runs when attacked and so he changed it to a bee (laughs)! Anyway that's how we got our insignia—the bee with the sailor hat, shooting a tommy gun and hanging onto his tools at the same time. Prior to the war there had been civilian construction workers in the Pacific building airfields and ports, but they were not prepared to fight. We were trained to build and also fight, and often we had to do both.

The first Seabees during the early war years of 1942 were experienced tradesmen: equipment operators, carpenters, iron workers, welders, electricians and plumbers. Thus, a lot of them were older than the average guy in the military. Most were married and many had kids at home. (We had one guy in our outfit who had seven children.) Because of this, the average age for Seabees in World War II was 32 or 34, much higher than in other services. Later in 1943, when I went in, they were taking younger people like myself and then training us on the job, but the early guys were oldtimers.

What we did was build anything and everything. A lot of our work in the Pacific was involved with building airfields and port facilities as General MacArthur and Admiral Nimitz "hedgehopped" their way up various island chains on their way back to the Philippines and then to Japan. Sometimes I was on KP, other times driving trucks loaded with coral or gravel to use in building roads or runways. We built airports, highways, bridges, sawmills and warehouses. Our most famous piece of construction was probably the Quonset hut, named after our base at Quonset Point, RI. We put those up literally by the thousands all over the world.

On Sunday night, December 7th, 1941, I had gone bowling with a friend over at Ten Pin Lanes. We heard about Pearl Harbor on the way home listening to the car radio. However, it wasn't until the next year, 1943, that I went into the military. I turned 18 during my senior year and they drafted me right out of high school. I never graduated. (Later on, after the war, I went back and took my GED and got a high school diploma.) I was sent to Buffalo to be sworn in and it was there that I was told about the Seabees, this new construction outfit that was part of the Navy. It sounded good to me, so I volunteered, and off I went to Camp Peary near Williamsburg, VA, for boot camp. It was tough training. We had Marine instructors and they were tough, but it also established in us a strong camaraderie with the Marines, something that the Seabees have always had and still maintain.

From Camp Peary we were sent to Davisville, RI, for advanced training, and were then sent to Gulfport, MS, where we were assigned to ships to be sent overseas. We boarded the ship for our trip to the Pacific on December 31, 1943, New Year's Eve. That first night, the ship just went out into the harbor and dropped the anchor. I guess the Navy was afraid that they might have too many men AWOL (Absent Without Leave) if they let them go into town partying on New Year's Eve (laughs). The next morning we weighed anchor, got into a convoy and headed for the Panama Canal.

We had an interesting experience in the Pacific after we had gone through the Canal. There were about 10,000 men on that ship (the

Mormac Sea) and it started having engine trouble. Finally, the engines stopped and we were dead in the water. The destroyer escorts directing the convoy stayed with us for awhile but then said that they would have to leave and stay with the main convoy, so now we were on our own. However, some of our Seabees were excellent engine mechanics. They went down into the engine room on that ship and got things running again. We finally caught up with the rest of the convoy at Espiritu Santo.

From there we headed west and stopped at Guadalcanal for a few days. That was a meaningful stop for me because my buddy, Joe Urbanik, had gone in there with the First Marine Division on August 6th. He told me later that the Seabees had come in the day after the initial landings, and had done a heck of a job in supporting the Marines. From Guadalcanal the ship headed for the Admiralty Islands where I was scheduled to be part of some of the first replacements for the 78th Construction Battalion. The Admiralties were about 1,000 miles farther north and west of Guadalcanal and were in MacArthur's area of responsibility. In February, we finally caught up with the 78th on the island of Los Negros and that's where my Seabee life really began.

The fighting was still going on when we got there. You could hear the shelling and the firing going on nearby and on the adjacent islands of Ponam and Manus. Periodically, especially at night, the Japanese would bomb us and everyone would scamper for their fox holes. In this part of the Pacific, we were supporting U.S. Army and Australian troops. MacArthur also had B-17 bomber support and so our main job on Los Negros was to build an airfield that could be used by the B-17s. It wasn't very glamorous work. I did everything from KP duty to driving trucks loaded with coral. We would dynamite the coral, load it into trucks with steamshovels and then haul it to the airstrip location and use it in runway construction. We worked 24 hours a day with 12-hour shifts and we got the job done. After Ponam was taken, we moved there and did the same thing except that the airfield at Ponam was used as a base for fighters. We also put up Quonset huts for living quarters, facilities for fueling the planes, and all of the other infrastructure needed for an air base.

It was hot, humid and muddy. The mosquitos could be terrible. The bombing kept you awake at night...but somehow you kept going. Then once the airfields became operational, you saw another dimension of the

The destruction on Los Negros.

war. The airplanes would start using the newly constructed fields to take the war to the enemy. B-17s and P-38s would often return from missions shot up and in trouble. Some would belly in and crash; men would die trying to get back to their base. But slowly, the Air Corps would wear the enemy down and MacArthur would move on to the next island and to the next objective.

After five months at Los Negros and Ponam, we were sent to Manus to build a large advanced Navy receiving and supply base. On Manus we did a lot of road-building and also built a hospital. Our base was up on a hill away from the port and one day there was a heck of an explosion down at the piers. We could hear it and see it. We thought an enemy attack must be on, but what had happened was that an ammo ship, the *Mount Hood,* had exploded while it was unloading. A lot of guys were killed. It's those kinds of deaths that really seem tragic when you are in a war, but they happen. Accidents and friendly fire killed a lot of guys during the war and we saw our share.[1]

After Ponam, the Navy sent us to New Caledonia, an island much farther to the south, for R & R (Rest and Recuperation). It had never been

Roland Swanson on Okinawa.

taken by the Japanese and had been a staging point for transporting supplies to the South Pacific all during the war. We were stationed at Mt. Dior, near Noumea, and had some time to relax, do equipment repair, etc. In early '45 we got orders to head out to another "island X" and this one was to be Okinawa. Okinawa was much further north than we had ever been before, and was the closest invasion thus far to the main Japanese islands. The fighting was bitter. We followed the marines in on the northern end of the island and began rebuilding the Yontan airstrip. The fighting continued on the southern end of the island for several weeks and at night we would see the sky lit up like a Christmas tree with tracer rounds from the machine guns and antiaircraft gunfire. The Marines took a heck of a pounding at Okinawa but the enemy received even heavier losses. The Japanese had been ordered not to surrender, and they didn't. We also got pounded by Mother Nature. Two typhoons went through while I was on Okinawa. But they were nothing compared with the near total devastation caused by the war. The bombardment, the flame throwers and the bombing leveled the town of Naha. Virtually nothing was left standing. Everything had to be rebuilt.[2]

Roland Swanson and Dick Giordon (from nearby Sugar Grove) on Okinawa.

Probably, the closest I came to being killed was on Okinawa. I got up in the middle of the night and went to the perimeter of the camp to make a pee call. When I came back a Marine guard challenged me and I froze. I had forgotten the password. He challenged me again and I heard him cock the gun. Finally, I yelled "Seabee!" and he said "Come ahead." Can you imagine them writing home that I had gotten killed trying to take a leak? Yet, it almost happened.

While we were there, a tragic event occurred near us on the island of Ie Shima. Ernie Pyle, the famous war correspondent, was killed there. After it happened, a couple of our Seabees were assigned to build a pylon memorial for him. I don't know if it is still there or not. Okinawa, of course, was to become the primary staging area for the invasion of Japan and so a tremendous build-up took place getting ready for that. That's where I was when the war ended. We estimated that there must have been 50,000 Seabees on Okinawa building everything that would be necessary for the last push of the war. What an experience. In a little over two years we had moved almost 4,000 miles across the Pacific chasing the Japanese, and then, all of a sudden, it ended. Most of us in Okinawa were pleased that the atom bomb had been dropped. For us, it brought the end of the war.

I worked at Sears, you know, after the war, put in 21 good years and am proud of what I did with that company. But as I look back on my life, nothing compares with the pride I have in having been part of the Seabees. At the time, I didn't particularly like it, but we were young and tried to make the best of it. We were disciplined, we followed orders, we respected command, it was a tough job and we did it. And I believe that we really made a difference in the outcome of the war. Since retirement, I've started studying more about the history of the Seabees. We were involved in nearly every amphibious landing, including Normandy, that occurred during the war. We built, we fought, we were good, we got the job done. I guess that's why I stay active in Seabee veterans affairs. By the way, we're sending petitions to the Citizens Stamp Advisory Committee in Washington to have them authorize a commemorative stamp for 1997 honoring the 55th anniversary of the Seabees. Could I get you to sign a petition?

[Roland Swanson went to work for the Sears, Roebuck Company after the war and worked there for 22 years. He's retired now but stays involved as an active layman at the Lutheran Church and in serving as an officer in the Seabees veterans organization.]

U.S. Army Port Company

We were the first 18-year-old draftees to leave town as a group. After Pearl Harbor, Congress passed a law lowering the draft age and it was waiting for us when we graduated from high school in the summer of 1942. My birthday was in November, I registered for the draft in December and in March of '43 I was called up.

Things hadn't been going too well for us in the war up to that point and most of us knew it. Therefore, it was with trepidation that we went down to the train station the day we left for the Army. There were a few oldtimers in their 30s but most of us were just 18. The median between the tracks at the old Erie Railroad Station was jammed with family and friends. Most of us had never been away from home. The farthest I'd ever been was to Cincinnati on a family vacation. There were a lot of tears, especially from our parents. Where were we going? Would we come back alive? You really didn't know at that point. Another thing we didn't know was that sixteen of us from our hometown would be staying together. The day we left, we didn't know that. But all of us would be trained in how to load and unload ships for the Army. The Army had decided to try and keep some hometown groups together, and the sixteen of us would be attached to the 245th Port Company and spend the war moving supplies from ship to shore in New Guinea, New Britain, and the Philippines. We were heading for the South Pacific to serve under the command of General Douglas MacArthur in his fight against the Japanese!

Bob Olson
Technician 5th Grade, U.S. Army Reserve

[Bob Olson, like most draftees, had no idea of where he would be going in the war. Like Roland Swanson, he too was sent to the Pacific. His job would be to help supply the fighting forces as they moved against Japan.]

Like a lot of the draftees from our area, we took the train to Fort Niagara. It was the induction center for our area of the country. It was also where most of us had taken our draft physicals. We got our uniforms there and then the Army put us on a train for our first post, Indiantown Gap, PA. Everything in those days moved by train and the Army was no exception. It was an overnight ride and the next morning we arrived at a small station in Lebanon, PA, just outside the base, and were lined up and marched to our barracks.

Basic training was pretty standard, I suppose. Lots of drill, long marches, calisthenics, rifle training, etc. But for us, it only lasted about six weeks. The Army needed laborers, guys to unload ships and Indiantown Gap had been set up just for that purpose. Here we were, probably 200 miles from the closest salt water, in the middle of the Pennsylvania mountains, and the Army had constructed the hulls of two ships in the middle of a field. There were decks, cargo holds, cranes, cargo nets, and piers all set up, and we quickly learned how to load and unload ships. It wasn't long before we were on the train again and this time headed for the west coast. We didn't know where we would be going from there but we knew what we would be doing. We were going to be stevedores for the United States Army.

Our first stop in the west was at Camp Anza, located about ninety miles east of L.A. in the dry, desert-like climate of Southern California. From there, the Army would drive us to the piers in Los Angeles and Long Beach to help unload ships returning from the Pacific. It was our first real look at the war. Some of the ships were hospital ships and troop ships, and we would help carry stretchers and assist the wounded returning for hospitalization in the States. We began to recognize that some of the wounds were mental and not physical. One day a guy walked off a ship in Long Beach, grabbed a bicycle and began riding around and around in circles talking gibberish. That was more scary than seeing the physically wounded being carried off the ship.

In September of '43, we were moved north to San Francisco, and on September 24th, sailed under the Golden Gate Bridge heading west. We joked as we went under the bridge, "The Golden Gate in '48!" Most of us didn't think we would be home before then. We still didn't know where we were going, but it was pretty obvious that it was going to be somewhere in the Pacific. Our ship, the *West Point*, was actually an ocean liner, SS *America,* which had been converted to a troop ship. There were 15,000 of us on that ship. What a mass of humanity. We were fed two meals a day at 10 a.m. and 4 p.m. and we had beans at every meal. Our group was berthed on the top deck; as a matter of fact, we were in what had been the bridal suite. Somehow the military had figured a way to fill every possible space with a body. There were 250 of us in that bridal suite. The ship was

UNLOADING SUPPLIES FROM A SHIP.

fast and sailed alone. It zigzagged, often changing its heading to avoid submarines, but its best defense against submarines was its fast speed. On October 10th, we sailed under the beautiful landmark bridge at Sydney Harbor in Australia. That bridge was magnificent and I've always recognized it since when I've seen it in pictures.

Of course, Australia hadn't been geared up for a war either, and so there were no large Army bases to put us in. The Aussies had taken a race track called Warwick Farms, just outside of Sydney, and transformed it into a tent city for American troops. This is where we stayed. We did a little work at the piers in Sydney, but for some reason, maybe union problems with workers at the piers, we didn't get much work there. Most of our time was spent around camp and on liberty. We got along good with the Aussies and drank a lot of beer—though we had a hard time getting used to the fact that they drank their beer warm. Of course, the Australian beer companies

Bob Olson, having a beer in the South Pacific.

hadn't been built with all these American beer drinkers in mind and so the biggest problem they had was running out of beer. We used to hang out at the Royal Oak Hotel in Lidcombe, New South Wales, and sometimes the locals would get mad because we would drink up all the beer on a Friday night before they had a chance to even get to the bar (laughs)!

After about a month, on November 20th, we boarded a liberty ship, the *John Carroll* and headed off for our first real assignment, Milne Bay, New Guinea. Milne Bay is on the eastern tip of New Guinea and was a staging area for MacArthur as he moved north and west along the New Guinea coast. It had been a target for the Japanese but they had failed to take it after their setbacks at the Battle of the Coral Sea and the ill-fated attempt to take Port Moresby over the Kakoda trail.[3] But what a mud hole it was. It was near the equator, hot and rainy. The only way we could keep our stuff out of the mud in our tent was to prop up our rifles and hang the barracks bags off the rifles. What a mess. It was hot, really hot, and we worked all day bringing supplies ashore on landing craft from ships offshore. (At one point, it got so bad that I was hospitalized with heat stroke.) After a few days our mail caught up with us and I got a Christmas "care package" from home that my Mom had sent and do you know what was in it ? A sweater and a shoe-shine kit. Did I ever get a ribbing from the guys when that came in.

On January 5, 1944, we got orders to move on to Finschhafen, on the northeast coast of New Guinea, where we would be for almost six months. MacArthur had made a shrewd decision. Had our forces attacked every Japanese installation on New Guinea, there would have been a tremendous loss of life. Instead, he decided to "leap-frog" around most of the Japanese-held areas and just hit selected bases where he could use airfields and staging areas for an assault on the Philippines. Our job at Finschhafen was to be a staging area for places like Hollandia, further up the New Guinea coast. We were right across a stretch of water from the island of New Britain and one of the Japs' biggest bases was at Rabaul on New Britain. [See Bud Fisher's story about his attack on Rabaul in Chapter 16.] Every night the Japanese would send a harassment bomber over to drop a few bombs. We called him "Piss Call Charlie." Almost every night, just before taking your last piss of the night, just like clockwork, would come the nightly Jap air raid. Just enough harassment to make sure we couldn't get a good night's sleep.

Strafing by Japanese airplanes, the nightly visit of "Piss Call Charlie," that's the kind of action we had in New Guinea. Certainly not what the infantry faced, but still enough to let you know we were really in a war. One day when we were loading troops for an invasion, I recognized a friend from back home—Vandyke Underwood. He was a foot soldier and it was the last time I would see him alive. He was killed in the invasion of the Admiralty Islands. [Roland Swanson would see his grave later on the island of Los Negros.]

The food, I suppose, was typical of Army operations. It was filling but not memorable. We had periods of eating C rations but most of the time we had cooked food and decent meals. Of course, in typical American fashion, we always had to be supplied with beer, the "mother's milk" of the military. One day when the beer ship came up from Australia and we went out to unload it, we found three members of the crew who had passed out in the hold from drinking too much on the way up. We had to unload the drunks in a cargo net before we could off-load the beer (laughs)! It was tough work, though, at Finschhafen: 12 hours on and 12 hours off, seven

Natives on New Britain.

days a week. MacArthur was on a schedule and we had to keep up. In late April, his forces successfully attacked Hollandia, 600 miles up the coast of New Guinea; and in June we were transferred to Cape Gloucester, across the strait on the island of New Britain. We knew now that we had beaten the Japanese in the southern Pacific. Our next mission was to get ready for the invasion of the Philippines.

In New Guinea we hadn't really seen many civilians, but that was to change in New Britain. There were a lot of natives around, short, dark, inquisitive people. Language was a problem, but they were friendly. They didn't like the Japanese and had apparently been mistreated by them. Life was laid back in these remote places. Everyone worked hard and the distinctions between officers and enlisted men were hard to find. Our company commander, Captain Connelly, was easy going...as long as we got our work done. I remember one day a general from the 40th Division came through the camp. Nobody got up and saluted, no one yelled "Attention!" To us it was not a big deal. The general was mad and asked for our CO. He found Captain Connelly over in his tent squatting next to a kerosene refrigerator he was trying to fix. "What are you doing?" the general asked. Connelly was a cocky guy and didn't even get up. "What's it look like?" he said. "I'm fixing my refrigerator. It keeps my beer cold!" The general went through the roof and for the next week, we had inspections everyday (laughs)!

Sometimes things happen that you know are wrong, but war does strange things to people. One day a Japanese soldier turned himself in. He realized that the Japanese were finished at Cape Gloucester and that there was no way he could get back to Rabaul—several hundred miles away on the other side of the island. He had been educated in the United States and spoke good English. When he was being interrogated someone asked him what he intended to do after the war. He said, "I'd like to go back to Philadelphia and start a business." One of the guards who was from Philadelphia heard that, went berserk and shot the guy right through the head. It shouldn't have happened, but what do you do with the guy who shot him? He'd been on the frontlines fighting the Japanese for months. I think they busted him, put him in the brig and then sent him home. What else could you do? War is hell and, as they say, "shit happens."

We were in New Britain for almost six months, but in December of '44 we got our orders to load up and head for the Philippines. After a brief stop in the Admiralty Islands, we boarded the USS *Clay* (APA #39) and moved north in a huge convoy. There were 800 ships...ships as far as you could see. We were headed for Lingayen Gulf in northern Luzon, the main island in the Philippines. MacArthur had outfoxed the Japanese again. They expected an assault from the south because the U.S. had already established a toehold in the central islands around Leyte. But MacArthur went around to the north, to the same landing beach that the Japs had used when they invaded Luzon. The landing on January 9, 1945, was a surprise to the Japanese. Our troops got ashore with relative ease and pushed 30-40 miles toward Manila the first day. We were ashore by D-Hour plus 9 minutes: off-loading landing craft, rolling barrels of fuel and carrying ammo boxes ashore. When the enemy found out what was going on, a few kamikazes showed up and I saw one hit a carrier, but it was too little too late. We were on the move and they couldn't stop us now.

After we got ashore, things got a little hairy. Late in the day some Zeros came in on a strafing run. We'd been so busy unloading equipment that we hadn't dug in. We were right near a cemetery and a lot of the graves were actually in cement crypts above ground. We dove into the graveyard for

The Beach on D-Day at Lingayen Gulf.

cover. One guy was so excited that he dove inside one of the tombs that had broken up...right in with the bones and skulls. We thought we'd had it for awhile but our fighters soon had the Jap planes on the run. The destruction at Lingayen Gulf was total. Only one bombed-out school building remained standing. The shelling from our ships and the bombing from our planes had leveled everything within a mile of the beach. Some of the greatest risks came from our own guns. Just as we were getting into our landing craft before hitting the beach, a Jap plane flew over. It seemed like all 800 ships opened up on him. He didn't have a chance. But for us it was trouble too. The shrapnel from the exploding AA fire was falling like hail. If it had hit us, we would have been goners.

The infantry moved fast, southward toward Manila and within a month, by end of February, we had followed them to the outskirts of the city. MacArthur had made Manila an open city when he evacuated the area in 1942 on his retreat to Bataan, but the Japanese decided to defend and destroy it. A lot of lives were lost taking Manila back. Our troops were successful in getting to Santo Tomas, the Japanese prison camp where a lot of Americans had been interred during the war. Were they happy to see us.

FILIPINO CHILDREN AT LINGAYEN GULF.

Because they were civilians, there were also a lot of women in the camp. For us, it was the first time in over a year that we had seen an American woman. Was that a sight for sore eyes! We were fortunate and were able capture Santo Tomas without a lot of loss in American lives.[4]

A lot of the Filipinos weren't as lucky. There was an old, walled city along the North Pasic River and the Japs dug in. We saw them suspend Filipino kids on ropes over the sides of the walled city and dare our troops to fire. When we finally took the Old City, the stench was incredible. The Japs had filled the towers on the four corners of the place with dead Filipinos. It was the worst thing I had ever smelled.

We stayed in Manila until the war ended, off-loading supplies and helping in the process of rebuilding that country. I actually didn't get home from the war, though, until January of '46 because, after the war ended, we were sent to Okinawa and then to Shanghai and the Yangtze River area of China to help maintain order and get the Japanese troops that were there back to Japan. I imagine a highlight for me before leaving the Philippines was the day I actually saw General MacArthur. We were in Manila, in an unloading area near the river, bringing supplies ashore, and he drove up in a jeep. The jeep came in the wrong way. It was supposed to go in another driveway. A guard from our outfit stopped it and ordered the driver to turn around. "Don't you see who I've got in here?" the driver yelled. "I'm driving General MacArthur!" "I don't care if you've got Jesus Christ in that jeep!" the guard yelled back, "I've got orders not to let anybody come in this driveway!" All of a sudden we heard MacArthur, "Sergeant, you heard the man, turn this thing around and get out of here!" he ordered. That was MacArthur. He could obey orders too. He was a soldier's soldier. He had given a lot of orders and sent a lot of men to their deaths in that war. But he had also made decisions that saved a lot of lives. We were proud to have served under him all along the way.

It took us a while to get home, but all of us made it: all sixteen of us who had left town and gone to the Pacific in the 245th Port Company. I'll never forget the day I got home. We had been sent to Camp Attlebury, IN, for outprocessing and to get discharged, and we heard that a train was leaving for Warren. We thought it was going to Warren, PA, right near home; but after we got on the train, we found we were going to Warren, OH, about three hours from home. So when we got to Ohio, we had to hitchhike home. Joe Prosser and I had the same ride and the guy dropped us off at the corner of Fourth and Washington Sts. After almost three years of living with him, I said good-bye to Joe and went on my own down to Third and Washington to get the bus home. The bus finally came, I got on, walked down the aisle, and there, sitting on that bus, were my Mom and sister. Oh, wow. Was that ever sweet. It was the best bus ride I'd ever had. I was home!

[After he returned to town in 1946, Bob Olson landed a job at a sheet metal fabricating shop. He worked his way up, learning the business, until he became President of a local sheet metal company. He retired in 1986 after having spent forty years in that business.]

Background and Commentary

[1]Los Negros, Paulus and Manus were all a part of the Admiralty Islands, an archipelago located north of New Guinea and just south of the equator. General Douglas MacArthur needed these islands to set up staging areas

for his march northward to the Philippines. Roland Swanson and his group of Seabees were assigned the task of building the ports, highways and airfields on these islands. On November 10, 1944, at 8:55 a.m., a great tragedy engulfed the fighting men on Manus when a tremendous explosion shook the harbor. The ammunition ship, *Mount Hood*, anchored in the harbor and loaded with over 300 tons of explosives, blew up. The explosion rocked the island and could be seen for miles around. When the counting was over, 45 men were listed as known killed, 327 were missing and 371 had been injured. Every man on the *Mount Hood,* except for seventeen members of the ship's crew who had left moments earlier to carry out some duties on shore, was killed in the blast.

[2]Northwest of the Admiralty Islands by 2,500 miles, at about the same latitude as Key West, FL, is the Japanese Island of Okinawa. This was not an outpost of Japanese expansionism. It was considered to be a part of Japan and the Okinawans spoke Japanese. American war planners knew that the fighting would be tough as they planned to remove the expected 70,000 Japanese defenders on Okinawa, so a huge invasion force of approximately 154,000 battle-hardened soldiers and Marines was transported northward to invade the island. The Japanese had decided to make the battle an especially bloody confrontation. Initially, they withdrew to the southern part of the island giving only token resistance, but then they dug in. With gun emplacements and bunkers dug into the hard rock of southern Okinawa as their defense, they yielded ground only inch by inch.

Knowing that this would occur, the Imperial Navy and Air Forces of Japan made one last, all-out kamikaze attack on the enemy. Hundreds of explosive-laden planes dived out of the sky on the American fleet anchored off the shores of Okinawa, attempting to sink the invasion force. The mighty Japanese battleship, *Yamoto,* sailed from Japan with only enough fuel for a one-way trip. Its mission was to break through American defenses and slam into the fleet which was landing supplies and troops on Okinawa, sinking as many ships as it could. It was all for naught. The *Yamoto* was sunk by American planes before it ever got to Okinawa.

During the heat of the battle, on April 12, 1945, the troops on Okinawa heard the sad news that their Commander-in-Chief, President Franklin Roosevelt, had died. He was the only political leader that many of these young fighting men had ever known. Their hearts were heavy with the news, but the fighting never stopped. On April 25th, 51 nations met for the first meeting of the United Nations, an organization which had been the brainchild of Roosevelt to head off future wars...but the fighting on Okinawa continued. On the same day, the new President, Harry Truman, was briefed on the destructive capability of a new weapon, the atom bomb. President Truman watched the casualty lists on Okinawa mount up. When the fighting ended on June 22nd, 7,374 Americans had been killed in the land battle and another 31,807 were wounded. At sea, 34 ships had been sunk by the kamikaze pilots, 763 carrier planes had been lost, and 4,907 American sailors were dead. President Truman had decided that in order to avoid further American bloodshed, if the Japanese would not surrender, he would drop the atom bomb.

[3] In July, 1942, the Japanese attempted an incredible feat. Thwarted by the Americans from invading Port Moresby, New Guinea, by sea in the Battle of the Coral Sea off the coast of Australia, they now decided to push the Australians and Americans out of New Guinea on the ground. They landed a large force of army troops at Buna, on the north coast of New Guinea, and started to cross the Owen Stanley mountain range on a jungle path, called the Kokoda trail, bound for Port Moresby, a mere 78 miles away. However, their unexpected action was met by an equally unexpected reaction. General Douglas MacArthur decided to defend Australia in the mountains of New Guinea.

MacArthur rushed Australian reinforcements to New Guinea and ordered American troops to be brought up as soon as possible. The first major ground battle in the southwest Pacific was going to be fought in the rain forests and mountain peaks of New Guinea. The Australian soldiers, "diggers," as they were called, came through. The Japanese got to within sight of Port Moresby, and then fell back. The combined force of the jungle and the Aussies had been too much. American GIs now joined in the fighting and began pushing the Japanese back over the mountains. By the end of January, 1943, and after the loss of 8,546 Australian and American soldiers killed in the fighting, the Allies would be in control of the eastern tip of the island of New Guinea.

One war correspondent at the time, Pat Robinson, described the terrible fighting conditions in the jungles of New Guinea this way:

> *The terrain from Kokoda on across the Owen Stanley Range is probably the wildest and most difficult battleground in the world....The mountains are so steep that troops could climb only by clinging to trees and vines lining the precipitous trails. It was not uncommon to see a soldier resting by straddling a stump or bush so that he wouldn't roll down the mountain.*

Years later an American writer and former Marine, William Manchester, would come to Port Moresby and the Owen Stanley Range and walk up the Kokoda trail. He wanted to see the terrain that he had heard so much about. He describes a portion of it this way:

> *At Ioribaiwa, Australian engineers built what they mordantly called the "Golden Staircase," which survives today—four thousand twenty-inch steps, held together by roots, up a twenty-five-hundred-foot ridge and down and up again, each step hacked into clay, much as mountaineers cut traverses in ice. Now, as then, the air here is hot and extremely humid. Overhead, shrouded in clouds, loom jagged peaks, one, Mount Victoria, as high as 13,368 feet. Below, the jungle is studded with bottomless bogs. Often the trail is covered with waist-deep slop.*

The combat conditions in New Guinea were horrible. Men died from dehydration, exhaustion and heat stroke, as well as from gunfire. It was a place no one had ever heard of, but upon this battle's success or failure lay the future of Australia and the United States. When the battle ended, the threat to Australia was over. MacArthur had won the gamble and his troops had defeated the Japanese in the worst jungle fighting of World War II.

[4] The Philippines was "home turf" to General Douglas MacArthur. He had lived in the country for many years and left Corregidor under duress to command American forces in the Pacific. For him, liberating the POW camps in Luzon was a priority. After the fall of Bataan, the Japanese had forced the survivors to march 65 miles to captivity through the blazing heat without food or water. Twenty-three hundred Americans had died on that torturous "death march" and the survivors were believed to be in a POW camp in Arloc Province. Troops headed in that direction to

Japanese currency to be used in occupied countries or countries which had been expected to be conquered, found by Bob Olson in Manila .

liberate their comrades. In addition, a crack team of the Alamo Scouts (Sixth Rangers) was sent ahead of the main Army attack forces, and surprised and overwhelmed the Japanese defenders at a POW camp near Cabanatuan, freeing 511 American prisoners. However, MacArthur's greatest concern was for the welfare of some 4,000 American civilians interned at Santo Tomas, the University in Manila that had been converted into a prison camp.

A special commando unit was created from the 1st Cavalry Division. Loaded into trucks and spearheaded by tanks, this group was ordered to advance ahead of the primary attack force and liberate Santo Thomas before the Japanese could kill or harm the prisoners. After a two-day dash south from Cabanatuan, during the night of February 3rd, an American tank crashed through the gate of Santo Tomas. A CBS radio correspondent, Bill Dunn, was in the group when the camp was liberated. "I was almost at the rear of the column when lights suddenly blazed inside the camp, and the wildest and most beautiful screams of joy I had ever heard erupted!" he wrote. Dunn met several people whom he had known in Manila before the war and they all were emaciated and gaunt from malnutrition. With rations barely averaging 700 calories per day, the average weight of the adult males in Santo Tomas had dropped to 112 lbs. He didn't recognize some of them at first. One of the men in the armored column that liberated the camp was looking for his wife who had been stranded in Manila at the outbreak of the war. Suddenly, he grabbed Dunn. "I found her. I found her!" he screamed. He gave Dunn a tremendous bear hug and then "danced away to break the news to others."

It would take another month of fierce fighting to liberate the city of Manila, but on Monday, February 5th, the last Japanese hold-outs in Santo Tomas surrendered. The GIs had brought with them an American flag which they gave to those who had suffered at Santo Tomas. At 9:30 a.m. on that Monday morning, the internees of Santo Tomas gathered at the flag pole at the camp, and raised the American flag over what had been their home for over three years. "As it caught the breeze, a breeze still tainted with the smoke of a hundred fires outside the walls, the hungry thousands, without signal, began to sing 'God Bless America' in voices choked with emotion." Tears were shed by civilians and soldiers alike. The Americans at Santo Tomas had not been forgotten. They were free again.

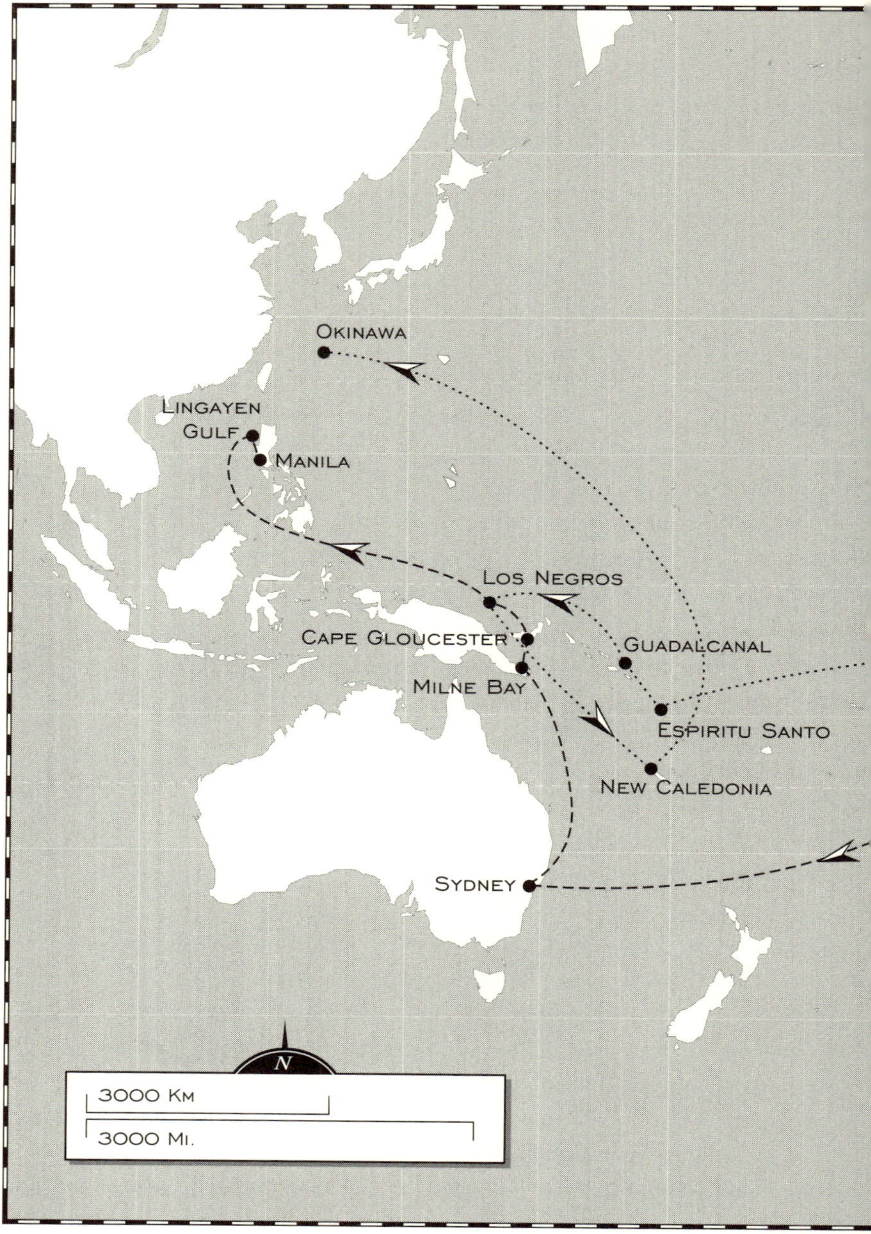

Travels of Bob Olson and Roland Swanson

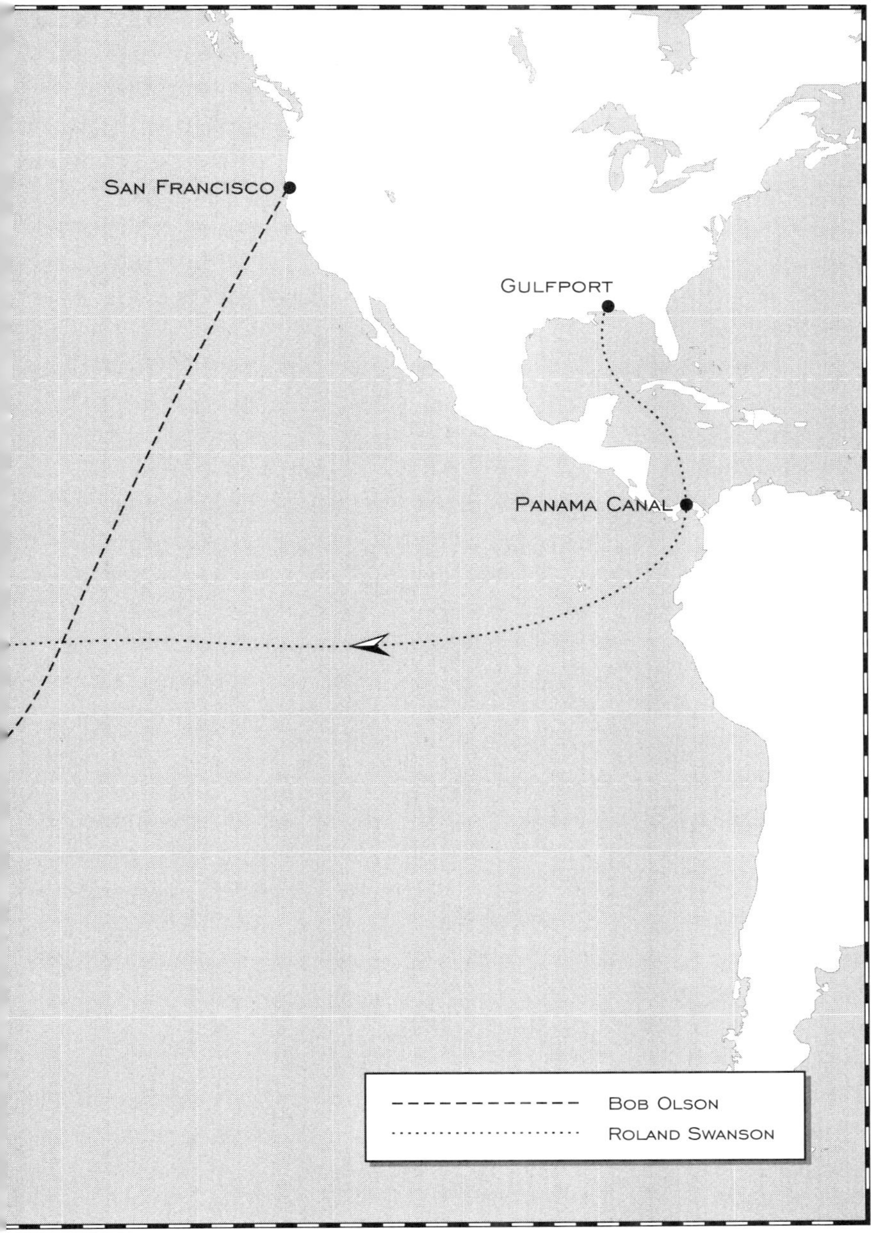

San Francisco
Gulfport
Panama Canal
Bob Olson
Roland Swanson

18. Fighting Beneath The Waves

The toughest part about being a submariner in WW II was coming back to homeport. You usually were given the news that some boat had not made it back, and chances are that some of your buddies were on it. During the war, 52 American submarines were lost and over 3,500 men gave their lives. Someone told me that this amounted to a loss of 16 percent of all officers and 13 percent of all enlisted men in the submarine service. If so, that was worse than the percentage losses incurred by the Marine Corps during the war. The Navy didn't tell me that side of the story when I volunteered for subs. What I remember hearing was a sales pitch for the hotel accommodations at the Royal Hawaiian Hotel on Waikiki Beach that we had as a rest camp between patrols (laughs)!

Most of our deployments were solo. We would be given an area somewhere in Japanese waters, and it would take us about 14 days of steaming to get there. We would operate on station for about 30 days, torpedoing all of the Japanese shipping we could find, and then we'd head back to Midway or Hawaii. We received radio messages but seldom sent a transmission in order to keep our position secret. I vividly remember returning from one deployment and passing the USS Trigger *as it was going out on patrol. We waved and exchanged greetings with the flashing light. We were the last people ever to see the* Trigger. *Where did it go down? Nobody knows. How did they sink? Depth charges, an accident, hitting a reef? Nobody will ever know. What we do know is that the submarines that operated in the South Pacific sank more than five million tons of Japanese shipping which made it nearly impossible for the Japanese to supply their far-flung empire. We sank over 30 percent of their Naval ships and over 60 percent of their merchant fleet. By doing that we helped end the war and secure the peace in the Pacific.*[1]

Lee Towne Adams
Lieutenant, U.S. Naval Reserve

[Lee Towne Adams almost unwittingly volunteered for submarine duty. Little did he know how risky this duty was...that is, until he arrived on station for patrol in the enemy-controlled waters of the Pacific.]

I was a junior at the University of Rochester when the war started and knew that I would be going into the military one way or the other. The Navy had established a V-7 training program for officers, which meant that they would let you graduate from college if you hurried, so I opted for that.[2] There was only one problem: I had a damn hard time proving that I was an American. I had actually been born in Canada while my father was working there as an electrical engineer. The Navy said, "Get your father's birth certificate showing that he was born in America and that will suffice." Well, he had been born in Farmersville, New York, in 1887 and there were no birth certificates back then and no school records from the one-room schoolhouse. Unfortunately, at that time, his mother had been a Baptist and she didn't believe in infant baptism, so there were no baptism records either. Also, for some reason, there had been no 1890 federal census and so there was no record there. But I did have two great-aunts alive who had been present at his birth and, based upon their affidavits, I was accepted as an American citizen and sworn into the Navy V-7 program.

Once accepted, I was sent in April 1943 to the Midshipman School at Columbia University in New York City. Here we had four months of drill and calisthenics, and training in seamanship, engineering, navigation and the like. We even had some boat-training on the East River. As I mentioned, the submarine recruiter who came to the school was quite a salesman and talked up the submarine service as a place of fine food and amenities and as the outfit that was winning the war. After he spoke, we went back to our rooms and my roommate, who had been captain of the football team at Mississippi Southern, said, "Well, that's what I'm going to do, join the submarine Navy. And you, you skinny little shit, you won't even be able to pass the physical" (laughs)! My retort to him was, "Five dollars says I can pass that physical!" Guess what? I won the $5. More than that, I passed the physical and he didn't. Two days later the Commander of the School called me in and asked me why I wanted to be in the submarine service, and I said, "I don't know" (more laughs)! The next thing I knew I was headed for New London, CT, where I spent a couple of months of familiarization training.

I don't think I've ever been more scared than I was at New London when the Captain of our old World War I training sub, the O-7, took that old relic down to 175 feet. In World War I it had only been rated for 150 feet. At 175 feet it was like raining inside that thing, leaking through all of the hatches and rivet holes. But after a while you got used to it. All of the psychological testing had pretty much weeded out anyone with claustrophobia. Living underwater is something we had to get used to.

From New London, I was sent to Portsmouth, NH, where the USS *Razorback* was nearing the end of its construction and I helped put it into commission. After some "shakedown" cruises, we took it through the Panama Canal and into the Pacific where we became a part of the Pacific Submarine Fleet homeported at Pearl Harbor. There were actually two submarine commands in the Pacific. The Central Pacific area was headquartered at Pearl Harbor and the Southwest Command was located in Australia. The types of boats were also segregated by command. We had Fairbanks-Morse 16-cylinder, opposed-piston engines and the Southwest Command had the General Motors straight 10-cylinder engines. By splitting us that way, the submarine tenders and repair facilities only had to stock one type of engine parts. Outside of engine differences, all World War II submarines looked exactly the same. They were all 307 ft., 11 ¾ in. long, and 270 ft. long from pressure hull to pressure hull. There was one other difference. The earlier boats were called "thin-skinned" boats and had a ⅝-in. steel pressure hull. Our boat, and those built later in the war, had a ⅞-in. pressure hull. The big difference was that the heavier-skinned boats were rated to 412 feet in depth and the "thin-skinned" boats could only go to 300 feet. The Japanese never knew about our greater depth capability and that saved us many a time because they didn't set their depth charges deep enough.

Although it may seem like we were cramped, compared to the World War I subs, we had room. There were bunks for eight officers and 65 enlisted men. Nevertheless, as the war progressed and more electronics were introduced, larger crews were assigned and this meant that there had to be some "hot bunking" and sometimes an officer had to sleep in the wardroom.[3] Our combat information center, periscope and firing control were located in the conning tower. When submerged, we usually cruised at 60 feet of depth, because at that depth we could get six feet of projection from the periscope. I wore a lot of hats on that boat, as the First Lieutenant, Supply Officer, Gunnery Officer and standing my usual share of watches.

Preparation for a trip was a big thing. We would usually load up with torpedoes, fuel and supplies at Pearl Harbor, and then head for our advanced base at Midway Island. We would top off with fuel and supplies at Midway and then head out on patrol for 60 days. It would take us two weeks to get into Japanese waters. For the first 1,500 miles or so we would stay on the surface because we could make about 12 knots. We also stayed in designated runway or "no-bomb" zones so that our own planes wouldn't hit us. Despite these precautions, we did have at least two of our subs sunk by friendly fire during the war. When we got about 1,000 miles from Japan, we would begin spending days underwater and nights on the surface recharging batteries. The batteries controlled our lives. We could stay under 48 hours at two knots, 24 hours at four knots and at seven knots we could only last one hour underwater before the batteries gave out. The one thing we really hated were nice moonlit nights because then we became much more vulnerable to enemy attack.

After a patrol, we would tie up to a submarine tender for repairs and be given two weeks rest camp while the boat was being repaired. On Midway Island, that camp consisted of a few square miles of sand and a bird refuge. And, oh the birds. Gooney birds, boatswain birds, birds galore—and the noise they made wasn't very restful. It was much more preferable to go to Hawaii and stay at the Royal Hawaiian Hotel. There were also women there and I struck up quite a fancy with a beautiful girl who was working at the Red Cross. We've now been married some 50 years.

Of course, rest camp soon came to an end. After a couple of weeks, we would start loading stores, torpedoes and fuel for another deployment. We would give the boat a six-day shakedown cruise to check out all the repairs that had been made, and then we would head back toward Japanese waters. About 25 percent of the crew would be left behind to act as a relief crew for other returning subs, so about every fourth run you would stay behind for that kind of duty.

We were in the business of sinking Japanese shipping, any kind of ship. On one occasion we knocked off a Jap destroyer and that wasn't easy. Destroyers had a shallow draft and you had to set the torpedoes for only six feet of depth. If the seas were rough, the torpedo would leave the water and lose its direction, so you could only attack a destroyer if the weather was calm. Overall, our boat sank or helped sink six different ships, and also sank a lot of smaller fishing and cargo boats. One time, off Okinawa, we had orders to capture some fishermen in order to get intelligence. We did that, sank their boats and then took them back to Saipan for interrogation. Probably the biggest ship we helped sink was a troop ship just north of the Philippines. It was on one of the few trips where we operated with other subs. There was a wolf pack of six or eight of us about 500 miles north of Luzon. MacArthur was invading the Philippines and the Navy figured that the Japanese would try to reinforce their troops from the north. That turned out to be the case, and when the convoy came, we were waiting and helped sink the largest troop ship in the group. There were probably 15,000 men on that ship. You didn't think about the loss of life. You didn't have time to. You had a job to do to help win the war.

On the operation where we got the destroyer, we thought that we would have an easy time picking off the rest of the convoy. After we sank the destroyer, we put a couple of fish (torpedoes) into a merchant ship and then, instead of sinking, it came right after us and started dropping depth-charges. And was he good. He chased us for seven hours. Of course, in that kind of situation, you have to turn off all systems in the boat except for the main propulsion generators in order to lessen the enemy's chances of hearing you. Without ventilation, the heat goes up and everyone starts to sweat. On that particular day, I remember the sound-powered phone ringing in the conning tower and a guy in the after-torpedo room had just counted the 101st depth charge. Near the end of the barrage, they set off four depth charges over us all at the same time and it drove us down through a thermal incline into warmer water. We were set up for cold water and so we started sinking like a rock. The only way we stopped our descent was with full trim change and all ahead full on the speed, with a bow-up angle of about 45 degrees. When we stopped our fall, the depth gage read 595 feet in the conning tower, so the back of the boat must have been at about 620 feet. We're lucky we made it.

During general quarters, I was the torpedo angle-solver and was in the conning tower with the captain. One officer ran a torpedo data computer, another computed the spread and course and the captain determined the range using the periscope. When it came time to fire, I would put the torpedoes in a proper spread for the length of the ship and the distance to the target so that we had the best chance of scoring a hit. Just before we fired, the captain would have the sound man take one ping, I would double-check the settings and then we would fire the first fish. I had about eight seconds to make any last minute adjustments for the second torpedo and the same for the third torpedo. We usually shot in a series of three torpedoes. In the case of the large Japanese troop ship we hit north of Luzon, we launched four fish. Two of them hit. Another one of our subs also got some torpedoes into it before it went down.

Sometimes you would have a close call that no one anticipated. One night we almost lost the boat during the evening movie. The largest room on the sub was the forward-torpedo room and most of the crew was forward watching the movie. We were cruising on the surface when one of the lookouts spotted a Japanese plane almost on top of us. We started an emergency dive and then discovered that the trim was improperly set. So down we went and, with the preponderance of weight in the forward torpedo room, the bow almost went straight down. The motion picture projector broke loose and slid down the deck and smashed into the forward torpedo tubes. Guys were tumbling and rolling all over each other (laughs). Then the word came over the loud-speaker system: "Everybody aft!" And people started crawling and scrambling uphill toward the back of the boat. The sub finally leveled off and we were okay. Truly, a night at the movies that I'll never forget.

Another scare that we had was really one of our own doing. We were running submerged off the southern coast of Korea, between some islands and the mainland. One of the cooks was doing some deep-fat frying (which he really was not supposed to do) while we were submerged. Something happened and it caught on fire. Then like a damned fool, he threw water on it and now there was that acrid smoke. Every man that left the after-battery compartment, where the worst of the smoke was, shut the damper on the ventilation system (like they were supposed to do to keep the smoke and fumes from spreading). But then, of course, the last guy out decided to open the damper and now we had smoke throughout the whole boat. Here we were right off the coast of Korea and now we had to surface in an emergency in order to clear the smoke.

I had been sleeping but was now wide awake because of the smoke. When we surfaced, we popped up about a city block away from a small Japanese ship which we had to assume had a radio and, unless we did something, would disclose our position. I was the gunnery officer and I told my guys to get out on deck, load that 4-in. gun and nail that ship. I gave them a range of 200 yards from the high periscope. The sub was pitching in the seas, it was a cold, January day and the men were moving fast just to stay warm. Wham. They put the first shot point blank into it and down it went. Was I proud of the gun crew that day! Here they were in an emergency, in their skivvies, in bare feet with no foul weather gear on a cold winter day...and they got it done on the first shot. Because we had to surface quickly, they barely had time to get into the control room. Just as they got there, the captain said over the 1-MC (PA system), "Battle stations, gun, surface!" We broke surface and out they went. You know, we had some good, well-trained sailors on that boat; otherwise we never would have made it that day. After disposing of the Japanese ship, we were able to open the big hatch on top of the forward-torpedo room, start the main engines and ventilate the ship of the smoke.

It took tremendous teamwork to operate a submarine. For example, when we dove, any one of a number of men could sink the ship. The men in the conning tower, usually five including the captain, had to get in and pull the hatch shut. The man on watch in the after-battery compartment had to slam shut the main air intake. The messenger in the control room had to correctly rig the bow and stern planes for the dive. The people in the engine room had to shut down the engines, go on battery drive, and shut the engine air exhausts. The chief on watch had to open the vents and flood the proper tanks so that we would go down. All of this had to be done in 35 seconds because by then you would be underwater. This takes tremendous training and teamwork and everyone was dependent on each other for the success of the dive.

One night at the Officer's Club at Midway, I got to talking with a Navy psychiatrist about the psychological makeup of the average submariner. What made them tick? How did the Navy figure out who could hack it and who couldn't? You know what he told me? He said that the one thing they'd found out is that the average submariner had blood pressure about 10 percent lower than the average person. Maybe that was the trick. We just had to take things as they came at us and not get rattled. I remember one time when my ass was really in a sling. I was the supply officer and responsible for properly provisioning the boat. Somehow I screwed up and for the last week and a half, all we had to eat was rice and horsecock (bologna) (laughs)! The captain was really pissed but somehow he figured we'd make it. Another time, the engineering officer screwed up and we had to travel at about two knots and use the auxiliary engine for the last two days so that we could stretch our fuel and get back home (more laughs). But that was the submarine Navy. Somehow you believed that you could do it and that, in the end, you would make it back![4]

[After the war, Lee Towne Adams went to law school and then came home and practiced law. He went on to become County Court Judge, a position which he held for 25 years before retiring.]

Background and Commentary

[1]On March 27, 1945, the skipper of the USS *Trigger* radioed that his boat had sunk a small Japanese ship. Nothing was ever heard from *Trigger* again. Of the 288 U.S. submarines that fought in World War II, 52 of them were sunk. Thirty of those were estimated to be the result of enemy action. The rest of the subs that disappeared did so for a variety of reasons: navigational error, mines, groundings on unknown reefs, and some from mistaken friendly fire. One sub that is known to have been sunk by depth charges from a U.S. destroyer was the USS *Seawolf,* which was sunk on October 3, 1944, when it was mistaken for a Japanese submarine.

Lee Towne Adams and his fellow crewmen operating from Hawaii and Midway Island had to travel 1,500 to 2,000 miles just to get to their combat operating areas. Adams was right about the risks of being a submariner. Of the approximate 16,000 men who made wartime patrols in submarines, some 375 officers and 3,131 enlisted men were killed or presumed dead. Their submarines never returned to homeport. That is a casualty rate of 22%, the highest for any branch of the military in World War II.

[2]The Navy also had a V-5 program for naval aviators which was another accelerated program to generate Naval officers. (See Bud Fisher's story in Chapter 16.) The Navy had always had college graduates in their officer corps and the V-5 and V-7 programs were a way to insure that this would continue in wartime.

[3]"Hot bunking" was the practice in submarines of two men using the

same bed. When one got up to go on watch, the other would take his place.

[4]American submarines, especially in the Pacific, made a significant contribution to the outcome of the war. In 1942, during the early years of the war, it was the submarine force that was able to maintain contact with the Americans defending Corregidor in the Philippines and also assist American units in other areas that had been cut off from traditional air and ship support by the Japanese. Submarines operating out of Australia were also active in landing commandos and guerilla groups on islands and areas where there was active resistance against the Japanese.

As the war progressed, the role of the submarine was primarily focused on sinking ships in order to cut off the lifeline of supplies to the island nation of Japan. The effect that these patrols had on Japan was devastating. After the war a study was conducted to assess the impact of the submarine Navy in the war against Japan. It concluded that American submarines sank 1,314 Japanese vessels totaling 5.3 million tons of shipping. The loss in human life for the Japanese was staggering. According to Japanese records, during the war 27,000 merchant seamen were killed and another 89,000 were wounded or incapacitated, a majority of these losses being caused by U.S. submarine attacks.

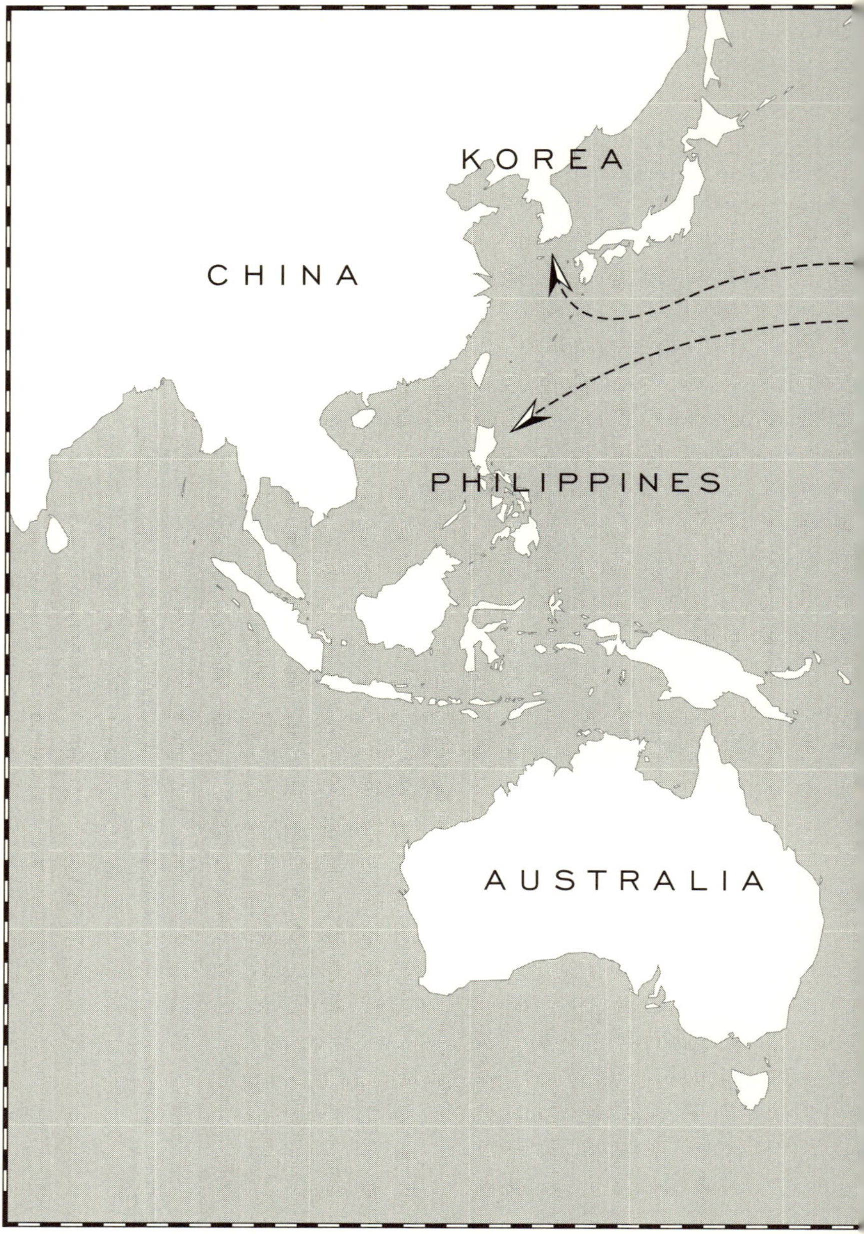

Travels of Lee Towne Adams

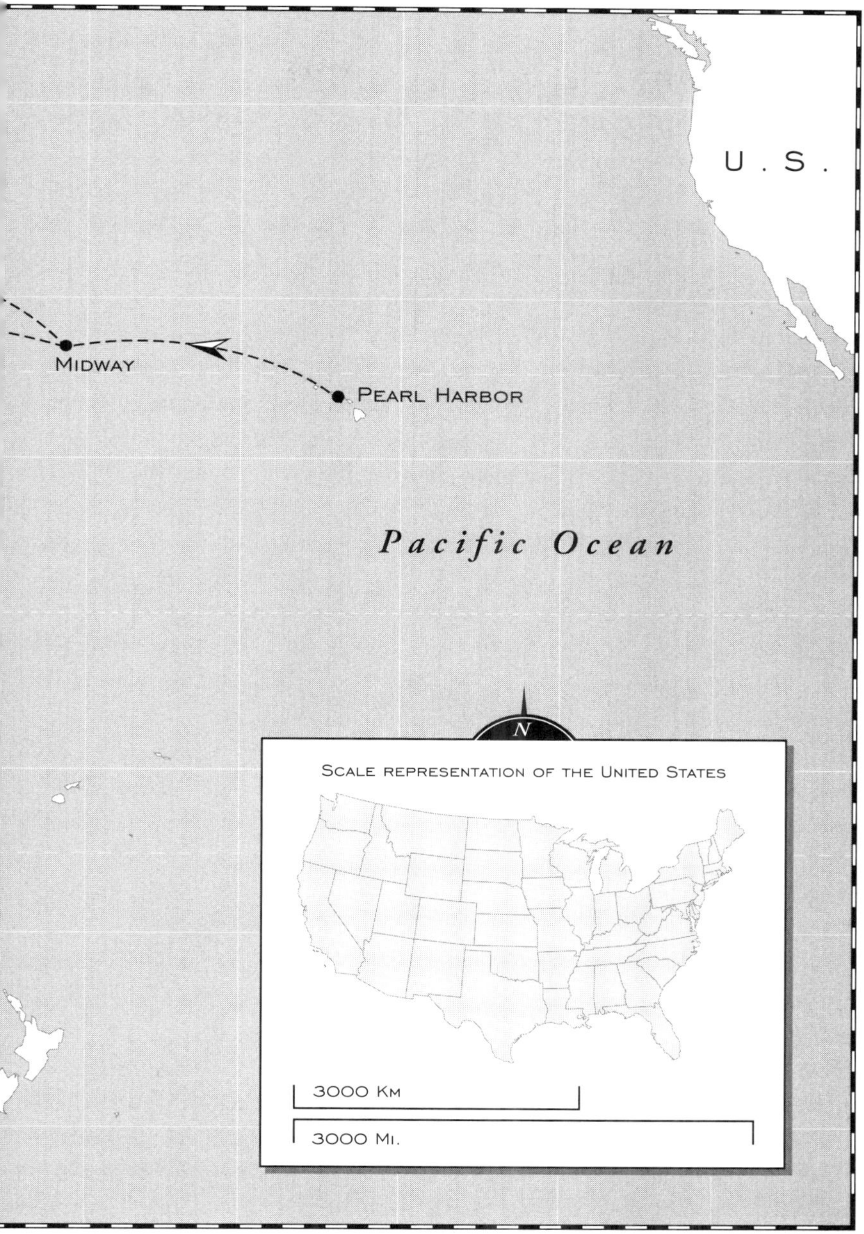
U.S.
MIDWAY
PEARL HARBOR
Pacific Ocean
N
SCALE REPRESENTATION OF THE UNITED STATES
3000 KM
3000 MI.

19. Battling The Kamikazes

We encountered the kamikazes right after the Leyte Gulf landings in the Philippines. It was a new development. The Japanese were on the ropes and by late 1944 were being pushed back and losing on all fronts. Their naval and air forces had been decimated and now their backs were to the wall. I suppose that we'll never understand what made them do it, what motivated those pilots to fly airplanes loaded with explosives into our ships, but they did it...I was there!

We probably saw five or six kamikaze airplane attacks on other ships and opened fire with our antiaircraft guns to try and give support in knocking down the planes. But the moment that really stands out in my mind was that morning, just at dawn, when we were attacked off Luzon. We had just delivered a supply convoy to Lingayen Gulf in support of the landings there and were steaming by ourselves. All of a sudden one of the lookouts yelled, "Enemy aircraft overhead!" and we looked up and there he came from out of the morning sun. I was on the port side of the bridge doing some navigating, and it looked to me like we were dead ducks. He was coming right at us. The Captain took evasive action and put the ship at "All ahead full, hard left rudder!" We began a hard turn to the left and the Japanese plane hit the water, just off the port bow. The explosion was huge and knocked the bow of the ship 30 degrees to starboard.

It was all over in a split second and, unbelievably, no one was hurt. The bow was covered with scraps of aluminum from the explosion and the Captain, who was standing on the flying bridge above me, got hit by a piece of severed control cable from the plane but it didn't even pierce his skin. We were safe, we were still underway, though going in a little bit different direction. We were never sure why he missed. A lot of the kamikaze pilots were young and inexperienced and maybe he just misjudged his attack. Perhaps we hit him with our antiaircraft fire. We'll never know why he missed, but, fortunately for us, he did.

It was a moment, a moment of terror, and now it was over. You didn't really get scared, you didn't have time to. Everyone just kept doing their job and waiting to see how it would come out. It was later that night that we didn't sleep so well. You began to worry that it might happen again the next day. The war was like that. Most of the time, it was just weeks and weeks of sheer boredom. Then it could be interrupted by a moment of terror. We saw other ships that went down from kamikaze attacks and heard about a lot of other ones that got hit. But we were lucky. In the four years that I was in the Navy I was on three different ships and we never took a casualty.[1]

Willard E. Perlee
Lt. Commander, U. S. Naval Reserve

[Willard Perlee would take two ships on the long, epic crossing from the east coast through the Panama Canal to the western Pacific. He had many memorable experiences including a near miss of his ship by a kamikaze fighter pilot.]

I graduated from Colgate University in 1940 and even then people were beginning to worry because the war had started in Europe. I decided to enlist in the V-7 Navy Officer program. The Navy asked me when I wanted to start and I said, "I want to delay it as long as possible" (laughs). So it was late in 1941, after I had finished my first year at Yale Law School, that I actually went to the Naval Training School for Officers, sometimes called the "ninety-day wonder school." The school was in downtown Chicago and we took our classes at Tower Hall, so named because it was close to the famous Water Tower near Lake Michigan.

Later, I was assigned to the Naval Intelligence Section in Boston, but soon found that too dull and applied for a transfer. The Navy obliged by sending me to the Naval Torpedo Station at Newport, RI. However, I was still bound to a desk and so I asked for another assignment. This time the Navy sent me to Cape May, NJ, where I was assigned the job of commissioning Yard Patrol (YP) 260, called the *Grey Gull.* YP-260 was actually a converted luxury yacht that had been owned by Samuel Carpenter, the President of DuPont. Carpenter had given his yacht to the Navy so they could use it for patrolling the Atlantic. It's hard for people today to believe it, but at that time German submarines were torpedoing our cargo vessels and tankers within sight of the U.S. mainland. There weren't enough Navy ships to provide them protection.

At any rate, I was assigned to skipper this vessel and, along with a crew of one officer and 12 enlisted men, we took that ship to the Philadelphia Naval Yard for refitting. It has never ceased to amaze me that the Navy would have given me such a responsibility. I had four years of college and one year of law school, had never been on anything more than a boat with a 30-horsepower outboard motor and now here I was, the Captain of a ship (laughs). But, when you have a war on, I guess that's what happens. Young people with very little training were entrusted with very expensive equipment and with supervising those who ran it. What we found out about the YP-260, however, was that the ship really wasn't suited for offshore patrol duty. We had two large gasoline engines for propulsion and, of course, gasoline is extremely volatile. We were like a floating bomb. Had we caught fire, we would have just worsened the situation. Realizing that we were unsuited for offshore patrol duty, the Navy assigned us to "protect" the anti-submarine net at Reedy Island, in Delaware bay.

In World War I, a German submarine had actually gone up the Delaware River and fired a torpedo at a ship in the Philadelphia Navy Shipyard and that upset the Navy to no end (laughs)! They decided that wouldn't happen in World War II, so they put in this anti-submarine net. To me it was a totally useless exercise because a 20,000-ton tanker moving at 10 knots has a surface suction along its hull that could have sunk our little ship. Therefore, we spent most of our time yelling at a good distance through a megaphone at merchant ships 50 times our size trying to identify them without getting shipwrecked ourselves. If we got close enough to be heard, we were in danger of being sucked in by their bow wave and having a collision. It was a joke. Fortunately for me, the Navy needed officers with experience and so, with my background of a few months on the YP-260, I was sent to Quincy, MA, to commission a new ship.

This was a somewhat larger ship, Subchaser (SC) 1268. It was about 110 feet long and had a crew of three officers and 26 men. This new assignment also provided me with another opportunity. I had been dating Florence McKeever (whom I called "Mac"), my high school sweetheart, for a long time and we wanted to get married. So before I left for the Pacific, while the ship was being fitted with sonar gear in Miami, I took the train to upstate New York and got married. We didn't have much of a honeymoon because, as Captain of the ship, I had to get right back to Miami after the wedding. Soon after getting back to Miami, I said good-bye to my wife, and the ship got underway for Key West where we honed our anti-submarine warfare skills by dropping miniature depth charges on our own submarines. If we hit one of them, a little "pop" would go off and the submarine would let us know that we had made a hit.

From Key West, we went through the Panama Canal, and then headed west across the Pacific. It's difficult to grasp the immensity of the Pacific. There had really been nothing in my experience up to that time to prepare me for grappling with such huge distances. It would take us about 30 days of steady steaming from Panama to get to Fiji or American Samoa. Then from there, we went further west and south to Noumea, New Caledonia, a French island east of Australia. That's why I said earlier that there were weeks and weeks of boredom. It took us that long to get any place. From New Caledonia, we escorted supply ships another 2,000 miles northwest to New Guinea where American troops were in combat with the Japanese.

By this time, I had become more acquainted with the ways of the Navy and one day saw an all-Navy directive which said that any Commander whose executive officer was qualified for command could apply for reassignment to the States in order to help commission new ships for the fleet. I think that the directive was actually meant to apply to skippers of battleships, cruisers and submarines, but I took a chance, requested a transfer, got caught up in the general flow of Navy paperwork and the next thing I knew, I had received orders to return to the States. The whole idea of this, of course, was to get home so that I could see Mac, and guess what? It worked (laughs)!

My wife was teaching in Westchester County, near New York, and the Navy sent me to Damage Control School at the Brooklyn Navy Yard, so we were able to see a lot of each other. Damage Control training was one of the more risky and frightening things I did in my Navy career. They made you fight oil and gasoline fires and the only way you could put them out was to keep spraying water or foam and advancing on the fire. If you retreated, you would be burned, so there was a great incentive to keep advancing on the fire. Mac and I were staying at the Roger Smith Hotel in White Plains and each morning, before I went to Brooklyn, I would take a towel from the hotel which I would use as protection around my neck when we were fighting fires. Of course, the towels got dirty from all of the flame and smoke at the school, and one day I got a note from the hotel

Will and "Mac" Perlee on the beach in Virginia before Will left for the Pacific.

management asking me to quit using their towels to shine my shoes (laughs). I never did tell them how I was using those towels!

After Damage Control school, I was sent to Hingham, MA, and assigned the duty of being Executive Officer and Navigator on a new ship being commissioned, the Destroyer Escort, USS *Lough* (DE 586). The DE was actually a cheaply built destroyer which had been constructed primarily to escort convoys of supply ships to the fighting fronts during the war. We couldn't go as fast as a regular destroyer and were limited in the amount and type of armament we carried. After commissioning, in May of 1944, we were sent to Norfolk and there picked up a convoy and escorted it to Bizerte in North Africa. After we returned, I found out that I would be going again back to the South Pacific. It was interesting how we found out. One day when I returned to the ship, they were painting it with what was called "Pacific camouflage"—colors of zigzag white, black and grey. None of us could ever figure out how it was supposed to hide the ship, but what we did know was that when your ship got painted with it, you were going to the Pacific!

I had already gone to the South Pacific once, and now I was to go again. We got underway, went through the Panama Canal, escorted a convoy to New Caledonia and then went on to Hollandia, New Guinea. From there we picked up a convoy of 80 merchant ships going to support the landings at Leyte Gulf in the Philippines. We had a rather close call on that trip. One day, just southeast of Leyte, we began to pick up a lot of battle talk on the voice radio and soon we began seeing smoke on the horizon. Our skipper, Blaney Turner, who had been a lawyer with an insurance company in Ohio before the war, was a rather aloof man but was also a very able commander. He always treated me fairly, although, because I was the navigator, I periodically had to tell him to "get the hell out" of places where we might be in danger of going aground. This happened to be one of those days when I felt compelled to speak up.

Captain Turner wanted to go at flank speed and get into the fight up ahead. He had several of the officers on the bridge and was discussing this. I let him know my feelings in no uncertain terms: "You're damned crazy if you do that!" I said. "We don't know what is going on up there and there's nothing the Japs would like better than to go after this slow-moving convoy!" Well, he finally decided to divert the convoy, and we turned 90 degrees and began to move away from the action. It was probably a good decision, because we found out later that what we had seen was a part of what was called the Battle of Leyte Gulf. The Japanese had decided to use a pincers movement from the east and west to cut off the beachhead at Leyte, and what we had seen was the naval battle on the eastern side of the island. A lot of American destroyers were sunk in that battle when they tried to make torpedo runs on the Japanese battleships and cruisers.[2]

When we actually got into Leyte Gulf with our convoy, there was still quite a bit of action going on. There was fighting on shore and the Japanese were bombing the harbor and the beachhead. Probably the scariest thing for us was when our ships were ordered to make a smoke screen in the harbor so that the Japanese bombers couldn't see what to bomb. The problem was that you couldn't see them but you could hear them. You just sat at anchor on your ship hoping that you were lucky enough not to get hit when the bombs dropped into the smoke.

The war moved quickly after Leyte. As I mentioned before, we escorted a convoy to Lingayen Gulf on Luzon for that amphibious landing and that is where we were attacked by the kamikaze planes.

Later on, we were attacked by kamikaze boats in Bantangas Bay, just south of Corregidor. We were there in an operation to support a Regimental Combat Team which had been landed to attack Manila from the south. The Japanese sent out these small, fast boats at night, loaded with TNT with the intent of driving right into our ships and sinking them. I've often thought that had the Japs combined those boat attacks with the aerial kamikaze attacks, they could have really inflicted some heavy damage on us, but they never seemed to coordinate the two. Our problem was that we had no guns that would deflect down to the waterline and so we were quite vulnerable. On the two or three occasions when we were attacked by these boats, the captain would head straight toward them at all ahead full and our bow wave and wake would swamp them. It was the only thing that saved us. A submarine chaser in our group wasn't so lucky. It was hit by one of these suicide boats and was sunk.[3]

As I mentioned, sometimes I had words with the Captain when I thought he was doing something wrong. Naval Reserve officers are more inclined to take liberties with persons of high rank than are Naval Academy graduates. One night, we were in heavy seas and were trying to get into a harbor on Mindoro Island in the Philippines. The harbor was protected by a mine field consisting of mines anchored at its entrance and they were under the control of the Army. The mines could be detonated by a control device on shore. We were not entirely free from worry that some inexperienced soldier would, upon seeing a ship in the mine field, detonate it and that would have been the end of us. We also thought that if we hit one of the mines hard enough, it might explode anyway. The Captain asked, "Mr. Perlee, can you navigate us in?" And I said, "Yes sir, as long as you keep underway. If you stop moving and start drifting, I'll have no idea of where we are." Well, of course, once we started in, something happened, and the Captain ordered the engines to "all stop." I was in CIC (Combat Information Center), right under the bridge, and when I heard the engines shut down, I yelled up the sound tube to the Captain on the bridge: "Captain, start those damned engines or I'll have you court-martialed when we get out of here" (laughs)! Well, he started the engines and we made it in somehow. After it was over, to his credit, he never mentioned the way I had spoken to him. I guess those kinds of things happen when you are in a tight jam.

Sometimes crazy things would happen. We received two commendations from our superiors in command which were really bizarre. On one occasion, at night, in Batangas Bay, we thought that we were being attacked by two kamikaze boats when, in fact, they were our own PT boats. We flashed a recognition signal at them, and they didn't respond so the Admiral ordered us to open fire. We did and hit both boats. We didn't realize what had happened until the next day and then we went in and rescued the American boat crews. Two men died in that friendly-fire accident. When we rescued the PT boat crews, we found that they had not been given the recognition signals and didn't even know that an American invasion was going on just south of Manila Bay.

As a result of it all, we received a commendation for our rescue efforts though nothing was said about the mistaken identity of the boats. On another occasion, we received a commendation for helping pull a supply ship, the SS *John Alden,* off a beach where it had grounded. The charts over there were notorious for being inaccurate and sometimes there would be coral reefs or shallow areas in places where the charts said you should have 100 feet of water. On the night the *John Alden* ran aground, the Captain of that vessel didn't even know he was aground until a palm tree knocked off the hat of his forward lookout (laughs). We went in the next day and, with the help of a tug, got the ship off the reef. In the process, we got into shallow water ourselves, bent the screws of the ship and eventually had to go into drydock to get them fixed. As I told the Captain, "Bending your propellers by hitting bottom is something you usually get court-martialed for. Thank God, we were successful and got him pulled off!" What really helped though is that the SS *John Alden* was loaded with 10,000 tons of beer for the troops in the Philippines (more laughs). That beer was needed and we had done a great job in making sure it was delivered.

As you look back on it, you're grateful for the experience. It was four years of my life, but, for most my age, it was four years out of everyone's life. Most of the time, we only knew what was happening to us in our little world. Periodically, I received newspaper clippings from home describing significant military action that had taken place near us, and we hadn't even known about it. From the Navy's standpoint, I suppose, we didn't have the "need to know," so a lot of this information was never communicated to us. Yet, it never occurred to me to question what I was doing. We all sensed that the United States was in a "do-or-die" situation and we just went ahead and did what we were asked. There was an interdependence, a common purpose, and you wanted to live up to the expectations of others and to your own expectations. I always felt though, and still do, that the primary reason we won the war was that we could out-produce the enemy. At least this was true with the Navy in the Pacific. Our folks back home just kept producing ships faster than the Japanese could sink them. That's ultimately why we won the war.

[After the war, Willard Perlee went back to finish law school and then came to town and started a law practice. He continues to practice law today and is now in partnerhip with his son, who is also an attorney.]

Background and Commentary

[1]By October, 1944, the Japanese leadership realized that the war had been lost. The Imperial Navy had been decimated, American forces were starting to bomb the home islands, and the American Navy had choked off shipping to and from Japan and its far-flung empire. Japan's military had courageously fought in every battle, but it was being pushed back, island by island. The noose was beginning to tighten; there would inevitably be an invasion of Japan itself.

Probably no culture was ever more immersed in a "do-or-die," macho, "never-lose-face" tradition than the Japanese society of that time. Japan was a modern nation in many ways, but still feudal in its soul. The old legends of the samurai, the soldiers of old who risked everything and paid whatever price to defend the empire, were stories emblazoned on the minds of every Japanese. Though industrialized on a very modern scale, the country still believed that the Emperor was God and that war was a divine mission on his behalf. It was a soldier's duty and honor to die on behalf of the Emperor.

The word kamikaze means "divine wind" and dates back to medieval times when a typhoon destroyed a Mongol fleet that was trying to invade Japan. When a pilot climbed into one of these kamikaze planes (or boats) that was loaded with explosives and a detonator, there was no coming back. He was resolutely committed to trying to destroy, in most cases, an American ship. Americans thought that these individuals were crazy. Some thought that maybe they had been hyped on drugs or alcohol in order to do this. On the contrary, they were just ordinary sailors and airmen following their traditions to this final end. It was called the *bushido* code of right thinking where one "acts immediately, decisively and correctly in all circumstances. Neither life nor death concern him. Thus, the samurai lives so that he is always prepared to die."[1]

[2]When Douglas MacArthur kept his promise of returning to the Philippines, his selected landing site was the small island of Leyte. The Japanese had expected him to initially attack on one of the larger islands, like Mindanao, so this element of surprise helped the Americans. The landing on October 20, 1944, went well and MacArthur waded ashore that day despite continued artillery and sniper fire coming from the enemy.

However, the Imperial Navy had been waiting for an opportunity like this to throw everything that they had one last time at the Americans. Two separate Japanese naval task forces approached in a pincers-like move in an attempt to concentrate their firepower and destroy the American beachhead. At one point, in a miscalculation, Admiral Halsey chased one decoy group of smaller Japanese ships to the north and was 300 miles from the beaches at Leyte during some of the worst of the battle. Nevertheless, the U.S. Naval forces who were left slugged it out successfully with the huge Japanese naval force of aircraft carriers, cruisers and battleships. The three-day action that ended on October 25, 1944, has been called the "greatest naval engagement in history." Three thousand Americans were killed. An American light carrier, two escort carriers, three destroyers and approximately 150 American aircraft were lost. But on the other side, the carnage was worse. Ten thousand Japanese airmen and sailors were dead. Four Japanese carriers, three battleships, six cruisers and 12 destroyers had been sunk. Hundreds of Japanese planes were blown out of the sky. The Imperial Navy was finished, never to be a major force in the war again. It was a good thing that Will Perlee's supply convoy decided to move to the east and stay out of this conflagration.

3 Batangas Bay is not far from the old American fortress of Corregidor, the Gibraltar-like island that protects the entrance to Manila Bay. It was from this island that valiant American and Filipino troops made their last stand against the Japanese after the enemy invasion of the Philippines in 1942. For weeks these beleaguered troops, with no hope of being relieved, fought the well-supplied troops and overwhelming firepower of the Japanese Army. General Douglas MacArthur, responsible for the Philippine defense, was finally ordered by President Roosevelt to leave Corregidor and take charge of U.S. forces in Australia. So, on one dark night, an American PT-Boat snuck into the bay, tied up at the north pier at Corregidor and then left the island with MacArthur, his wife and young son on board. After three or four days and after nearly being discovered by Japanese patrol craft on several occasions, the PT-boat finally got the MacArthurs to Mindanao in the south, and from there they were flown to Australia.

General Jonathan Wainwright, MacArthur's best field commander and the man who had led in the defense of Bataan where most of the fighting had occurred, was now left with the impossible job of defending Corregidor. Finally, with food and ammunition gone, on April 9, 1942, he was compelled to surrender to the Japanese. It was the greatest defeat that had ever been experienced by the military forces of the United States.

Today you can take a very moving, emotional, one-day trip from the piers in Manila to the old fortress at Corregidor. You can see the bombed-out buildings, the old mortar fortifications, the parade ground used for military drill and you can see the bombed out north pier with a bronze statue of Douglas MacArthur looking across the bay at Bataan with the words engraved on the monument: "I shall return!" Then, at the end of the day, you can take a trip into the Malinta Tunnel where MacArthur and his colleagues survived weeks of bombardment from the Japanese. The Philippine government has reconstructed some of the lateral tunnels and, as you walk along, a very tasteful, yet powerful, sound and light presentation shows you the hospital, communication center and barracks where the embattled soldiers lived their last days before surrender.

MacArthur never forgot those troops and their leader, Jonathan Wainwright. When the war ended, he sent out an order that every effort be made to find Wainwright. If he could be found, MacArthur wanted him to attend the formal surrender ceremony being scheduled for Japan.

Wainwright was finally located at a POW Camp in Manchuria, was transported back to the Philippines and finally arrived in Yokohama, Japan, in time for the ceremony. Perhaps the most memorable picture of World War II is the photo of General MacArthur signing the surrender document on the USS *Missouri* in Tokyo Bay flanked by two tall, emaciated men who had suffered from malnutrition as prisoners during the war: British General Sir Arthur Percival, who surrendered the garrison in Singapore in 1942; and General Jonathan Wainwright, the American General whom MacArthur had left behind at Corregidor knowing that he could send him no help. MacArthur used five pens to sign the surrender document that day. It had been difficult for him to express his deep emotion for Wainwright and for what he had done at Corregidor; but that day, with great symbolism, he let the world know. After signing with the first pen, he turned and handed it to General Jonathan Wainwright.

The Travels Of Will Perlee

20. The Hell Called Iwo Jima

Tell you about Iwo Jima? Let me tell you about hell. We looked at that island from the ship as we began to climb down the cargo nets into the assault boats. We didn't think anything could have survived the bombardment. For two days the Navy had pounded that island with guns and napalm. It looked like a giant matchbox on fire. It didn't look like anything could have survived. We'd been told that we should be able to take the place in 72 hours, and at that point, it looked like we could. It eventually would take us 72 hours just to reach the first airfield which was about a half-mile from the beach. It would take 30 days to secure the entire island.

As you look back at it, it's hard to know how you kept going. I got to Yellow Four beach about two hours after the first guys landed. Things were a mess. We were under mortar- and machine-gun fire. Nobody had even moved off the beach. We hunkered there with the dead and wounded and kept unloading ammo and supplies when we could. Finally, close to noon, the first group pushed over the top of the first crest of black sand. By the end of the day, we may have made 500 yards. It was hard to dig foxholes. The whole island was volcanic ash and the deepest we could dig was about a foot or two before the sides would start caving in. Under the cover of darkness, the Japs started moving and the fighting got worse.

We finally took the place. It cost the Marines 6,000 dead and 25,000 wounded to do it. The Japs wouldn't surrender. Before it was all over we had killed an estimated 22,000 Japanese. Only 200 were taken prisoner. A lot of them were buried alive in the underground bunkers and caves they had built. Someone told us that they'd been told never to surrender to a Marine because you couldn't become a Marine unless you'd killed either your mother or your father. I guess they must have believed it.

How did we do it? We were Marines. I was in the 4th Division. We'd been through Saipan, Tinian and now Iwo. We stuck together. You never let a buddy down. You did your job. You did it well. You were proud of your outfit, proud of the Corps, proud of your country. We knew that we could take Iwo Jima and we did. We paid for it with our blood. Why we ever gave that island back to the Japanese is beyond me. When I think about it, I think about all of those body bags and ponchos full of dead Marines at the cemetery near the beach. That is a place bought by the courage and sacrifice of the Marines. We should have kept that place just so no one could forget what it took to win World War II.

George Elder
Sergeant, U.S. Marine Corps

[The Marines experienced tough fighting throughout the Pacific but it was especially bad on Iwo Jima. George Elder is lucky to be alive. He survived Iwo Jima.]

I was a Marine in the 4th Division, part of the signal corps. Our job was to establish communications between command headquarters and command posts up front. We carried carbines and sometimes had to fight, but our primary job was to run telephone wire from one outpost to the next as the front moved. When I arrived in the Central Pacific in 1944 we were assigned to the assault on Saipan. All of the islands were tough but none as bad as Iwo Jima. Saipan was my first baptism in combat and it was probably the most scared I had ever been in my life. I'll never forget my first night on watch. The Japs were known for midnight *"banzai* charges" and it seemed to me that everything out there was moving. I kept looking at something that looked like a man, I could have sworn it was a Jap. I fired and nothing happened. One of my buddies came up and said, "What ya doin? That's a tree out there" (laughs)! But it wasn't funny then. I was a damned scared 18-year-old kid. Even three months at boot camp in Paris Island couldn't have prepared me for that.

My friend, Gunny Nelson, and I signed up together to join the Marines. It was April 1943 and we had just turned eighteen. It's hard to explain today what it was like back then. Everybody wanted to fight. We knew that our country was up against the wall and that we had to defeat Hitler and the Japanese. We decided that we wouldn't even wait for graduation, so as soon as were eighteen we quit school, left the senior class and enlisted in the Marine Corps. Our parents and teachers probably didn't approve but no one really questioned what we did. Back then, going into the military was the right thing to do. We didn't even have an easy time enlisting. When we got to the enlistment center in Buffalo, the Marines had already reached their quota for new recruits for that day. So Gunny and I stayed overnight at the Ford Hotel, were the first in line the next day, passed our physicals and ten days later reported for Marine training at Paris Island, SC.

At first, we really didn't know why we were taking those islands in the Pacific. Later on we learned that they would become air bases for the bombing of Japan. But we didn't need to know the overall military strategy; we were Marines and did what we were told. We had been trained in an incredible "buddy system." Your buddy was your best friend. Another Marine was like your brother. If a guy got hit and went down, you helped him. If he was wounded, you tried to stop the bleeding or get a medic. If he was killed, you somehow got his body back. When you saw the wrapped ponchos in the cemeteries, you cried. Somehow it got us through. We had a job to do and nobody ever let anybody else down. It was a dirty business, it was an awful business but we were determined to get it done...and we did.[1]

Saipan and Tinian were fairly large islands, maybe 20 miles long. They were tropical, with sugar cane fields, palm trees, sandy beaches. Both were to become bases for the B-29s that bombed Japan. [See the story of Carl Lenz in Chapter 22.] Tinian was especially memorable because the actual landing went real easy. We hit two small beaches on the northern end of the island. The beaches were so small that the Japs probably figured we would never try to get ashore there. Resistance was light but stiffened quickly when we turned south toward Tiniantown, the small village at the other end of the island. The Japs had really dug in there. Our planes and ship bombardment had leveled the whole town...there was nothing left. But the enemy was underground, dug in and playing a defensive game. It got down to hand grenades and flame throwers, soldier against soldier. The tanks helped but it was individual effort that finally won the island. Our division had incurred some significant casualties, but virtually every Japanese soldier had been killed. The Jap soldier had been told to go to his death for the Emperor, and he had done so.[2]

The greatest disaster at Tinian came at the end. The last outpost of Japanese strength was on top of a cliff area. A lot of the civilians on Tinian had also hidden in the caves dug into these cliffs and the Japanese had convinced them that we would kill them all if they surrendered. We began to see individual soldiers dive off the cliffs to their death. One group of about forty soldiers and civilians tied themselves together and set off a grenade which in turn detonated a huge explosion. Arms, legs and parts of bodies flew everyplace. Finally, we got a loudspeaker on a truck up near the cliff and a couple of the prisoners and civilians we had captured got on the microphone and told the people on the cliff that we wouldn't kill them and that they should come out. Slowly, most of the civilians filtered down onto the plain below the cliff. Most of the remaining Japs either committed suicide or were killed by us when we took the cliff.

This should have been a lesson for us when we hit Iwo Jima in February of 1945. The closer we got to the Japanese homeland, the tougher it would be and Iwo was only 700 miles from Japan. There would be few Japanese surrendering at Iwo Jima. Iwo was a killing field. It was black, volcanic sand. A sulfur smell mixed with the smells of gunpowder and death. There were few trees and those that had been there were blown away. The sand caved in on you and you couldn't dig a deep foxhole. The only protection came from a series of sand plateaus or levees that Mother Nature had left behind. But every time you went over one of those, you were totally exposed to enemy gunfire. The Japs had dug in artillery and mortar on Mt. Suribachi on the southern end and we were like sitting ducks out on those black sand beaches. It took the 28th Regiment of the 5th Marine Division four days to take Mt. Suribachi and finally those guns were silenced.[3] But the main enemy defenses were on the northern end of the island. General Kuribayashi had put his headquarters there and that whole end of the island was honeycombed with caves, buried pillboxes and concrete bunkers. Once again it was hand grenades and flame throwers that had to do the job. You counted your advance in feet and yards as you moved from one Jap position to the next.

We would move with the front, running telephone lines from the command post to company and platoon positions. You got numbed to death after a while. Just as I got ready to go over the top one day with a wire run, I saw a marine lying down near a crater. I thought he should move back and out of the line of fire. I slapped him on the back and told him to move back. The body rolled and the back of his head was gone. "Sorry, buddy," I said as I moved past him heading for the front. You had to stay cool and not panic. My good buddy, Roy Clark, who also made it out of Iwo, was an excitable kind of guy. One day we were in one helluva mortar barrage and I could see he was getting uptight and was ready to move. "Don't move, Roy," I said, "you'll get killed for sure. Just smell the smoke, smell the smoke." He must have started concentrating on the smell because he stayed put. He always thanked me for that advice later on.

I'll never forget the day that the first B-29 came in. The 5th Division had finally taken Suribachi and we had just secured the first airfield. Hell, we had just barely pushed the Japs off and they still controlled one end of the field; and here comes this huge airplane. We'd never seen such a big one...it was a monster. It was in some kind of trouble and was making an emergency landing on a trip back from Japan. He made it in okay, but, as I remember, the plane sort of got busted up on landing. That was why we'd invaded in the first place, to give those guys a place to make emergency landings. [See Chapter 22 for the story of Carl Lenz's emergency landing in his B-29 at Iwo Jima.]

Come to think of it, I did get wounded on Iwo. Got hit by a machine gun or rifle shot in my heel and it knocked off part of my foot. But on Iwo you didn't stop for that. The litter stations and field hospitals had a lot bigger problems to deal with. I didn't even get a purple heart for that. Those kinds of wounds didn't count on Iwo Jima. (The purple heart that's in my records came from broken ear drums I got on Tinian when a truck I was riding on hit a land mine.) What do I remember most about Iwo Jima? Just one thing, I got my ass out of there alive. There were a lot of days when I didn't think I would. I think it was near the end when somehow I met Mike Zanghi from back home. He made it out of there in once piece, too, and I'm sure he felt as lucky as I did.

It really pissed me off when we gave that island back to the Japanese. I know that the war is over and we should forget...but I can't forget. I left too many friends in graves on that godforsaken piece of real estate to ever forget. We bought that island with American blood and we should have kept it. There's another thing that bothers me too. You know those special license plates that they have now? There's one that says "purple heart" on it for veterans who were wounded. Can you believe that the state wants me to pay extra money for that plate? I'll be goddamned if I will. For what we did on Iwo Jima, they should give us those plates for free!

CEMETERY AT IWO JIMA.

[George Elder was wounded and received the Purple Heart. He came home and, for a few years, owned and operated a grocery store and gas station. In 1950, he went to work at the ball-bearing plant in town where he was employed for 39 years before retiring.]

BACKGROUND AND COMMENTARY

[1]The United States had divided the Pacific Command into two regions: the Southwestern Pacific, under the command of General Douglas MacArthur; and the Central Pacific, under the command of Admiral Chester Nimitz. This was considered necessary because of the tremendous distances involved in this theater of war. Initially, Nimitz had started his operations by stopping the Japanese advance toward Australia in the Battle of the Coral Sea and in the fighting at Guadalcanal in the Solomon Islands. His troops were primarily Marines and they would bear the brunt of the island fighting throughout the Pacific. Nimitz, like MacArthur, realized that great numbers of Japanese troops could be avoided and isolated on the hundreds of islands where they had been sent around the Pacific. For

example, although air attacks were made on the massive Japanese installations at Rabaul and Truk, no ground troops were ever committed there. Instead, Nimitz leapfrogged toward Japan, going into the Marshall Islands at Eniwetok and Kwajalein and then jumping further north and taking the Mariana Islands of Saipan and Tinian and retaking Guam.

The fighting that did take place was harsh and bloody, and the Marines took the brunt of it. The tenacious defense and unwillingness of the Japanese to surrender made American casualties high, and this was one of the decisive factors in President Truman's decision to use the atomic bomb to end the war. (Saipan today is a major recreational and resort area for Japan. Saipan and the Marianas are to the Japanese what Florida and the Carribbean are to Americans. Today, on those battlefields, you will find hotels, swimming pools and nice restaurants.) Many of those who fought on Saipan and throughout the Pacific feel that their efforts have been largely forgotten since relatively few Americans travel in this area of the world. As a remembrance to those who died in the Pacific, a recent memorial to our soldiers, marines, sailors and airmen was erected on Saipan and dedicated on the 50th anniversary of WWII landings in the Marianas on June 15, 1994. On the granite of this memorial is inscribed the following:

> *...A grateful nation honors and mourns its fallen sons in the World War II battles for Saipan and Tinian, and the Battle of the Philippine Sea. Their supreme sacrifice in the bright morning of their lives contributed to the victory won and the peace that followed...*

[2]Operations in the Mariana Islands were necessary in order to provide bases for the B-29s which would be used to bomb Japan. The landing on the island of Tinian was one of the best-executed amphibious landings of the Pacific war. The 9,000-man Japanese garrison was taken by surprise. Virtually every Japanese soldier went to his grave but only 327 Americans were killed. On the other islands of Guam and Saipan the killing was more gruesome. On Saipan, 31,000 out of 32,000 Japanese troops were killed in the fighting and 3,426 Americans lost their lives. An estimated 20,000 civilians also died during the battle. Guam also produced bitter fighting, with approximately 19,000 Japanese killed and some 1,435 Americans

killed or missing in action.

During this stage of the war, as had been true at Guadalcanal and other islands in the South Pacific, the Japanese conducted *"banzai* charges." Instead of surrendering, they would line up in the middle of the night, often having had their fill of food and sake, and charge the American lines yelling *"banzai!"* In its most literal translation, the word could be interpreted as "hurrah," but it was far more than that for the Japanese soldier. He had been trained to go to his death for the Emperor and this was an affirmation that he was doing so gladly and willingly.

However, in most cases, these *banzai* attacks ended up being a form of organized annihilation. The Marines and soldiers who heard the Japanese coming would wait and then mow them down with machine-gun fire and artillery bombardment when they got close. Thousands of Japanese troops were killed in these suicide attacks. Later at Iwo Jima, and especially at Okinawa, the Japanese had corrected these tactics. They would make the Marines come and dig them out and force them into hand-to-hand combat. Most of the Japanese soldiers still died, but at least they took more Americans with them with these new defensive tactics.

The Japanese soldier's allegiance to the Emperor was combined with the philosophy of *bushido,* of manliness, of never losing face, which made surrendering a nearly impossible option for them. It was better to commit *hari-kari* (suicide, usually with a sword), than to surrender to an American.

[3]Perhaps the most recognized photograph of World War II was taken by AP photographer Joe Rosenthal on the top of Mt. Suribachi as a group of American Marines raised the American flag after they had taken the summit. The photograph was recast in bronze and can be see today as the U.S. Marine Memorial along the Potomac River in Arlington, VA. Ironically, the fighting still to come on Iwo Jima was so fierce that three of the six men in the flag-raising photograph were killed before the battle for Iwo Jima had ended.

21. Liberating The Death Camps

Toward the end of the war, the front was sort of like organized confusion. We were in the 12th Armored Division and assigned to Patton. We were sweeping so fast across southern France and southern Germany that a lot of times you didn't know exactly where you were. You just followed the truck or tank ahead of you, kept moving and measured your success in how many miles you had gone that day. The Germans were surrendering in droves then, and you just sped by them as you headed east while they walked toward the rear of our lines going the other direction.

We had no idea of what Landsberg and Dachau were except a couple of towns we were told to take. No one had prepared us for the death camps. I just saw the edge of the prison in Landsberg and there were half-dead-looking people walking around in a daze in their black and white striped prison uniforms. They were nothing but skin and bones. The infantry had arrived first and we in the artillery got there a couple of days later. It was enough though to make you sick.

A few days later we came into Dachau. By the time we got there the Army had cleaned up the worst of it, but there were still dead bodies stacked around like cordwood. I remember one dead German guard who was lying along the side of the road. Apparently, the prisoners had killed him when they had been liberated; their anger and hatred couldn't be contained. We walked into the "shower rooms" where they had stripped and then gassed the people. It was as clean as a kitchen...immaculate. It was hard to believe what had gone on there. Then we walked out behind the furnaces, and there, in the incinerator piles, were pieces of human bone, unburned feet and limbs sticking out of the piles, shoes scattered around. It was a horrible feeling. You got sick looking at it and felt like puking. All you wanted to do was to get the hell out of there!

What kind of distorted people had done this? How could one human being treat another one this way? There were days during the war when you were slogging through the mud or trying to sleep in the snow and cold when you wondered if the fighting was really worth it. When we saw Landsberg and Dachau, we knew it had been worth it. This was the work of Hitler and the Nazis and we had brought a stop to it.[1]

Joe Zanetta
Captain, U. S. Army Reserve

[Joe Zanetta saw the end of the war in Europe. When he saw the death camps, he knew, without a doubt, that he had been fighting for a just cause.]

I graduated from high school in 1935 and so was 24 when I was drafted. It was 1941, before Pearl Harbor, but Roosevelt knew that trouble was coming and the draft had started. The Army sent me to Fort Bragg, NC, for basic training and from there I was sent to Camp Forest, TN, where I was assigned to the 75th Tank Destroyer Battalion. I was a radio operator and basically what we did was drive around in self-propelled wheeled vehicles which had 75-mm antitank guns mounted on them. (Later, we would get them with half-tracks.)

In the fall of 1941, we were sent on maneuvers to Louisiana and took part in some big war games. Guess who was in charge? A major by the name of Eisenhower. He really knew what he was doing and I suppose that experience helped him in his rapid climb up the chain of command. After those maneuvers, we were sent back to Camp Forest where I'll never forget one Sunday when I had KP. We were in the kitchen cooking and cleaning pots and pans with the radio on, when they announced the Japanese attack on Pearl Harbor. We all knew right then that we would be seeing a lot more of the Army that we had ever hoped to (laughs). We had all been drafted to serve for one year, but we knew now that was a joke.

One of the officers in my outfit, George Hartung, really liked me and he kept telling me that someday he was going to do something for me. I didn't know what he meant, but then, sometime in May of '42, he told me that I had been accepted for Officer Candidate School (OCS) for the Artillery at Fort Sill, Oklahoma. There were a lot of us then who were being commissioned because the Army was severely short of officers. "Ninety-Day Wonders" they called us because after 90 days we were supposed to know how to lead men into combat. It was like basic training all over again, but worse. We did calisthenics and obstacle-course running. Classes went on all day, with ten minute breaks between. Of course, they scheduled the classes so that you would have to double-time between them in order to be on time (laughs). I suppose we needed all of that training and more.

The organization of an Armored Division was really pretty simple. There were three combat commands: an "A," a "B" and a "reserve" command. Each command had three battalions of about 1,000-1,500 men each who were divided into "infantry," "tank" and "artillery" outfits. So when we moved, we didn't just go with tanks. We had infantry and artillery to support the tanks and vice versa. There were several types of battalions including a headquarters battalion, a signal battalion, an ordnance battalion, and a maintenance battalion. Our outfit, the 494th Headquarters Battalion, had about 650 men in it. Although I had been trained in artillery at OCS, they wanted me to be in communications because of my prior experience, and so that is where I ended up.

Because of the makeup of the Division, we could be split up and moved around. Some of the 12th Armored Division ended up fighting with the 5th Army under General Mark Clark and other parts of it with the 3rd Army under General Patton. We got moved around as the Allies began their sweep into Germany. We had some real characters in the division. The Army needed bodies. We were told that in the Armored Divisions, 30% of our men had previously been deferred for physical disabilities. Supposedly, we had priority manpower right after the Air Corps. Can you imagine what the rest of the Army must have been like (laughs)? After Pearl Harbor, it became pretty tough to get a physical waiver or 4-F. They wanted everybody. If you were a warm body, you got drafted (more laughs).

I could have been sent overseas in 1943, but instead I was sent to Camp Barkley and Camp Campbell, TX, to train some more. The Germans had made duck soup out of some of our armored outfits and so the decision had been made to give us more training to prepare for combat. The German 88 loved to see us coming. It was the best weapon in World War II, and we had to figure out better ways to defend against it and get better equipment to fight it. [See Chapter 4 for a more complete description of the German 88-mm artillery gun.] It's always been my view that man-for-man the German soldier was better than we were. They had been trained their whole lives for combat, and we hadn't. We were good soldiers but in the end, what we primarily did was just overpower the Germans with our numbers and force of arms. Nevertheless, we were well-trained and the time it took for this training is what kept me out of North Africa. I'm just as glad it did. I didn't want to be a dead hero (laughs)! Actually, the liberty was also pretty good in Abilene and we didn't mind it when we had time off.

It wasn't until September of '44 that we headed for England. From there we shipped out to Rouen, France, for our trip to the front. By that time, the Germans had been pushed back east of Paris and we made our first contact with them in the Alsace-Lorraine area. We actually lost our first men near Colmar, France. We were rolling down a road and there was a German 88 that had us zeroed in. We weren't supposed to engage the enemy and had been ordered to continue down the road and set up headquarters. But four of our tanks turned their turrets toward the 88, tried to take it out, and "smash!" they were hit by the krauts. The fifth tank had learned his lesson by then and just kept going as he'd been ordered, and the Germans left him alone. Why? Who knows. But it shows you the effectiveness of the German 88-mm gun. The enemy actually fired five times and knocked out four of our tanks. It was a good gun.

The closest I came to getting it was at Speyer, Germany. We had intelligence that we were close to a German Panzer platoon and I was running around trying to set up bazooka positions just in case they attacked. The next thing I knew, we were under direct fire. They weren't lobbing the shells in, they were shooting them straight at us. I hit the deck, we called in the Air Corps for a strike, and that quieted down the German attack. You feel lucky after an experience like that. We had occasional artillery attacks but nothing as concentrated as that day at Speyer.

During part of the time in France and Germany, we were assigned to General Patton's 3rd Army and became known as the "Mystery Division" because he had us remove all insignia and markings which identified us as a part of the 12th Armored Division. Apparently this was done to confuse the Germans, but it also confused a lot of the American troops that we worked with. Patton was true to his reputation: we were always on the attack. One day in March or April 1945 we actually advanced 100 miles. That is an amazing feat when you realize that we were confined primarily to small, two-lane roads most of the time and they were just jammed with vehicles. When we were moving fast, we often lost track of where we were.

The reconnoiter outfits were up front and sometimes out of radio range. Other American armored and infantry battalions would sometimes be on the same road. It was organized confusion. The maps were often inadequate, and most of the time you just followed the guy in front of you.

We kept in contact with our battalion, but that was about it. We had some small L-4 airplanes, sort of like Piper Cubs, and they were probably our best source of information on what was happening up ahead. Sometimes, the Germans were retreating so fast that you didn't even know where they were. I heard of one recon group that entered the town of Augsburg, way ahead of our advancing troops. The Germans were still in the town, but were so surprised that they didn't even fire on that recon patrol (laughs). Somehow our guys rolled right past the German column, pulled off the road and escaped.

There were so many prisoners near the end. You had to feel sorry for them. We didn't even stop to take prisoners, just sent them toward the rear. As dark came they would carry white flags or scarves and most of them would be holding their hands above their heads. They were tired with sad and emotionless faces. It had to be the ultimate humiliation when they walked through their own cities and towns with their hands over their heads. They were good soldiers but Hitler had bit off more than he could chew and now the war was over for them.

There was one big difference between the German and American armies. Every time we would be headed into a major engagement, our senior officers would call us together and give us the general picture of what they thought the situation was. We would then get our guys together and pass the word down the line. Then if we got into trouble and things weren't working out quite right, at least the men would have a general idea of what we wanted to accomplish. The Germans didn't work that way. Only the guys at the top knew. The individual soldier just carried out orders. On many occasions, the American soldier did better because he was more well-informed and felt a part of the process. If things didn't pan out on a German operation, the soldiers would be running around like lost sheep.

A good example of this was the briefing we received about the Autobahn. Because it was a four-lane highway, the Army knew that it would be the fastest way to advance through Germany and they told us to get to it as soon as possible. They also told our Air Corps not to bomb it so that we could use it. I'm not sure that we took the designated route to get to the Autobahn, but once we got there, we found that it was in good shape and hadn't been destroyed. That's when we really rolled. It was a good thing we'd been briefed on what our objective was and why we should try to reach it.

The Germans were clever in a lot of things. For example, at one point we found a whole German factory used for manufacturing airplanes located in some woods. It was completely camouflaged and you couldn't even see it from the air. We found it because somebody told us about it. By that time it was out of business, but the machines and everything were in place. They were ingenious when it came to things like that. They also knew how to build hotels. I stayed in more hotel rooms in Germany than I did in the States (laughs). I remember one hotel that we took over near Burgau as an officers' quarters. There were four or five beautiful German women in the place and they wanted to work for us. We expected them to cook, clean, etc. but they were interested in another kind of work and were upset that we wanted them as chambermaids (more laughs). We let them go. That was a "No-No" in an officers' mess.

My most vivid memories of the war, though, were the death camps. What we saw was an unbelievable scene of horror, like something out of hell. I can't believe that many of the rank-and-file German people could have known what the Nazis actually had been up to in those camps. It would have had to be as incomprehensible and horrifying to them as it was to us. We had read about camps like this through the *Stars and Stripes* newspaper but we had heard nothing through the chain of command. (That was a standing joke during the war. You could find out more about what was going on in the war by reading the newspaper than by listening to official army stuff.) But you always took newspaper stories with a grain of salt, just like you do today.

Nothing could have prepared us for what we saw at Landsberg and Dachau. I can still smell the death in the air at Dachau. The people who were still alive were so skinny and starved that they could hardly stand up. They were housed in big barrack-style buildings and slept on wooden benches, some with flimsy mattresses. There was barbed wire all around the camp with no way of escape. We really weren't prepared for it. You asked yourself, "What'n the hell was this guy Hitler thinking of when he did something like this?" They had even taken gold teeth and rings off the bodies for their salvage value. Somehow we hoped that the people who had done this would be brought to justice, but how could justice ever be done for this kind of inhuman treatment? [2]

We didn't stay long at the camps. We didn't want to. All we wanted to do was get out of there. Most of us said, "By Jesus, you know, this could have been us!" It was a horrible feeling, horrible. But it happened. I saw it, smelled it, experienced it. There will always be bad people out there. The death camps were the epitome of evil. I just hope the world never sees anything like it again. We rejoiced when we heard that Hitler was dead and that the war was ending. He had been the architect of the greatest evil of all time.[3]

[Joe Zanetta returned home after the war and worked for the Standard Brands Company for 37 years before retiring. He was called upon to serve his country one more time. As a member of the inactive Army Reserve, he was called back to active duty during the Korean War. He served in Korea for 14 months as an officer in a self-propelled artillery company.]

Background and Commentary

[1]When Dachau was liberated, 30,000 people were set free. Yet, the concentration camp at Dachau was small by Auschwitz standards; its gas chamber could kill only about 350 people per hour, about 10 percent of the killing capacity of Auschwitz. It also had a heterogeneous group of inmates. Some were Jewish inmates but many were political prisoners of the Nazi regime. There were also homosexuals, Jehovah's Witnesses and other "anti-social" types who were prisoners at the camp. Dachau was the first concentration camp established by Hitler. It was only ten miles from Munich, where Nazism had been born. Here people would be used as live guinea pigs and experimented on by Nazi doctors. It was the model upon which Auschwitz would be built with its massive gas chambers. It was in camps like this that Hitler had decided to wipe out the "dregs" of society so that the "superior" Nordic/Aryan race could dominate the world. In short, these camps illustrated what can happen when a society goes mad. In total, Hitler would kill about 10,000,000 people in these camps,nearly 6,000,000 of them Jews.

On April 29, 1945, the infantry fighting ahead of Joe Zanetta came into the town of Dachau. None of the men had been briefed on what they might find. The first thing they found was a train—a train full of Jews and other political prisoners who had been sent to the concentration camp at Dachau. The train wasn't moving and had been pulled into a railroad siding just outside the camp. As Colonel Robert Wiley came across the train of box cars and gondolas, he met one of his scouts coming back from the tracks. He asked the man what was going on. The old, seasoned soldier, who thought he had seen everything in his trek across France and Germany, broke into tears. He couldn't speak. All he could do was point toward the train. Wiley went forward and what he found was incomprehensible—corpse after corpse of 60- and 70-lb. former human beings, jammed into the railroad cars of the train. Wiley ordered his troops to check every railroad car. They found no one living. There were 2,310 dead bodies in that Dachau-bound train.

As the troops approached the concentration camp, they came under fire from the SS troops inside. The Americans fired back, broke down the gates and went in. The prisoners soon realized what was happening and came running out of their huts. The SS guards opened fire on the prisoners. When the American troops saw this, they went berserk. Nothing in their experience had prepared them for something like this. They leveled their guns at the guard towers and fired away. Finally, the remaining German guards began to surrender...they gathered before the American troops. A GI went crazy, "They're vermin, sir," he said to a Lieutenant. "There's no death that's bad enough for them." Then he lifted his machine gun and opened fire. One hundred and twenty-two Nazi SS prison guards fell like wheat. Colonel Wiley heard the gunfire and rushed over. He launched himself through the air and kicked the U.S. soldier in the head, knocking him over. The gunfire ceased.

Things were getting out of control and Wiley knew it. He saw an Army Chaplain come through the gate and called him over. The Colonel didn't know if he was Protestant, Catholic or Jewish...it didn't matter. "We need a prayer to calm us down," he said to the chaplain. The Chaplain started to pray, taking some of his thoughts from the book of Isaiah: "Comfort ye, comfort ye my people, saith the Lord your God," he said. "We thank you O God for preserving us to this moment of deliverance...We pray that you return us speedily to our homes and to the embrace of our loved ones"...and then he said, "Amen." Wiley and the Chaplain were in tears. A profound calm settled over the crowd. The killing at Dachau was over.

[2]Joe Zanetta didn't know it at the time, but one of the famous personages from his hometown, Supreme Court Justice Robert H. Jackson, would become the prosecutor for the Americans at the Nuremberg War Trials where those responsible for the camps like Dachau would be judged for what they had done. Jackson's rise to prominence in the Roosevelt administration is one of the classic political stories of that era. He had known Franklin Roosevelt through politics, when Roosevelt had been Governor of New York. Bob Jackson was a good attorney but from a small town, a place from which it was difficult to be discovered by political bigwigs. But Jackson was persistent and, in 1934, finally landed himself a medium-level job in Washington with the Roosevelt administration as General Counsel to the Internal Revenue Division of the Treasury Department. Within a relatively short time he had been promoted to Solicitor General and soon became Attorney General of the United States.

During those years, Jackson often came home for holidays and would work on some of his Washington tasks during the early mornings on a park bench in town. One of his good friends, Fred Dunn, a former mayor, saw him there one morning and Jackson asked, "Hey, Fred, do you think the American people would buy it if we started sending the British war supplies in exchange for some bases in the Caribbean?" Fred, a good Democrat and strong backer of Roosevelt, said, "That's a hell of a good idea, Bob. I'm sure they would!" Always, after that, Fred Dunn would say that he had helped write the Destroyer/Bases deal with Britain—a part of Roosevelt's lend-lease policies—sitting with Bob Jackson one Sunday morning on a park bench on the west side of town.

In 1941, President Roosevelt appointed Robert Jackson as an Associate Justice of the U.S. Supreme Court, where he continued his tradition of excellence in public service. At the end of the war, President Harry Truman asked Jackson if he would be the American prosecutor at the Nuremberg War Trials in Germany. Jackson accepted, went to Nuremberg and drafted the charges which were made against 22 German leaders who were deemed to have been most responsible for Nazi atrocities during the war. At the end of the trial, which lasted from November 1945 to October 1946, the court acquitted two of the defendants, sentenced twelve to death, three to life imprisonment and the rest received various terms of imprisonment. Perhaps the most notorious defendant who was sentenced to death, and one who was unrepentant until the end, was Herman Goering, Hitler's right-hand man. It was Goering who had started the Gestapo, developed slave labor as an economic tool for the Third Reich, and established the first death camps, like the one Joe Zanetta saw at Dachau. It would be a lawyer from Joe's hometown who would finally bring Herman Goering to justice.

[3]In January 1943, at a major war conference in Casablanca, Morocco, between the British and Americans, Prime Minister Winston Churchill and President Franklin Roosevelt decided that the only acceptable terms for ending the war would be "unconditional surrender." In their view, the brutal aggression of the Axis powers required a complete new start for the governments of those countries. There would be no partial peace as there had been at the end of World War I. There would be complete peace and total victory before the war could end.

Hitler realized this and so fought on until all hope was gone. His actual end reads somewhat like a third-rate soap opera. As he cowered in his bunker in Berlin with the German Army collapsing all around him, he wrote a brief defense of his Third Reich, blamed Germany's loss on his generals, urged his successors to continue his policies of exterminating the Jews, and then turned the reigns of government over to Admiral Doenitz of the German Navy. He then married his mistress of many years, Eva Braun. The next day, April 30, 1945, he and his new wife committed suicide. On May 7th, the Germans signed surrender papers in Reims and on May 9th, they signed again in Berlin. Hitler's Third Reich had come to an end. The war in Europe was over.

22. Bombs Over Tokyo

It was July 9, 1945, and we were over Sendai, Japan, on a night bombing mission. I will never forget it. It was a B-29 incendiary raid and I was a gunner in the left blister. When we got there, the city was already in flames. We were making our bomb run at about 12,000 feet with directions to hit that part of the city not already burning. I remember seeing a large temple surrounded by a moat; the city was in flames around it. All of a sudden we were picked up by searchlights. It was frightening. We couldn't get out of the light. I shielded my eyes looking for planes but couldn't see anything. Because we were illuminated, I thought for sure that we would be rammed by a night fighter... not that I could do anything about it (laughs). The pilot thought the same thing, and, to escape the lights, banked right and piled into the cauldron of smoke rising over the city. There was an awful lot of smoke and heat, even at 12,000 feet, and the plane bucked and bounced from the heat currents caused by the fire. The bomb bay doors were open and we dumped our bombs into the fire storm below.

The smells in the smoke were indescribable. It was nauseating to smell a city burning. You could tell that there was more than wood in that fire. Garbage, flesh, wood...whatever a city is composed of was burning. That experience initiated me into the horrors of war. I was only 19 at the time but I realized that what we were doing was bad and evil. There was no specific military target. We were bombing Japanese cities indiscriminately. We were bombing, burning, searing thousands of innocent people. Later, after I returned to the States, these memories flooded back and they became a major influence in my decision to enter the ministry and become an advocate for the Gospel of peace.

Carl Lenz
Sergeant, U.S. Army Reserve

[How would you react as a 19-year-old if you were flying these missions? It is a good question to keep in mind as you follow Carl Lenz's story of flying his bombing missions over Japan. It was the ferocity of those raids that ultimately ended the war.]

I was 17 when I signed up. It was 1943, and I knew that when I reached the age of 18 I would probably be going into the military. So I went down and signed up in the Army with the understanding that I would be going into the aviation cadet program. I loved airplanes, always have, and so I volunteered for duty in the Army Air Corps.

Actually, my Mom and Dad had to go to high school graduation for me and pick up my diploma. I was called up three days after my 18th birthday in May of '44 and it was just a month before graduation. The Army sent me to Keesler Field in Mississippi for basic training. I, of course, wanted to be a pilot; most of us did. But they gave us tests, and my name came up not "pilot," but "navigator!" Then the Army told me, "Sorry, we have too many navigators; we need gunners!" so off I went to gunnery school at Buckingham Air Base near Ft. Meyers, FL.

Florida was a new experience for me. Heck, I'd never been south of Pittsburgh. We finally graduated in October of '44 and they called me in to tell me that I was such a good gunner that I had been selected for gunnery instructor school at Laredo, TX. After being qualified as a gunnery instructor, I was sent as an instructor to Clovis Air Base in New Mexico. Did I want to instruct gunners? Are you crazy? I wanted to fly in combat just like everyone else (laughs). Luckily, a crew that was in New Mexico was short a left gunner. I went to the pilot and said, "I'd like to go and fill your vacant gunner position." It sounded like a good idea to him, so he got my orders changed and soon I was airborne, heading west in a brand new B-29.

The B-29 was an amazing ship. It was 99 ft. long, had a 141-ft. wing span, four 2200-HP Wright engines, a gross weight of 70 tons and could fly faster and farther than any bomber that had been used prior to that time in World War II. It was truly a new generation of airplane. It could fly 250-350 mph, about 100 mph faster than the B-17, and it could carry a bomb load twice that of most other WW II bombers. More importantly, it could fly higher and farther than any bomber then built. We could go over 1,500 miles from base and return; and, with superchargers and a pressurized cabin, we could climb to 35,000 feet, as high as the jetliners go today. It was some airplane.

The guns themselves were an engineering marvel. In most World War II bombers you would physically move the machine guns and try to hone in on a target. You had to lead the target to compensate for its speed and

Carl Lenz (back row, far right) with his B-29 training crew before leaving for the Pacific.

concentrate on where the tracers were going. Our guns in the B-29 were computer operated. (We must have had some of the first computer guidance systems for weapons of this type.) You didn't have to lead the target, you just got him inside a group of red dots and the computer corrected for his speed and the speed of your own airplane. It was slick and, needless to say, 19-year-old kids like us were proud and impressed![1]

The plane that we went over on was called the *Up 'N Comin'* and we flew west: first to Sacramento and then on to Hawaii. Talk about the whole country being involved in the war–inside the door of that plane was a plaque that read: "Built with warbonds purchased by the people of Gardner, Massachusetts." It gave you a homey, intimate feeling about the plane. After two days in Hawaii, we left for Kwajalein, a small island or atoll near the equator that the marines had wrested from the Japanese in 1944. Our pilot, Jim Allen, had received our orders in the States but was instructed not to open them until we had left Hawaii. Once airborne, we found that we were heading ultimately for Tinian, an island 1,500 miles south of Japan in the Mariana Islands. We were to be a replacement crew

A ground crewman relaxes before loading a bomb on a B-29 in Tinian.

for the 58th Wing of the 20th Air Force which had just been moved to the Pacific from the CBI (China-Burma-India) theater. "Replacement" often meant that we would be replacing a plane that had gone down in combat.

It was late in the war. We arrived at Tinian in May, 1945. However, the Battle of Okinawa was still underway and most of us believed that the war with Japan was far from over. We were eager to get into the action. Actually, by this time, the threat of being shot down by Japanese fighters had diminished. Instead, the Japanese were concentrating on kamikaze or suicide action with their remaining fighter aircraft. Although several B-29s had been intentionally rammed and brought down by these kamikazes, our greatest concern came from the danger of flying through flak from ground-based antiaircraft guns. This bombardment from the ground was especially intense around big cities like Tokyo and Osaka. The Japanese had left many of their smaller cities virtually unprotected with very little antiaircraft defense. To avoid flak, during our daytime raids we would fly high, between 25,000 feet and 30,000 feet, and in formation. By staying together, we had better defense against fighters, and we were too high for most of the flak. But at night, during the incendiary fire raids, we would fly single file at 10,000-12,000 feet and there we would really get pounded by the Japanese antiaircraft guns. If anyone has told you that he flew through flak and wasn't scared, he would be lying. It's really terrifying.

Before the war finally ended, we had flown 13 missions over Japan and probably bombed 10 different cities. I remember one, specifically, on July 25th. It was a daylight bombing raid on Osaka, a large industrial city on the east coast of Japan. Always for daytime raids, we got up early, around 2 a.m. We had to be briefed, get to the plane, and be airborne by 4 a.m. After all, we were over 1,500 miles and eight hours flying time from the target. It was eerie in those early morning hours. We would wait our turn for take-off, sit on the wing of our ship, and watch the other airplanes roll down the runway. Then it would be our turn. There were two runways at our air-field on Tinian, and, with a plane taking off every 30 seconds, the sky would be full of aircraft.

With all four engines roaring, full of 6,000 gallons of avgas and 10 tons of bombs, we started down the runway. Our pilot finally pulled the nose up and we lifted off the runway just as the numbers at the other end slid past us. It seemed like a normal takeoff, but I soon saw some soldiers standing near the end of the runway running away from the plane. They obviously thought we were in trouble, and we were.

The end of the runway at Tinian was on a cliff 50-70 feet above the water's edge, and we dipped below the cliff edge as our pilot tried to gain airspeed. We were now close to the water and I saw the whitecaps. "Oh, oh, here we go!" I thought. I had already called on the intercom to tell the cockpit that our flaps and gear were up, but I ducked down to look again and sure enough, the left gear was stuck partially down. It was obviously causing drag and pulling the plane down. I called the new information in. When he heard my report, the copilot looked down and saw that the gear switch had not locked on "up" and the gear had only partially retracted. He flipped the gear switch again and this time "locked" it in place. Then the gear began to retract slowly, ever so slowly, and we began to gain altitude. The tailgunner had been sitting in his takeoff position way aft on the Auxiliary Power Unit (APU) which we called the "put-put." After our near dunking, he finally crawled forward and the seat of his flight suit was soak-ing wet. We had been so low that the propwash had sent spray from the ocean through the camera hatch, into the tail of the plane and he had gotten his fanny wet. What a way to begin a trip (laughs)!

It was a good flight to Osaka, but we had to wait to rendezvous with the rest of our group and squadron and to wait for the P-47 fighters that would escort us over the target. As we neared the target, the flak really got heavy. One of the fighters was flying about a mile from us as we started the bomb run and in a second he was gone...poof, a direct hit by a flak shell. My adrenaline was really running then, it could just as well have been us. Just as we let our bombs go, I saw heavy flack about 100 feet above us. The lead plane in the squadron dove for a lower altitude and we followed. We ended up leaving Osaka straddled between two layers of flack. In addition to the P-47, we lost one of our bombers over Japan that day. It was the worst day for antiaircraft fire that we had seen during the war. After the war, my Mom asked me where I was on July 24th, and I told her "over Osaka on a bomb run." (We were one day ahead of her time back home.) Then she told me that on that same night she had the experience of a bright light appearing in the corner of her bedroom, and a voice told her not to worry because I would be all right. Weird, real, crazy? Who knows, but I came out of it okay.

After the Osaka raid, we were, of course, exhausted and tired from the flight and from the trauma of making the bomb run through that terrible flak, but our day wasn't over. The engineer informed us that we were low on fuel and that we couldn't get back to Tinian. We would have to make an emergency fuel landing at Iwo Jima on the way back.

Iwo Jima was a godawful place to see. It was all black sand and volcanic rock. It smelled of death from the recent fighting, and fissures in the rock oozed with sulfur fumes. Hardly anything grew on the place. It wasn't a place to take a vacation. But thanks to those Marines who had taken the island in the spring, we had a place to land in an emergency like this. [Read the story in Chapter 20 of George Elder, one of the Marines who helped take Iwo Jima.] Actually, the United States had decided to take the island for just that reason. It was about 700 miles from the Japanese mainland and the Japanese could launch air strikes at us from Iwo as well as alert the mainland to many of our bombing raids which had to fly close to the island. The Air Corps also needed an emergency field where bombers could land if they got into trouble during the raids on Japan. Some 6,000 Marines died taking Iwo Jima. Thanks to their sacrifice, the crew of our plane, *The Journey for*

Margaret, had a place to land on July 25, 1945.

The landing that day at Iwo Jima had its own excitement. By the time we got to the island, we were about out of gas. The pilot called in for landing instructions and was told to "hold" because other airplanes were also low on fuel and trying to get in. He radioed back that we were so short of fuel that we had to declare an emergency landing. The tower said, "Ditch it. We can't get you in." Well, if you knew our pilot, you could understand why we liked him. Jim Allen was quiet, but tough, brooding, yet a hell-bent-for-leather kind of guy. He wasn't about to ditch that B-29 and he squeezed into the landing pattern without permission and we landed at Iwo. The air controllers were irate, to say the least, but we were on the ground and safe. Over 225 B-29s had diverted to Iwo Jima that day because of similar problems. What an ending to an incredible day. We almost hadn't gotten off the ground on take-off, we almost got shot down over the target, and we almost ran out of fuel. You don't have many days like that in a lifetime.[2]

The day we heard of the Japanese surrender was unforgettable. We had a mission planned for that day. The plane was loaded with avgas and bombs and we all went to the usual briefing to discuss the mission, identify the target, etc. After that I took a nap because I knew that we would have to awake at midnight and get ready for the trip. I woke in a cold sweat at 6 a.m. "I'm late for the flight!" I said, and jumped out of bed. Somebody said, "Go back to bed, Carl. We don't have to fly today. The war is over!" I couldn't believe it. None of us thought that the Japanese would surrender. After the war ended, we flew search and rescue missions for another month or so out of Iwo Jima before heading home.[3]

As I look back at the whole experience, I realize how much it changed all of us. We were 19- and 20-year-old kids when we left, but we were grown men when we came home. When I got to college, I found that I really had little in common with the younger people in my classes. They hadn't seen what I had seen, and there was no way you could communicate that experience to them. As I mentioned, the fireraids had a tremendous effect on me. For my first two years in college, I couldn't sleep well. I would often wake up in the middle of the night and hear the drone of B-29 engines and see the fires from the cities of Japan. We've all heard about "flashbacks" and combat memories experienced by the Vietnam veterans,

HIGH and MIGHTY

OLD MAN MOSE
SKY BLUES

[ABOVE AND OPPOSITE] NOSE "ART" ON B-29S FLYING OUT OF TINIAN. IN THE ABOVE PHOTO, THE CREW HAD TO PAINT A STRIPE OVER THE "IMPORTANT PARTS" BEFORE THE CHAPLAIN WOULD LET THE CREW FLY IT HOME AFTER THE WAR ENDED.

and I guess that is what I was having. I imagine that a lot of WW II veterans went through it, just like I did, but I guess we all thought it was just a part of what had happened and we didn't make a big deal out of it.

I had those bad dreams and sleepless nights for close to two years, but then I had a religious experience which changed it all. I went to a Church retreat and heard a minister named Calvin Reed. I can't even remember what he said, but I do remember what he read. He read the 12th chapter of the Book of Romans. It starts, "I beseech you, therefore brethren, by the mercies of God, that you present your bodies a living sacrifice..." It struck me like a bolt of lightning, and I knew then that somehow I was supposed to live a life of ministry, of helping others. When I realized that, the sleepless nights went away, the darkness ended, and I went on to a very exciting and gratifying 40-year career as a Presbyterian minister.

We still get together, you know. Of our eleven crewmen, there are seven of us still around. We had some bad times as a B-29 crew, but we also had a lot of good times, and we can sit around all night and talk about the fun that we had. Our wives listen patiently as we talk about our adventures and laugh about the "nose art"...all of those girlie pictures painted on the noses of those B-29s. I suppose that military men in combat live on basic instincts, and sex is certainly one of those. I'll never forget the chaplain coming by a plane one day just before it was scheduled to fly home. "You can't fly back with that naked woman on your plane," he said. So the crew painted two narrow stripes over the critical parts, put some artful language on the stripes to show their displeasure, and then flew her home (laughs). Yeah, we had some great times in those days, and most of us have stayed friends for life even though the war ended over 50 years ago.

One thing the war never did was spoil my love for flying. I still love to fly. I still love airplanes. There are a lot of days when I wish I were still out on that tarmac with those four huge radial engines rumbling, crouched inside that big 70-ton bird waiting for it to roll down the runway on the beginning of a 15-hour, 3,500-mile trip. Those were the days. Though I can't do that anymore, I can still remember and I can look up on the wall in my den and read that favorite poem we had framed which says it all:

I have slipped the surly bonds of earth,
And danced the skies on laughter-silvered wings:
Sunward I've climbed and joined the tumbling mirth
Of sunlit clouds, and done a hundred things
You have not dreamed of: wheeled and soared
And swung high in the sunlit silence, hov'ring there
I've chased the shouting wind along, and flung
My eager craft through footless halls of air;
Up, up the long delirious burning blue
I've topped the windswept heights with easy grace
Where never lark, nor even eagle flew;
And while with silent, lifting mind I've trod
The high, untrespassed sanctity of space;
Put out my hand, and touched
The face of God.

John Gillespie Magee
RAF, 1923-1942

Carl Lenz's plane, *Journey for Margaret*, named after the captain's wife.

[After the war, Carl Lenz went to college and seminary. He became a Presbyterian minister and spent forty years as a pastor in various churches. He is retired now but, from time to time, on Sunday mornings, he substitutes as preacher in churches in the area.]

Background and Commentary

[1]Plans for the B-29 were actually started in 1939. Charles Lindbergh, the famous pilot who was the first to make a solo flight across the Atlantic, met with General "Hap" Arnold, head of the U.S. Army Air Corps, and urged him to begin upgrading American fighting aircraft. Lindbergh had been in Germany and had flown some of the new planes operated by the Luftwaffe. He knew that America was behind on aircraft technology. For awhile, he served on a special board, created by Arnold, which began the research to build a new bomber with twice the range of the B-17. (Lindbergh soon left to become a spokesman for the isolationists who were opposed to America's involvement in the war.) In September 1940, Boeing Corporation was awarded the bid to build this new bomber, the B-29.

America was fortunate that this planning had started before its entrance into the war. The first prototype didn't fly until 1942, and it eventually crashed, killing the test pilot. Production didn't start until late fall, 1943. To accelerate production at Boeing's Kansas plant, the planes were partially built inside and then taken outside where workers in gloves and overcoats finished their construction in the cold winter weather of the midwest. But the effort was worth it. By April 1944, Hap Arnold had B-29s flying out of China and bombing Japan. It was truly a new generation aircraft, an awesome machine. It was the first fully pressurized bomber in which the crew could work without oxygen masks and heated flight suits. It was full of new electronic gear and had remote-controlled .50-caliber machine gun turrets. Most importantly, it had a 4,100 mile range and could carry 20,000 lbs. of bombs. The B-29, *Enola Gay,* would ultimately carry the big bomb, the atomic bomb, that would be dropped on Japan and end the war in the Pacific.

[2]Carl Lenz and the men who flew the B-29s have nothing but praise for the Marines who died taking Iwo Jima and for those who had been wounded or killed while building the emergency airfields there. At D-Day plus 13, while the fighting for the island was still on and runway construction was still underway, the first B-29 landed on Iwo Jima. The plane was nearly out of fuel and couldn't get back to Tinian. It circled the famed Mt. Suribachi, put on full flaps, hit the hard-packed volcanic runway, and with full braking action lurched to a stop...safe on Iwo Jima. Across the field, Japanese mortars were falling; the battle was still on. Hundreds of jubilant

Seabees and Marines surrounded the plane as the crew tumbled out of the doors and hatches of the aircraft. Some of the crewmen squatted down and kissed the black, volcanic ground on which they had just landed. The troops on Iwo Jima were ecstatic. This is why their friends had died...so that these air crewmen, on their 4,000-mile bombing missions, would have an emergency place to land instead of having to ditch in the Pacific Ocean. By the time the war ended, approximately 2,400 B-29s had made such emergency landings and had found the safe haven of Iwo Jima.

[3]It was the B-29 raids which finally brought down the government of Japan, but at incredible cost. The incendiary bombing raids claimed the lives of thousands of Japanese civilians, and the cities of Japan were made a wasteland. The famous March 9, 1945, raid on Tokyo resulted in immense loss of life: 334 B-29s flew over Tokyo that night dropping tons of incendiary bombs. It was a windy night and the wind fanned the flames into an incredible conflagration. When the bombing was done, 85,000 Japanese citizens were dead and a million were left homeless. The aircraft intentionally avoided the Emperor's palace, but all around him, the Emperor could see the flame, the destruction, and the horrors of war. Yet, Japanese resolve held. There was no surrender.

Some top-secret bombs had been taken to Tinian. There were three of them. Each weighed 9,000 lbs., and it was hoped that these instruments of destruction would bring Japan to her knees. In September 1944, Paul Tibbets, a 28-year-old Colonel, had been sent back to the United States for special training on how to deliver the firepower of this awesome weapon. At 2:45 a.m. on August 6, 1945, Tibbets taxied his big B-29 out onto a runway at Tinian. The plane had been named *Enola Gay,* after Tibbets' mother. A Navy Captain by the name of Thomas Parsons was along. His job was to arm the weapon after the plane was in the air. No one wanted to take the chance of a crash on take-off with a live atomic bomb on board. Tibbets' plane slowly climbed off the runway at Tinian and headed toward Hiroshima, Japan.

Tibbets had trained for almost a year for this mission. The sky was clear over Hiroshima. He was high, cruising at 31,000 feet. He had to put eight miles between the point of impact and his airplane, or the explosion would blow him out of the air. The bombardier took over as the plane flew toward the heart of the city. The bombardier looked down through his bomb sight and found the target. At a little after 8:15 a.m., the bomb dropped from the belly of the big airplane. Forty-two seconds later it would do its work on the city of Hiroshima. The B-29 lurched forward, free from its 9,000-lb. burden. Tibbets dipped the nose, put the bomber in a dive to pick up airspeed, and turned away from the target so that he could gain the eight miles he needed before impact. The bomb exploded. Over 60,000 people in Hiroshima were killed instantly. A huge mushroom-shaped cloud erupted over the city. The power of the universe had been released over Japan. The crew of the *Enola Gay* was awestruck. Never in the history of warfare had there been an explosion of this magnitude.

Still the Japanese government waffled and voted to continue the war in hopes that the Allies would accept better terms than an unconditional surrender. The United States decided that it should tell the rest of Japan about the bomb and urged its citizens to pressure their leaders to end the war. Over the next two days, 16 million leaflets with this message were dropped on 47 cities in Japan. The war went on.

On August 9th, the second bomb was loaded on a B-29 at Tinian. This time the pilot headed for southern Japan, for the city of Kokura. Kokura was clouded over and so the plane turned toward Nagasaki, the secondary target. This was an ironic tragedy in itself. Nagasaki was probably the most westernized city in Japan. This was the city that had initially received the first Christian missionaries to Japan. Now, it was to become the victim of technology produced by the industrialized west. It was also cloudy over Nagasaki that day, but on the third pass over the city, the clouds broke open. The bombardier saw the target, pushed the button, and the second atomic bomb fell from the sky on the unsuspecting people below. This time, only 35,000 people were killed. The mountainous terrain around Nagasaki contained the power of the blast within the bowl-shaped valley which formed the heart of the city.

The Imperial Council met thoughout the night in Tokyo, and this time the vote was three to three to discontinue the war and accept surrender. The Emperor broke the deadlock. It was time for Japan to surrender. The Emperor went on the radio to announce his decision to the people. It was the first time that his subjects had ever heard his voice. He was speaking as a defeated monarch, but because he spoke with the authority of God, the people obeyed. The nation of Japan laid down its arms. On September 2,

1945, on an American battleship anchored in Tokyo Bay, General Douglas MacArthur would officiate over the signing of the papers confirming the unconditional surrender of Japan. World War II was over.

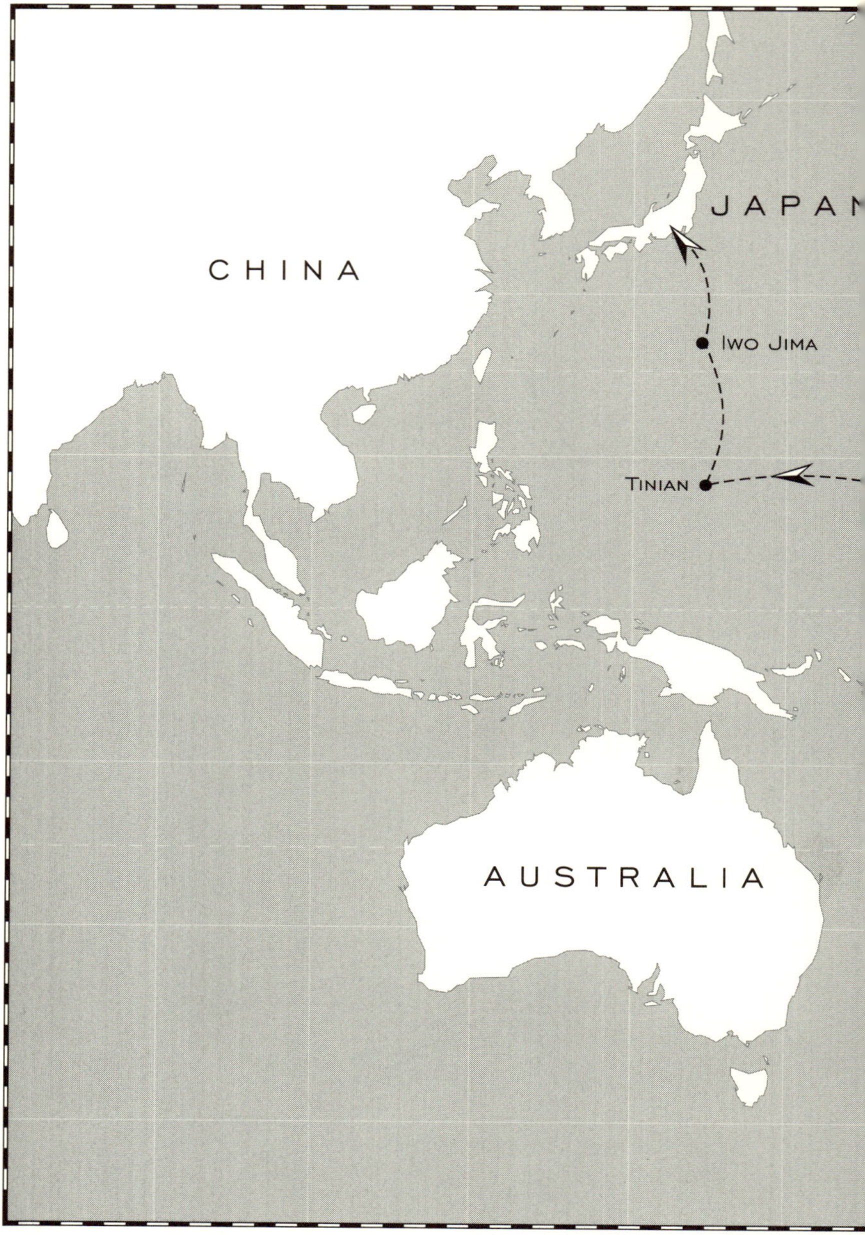

Travels of Carl Lenz

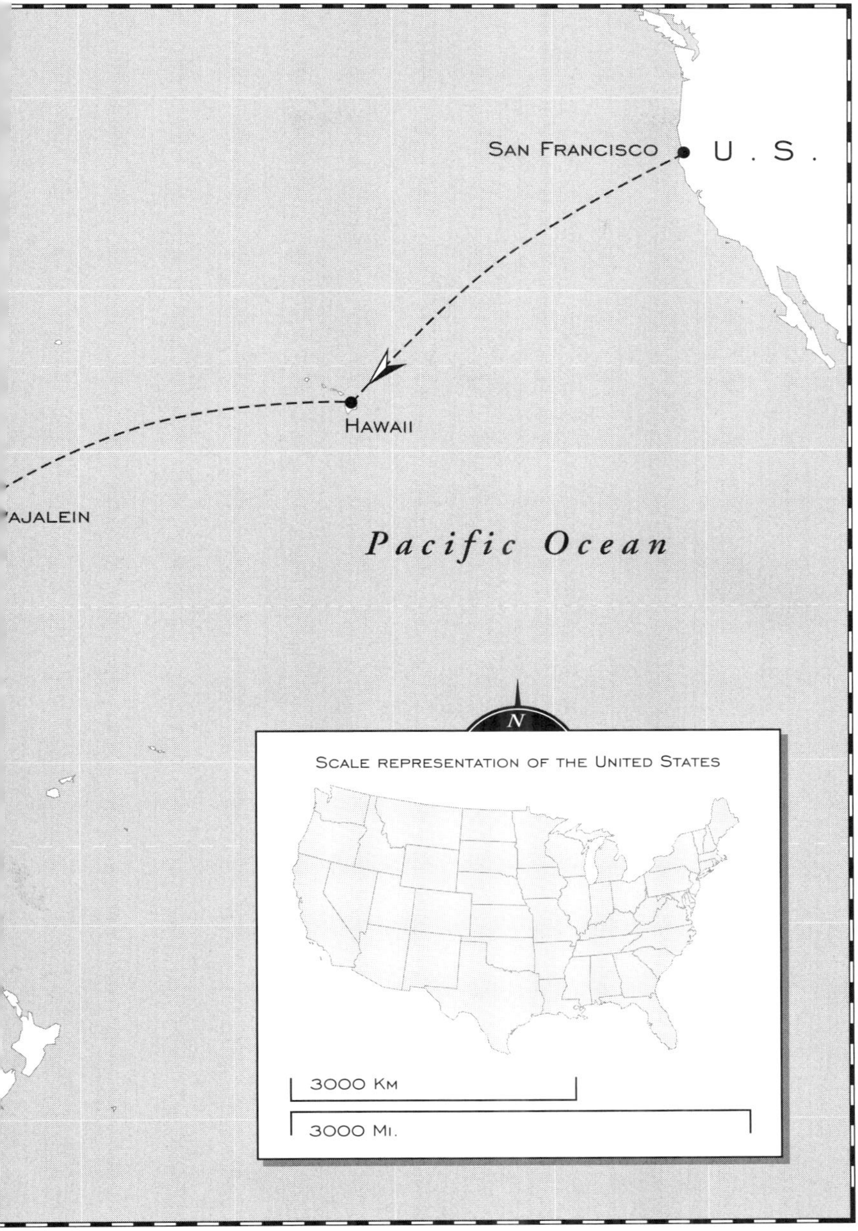
San Francisco
U . S .
Hawaii
AJALEIN
Pacific Ocean
N
Scale representation of the United States
3000 Km
3000 Mi.

23. Reflections On The War

What are we to make of these stories from World War II? Is there any common ground in this amalgam of accounts from 28 people who went off to war and then came back to this little town?

Bob Kerr's wife certainly had a point: this was their "big show." Most of them, since the war, have had successful careers and several were leaders in the community. Yet, as they near the end of their lives, it is this experience, the experience of going to war as young people, that they most want to remember. What they did after the war was just typical living, working, building a business, raising kids. What they did in the war is somehow for them more unique, more life-forming, more monumental.

What I did not find among these veterans was braggadocio or self-centeredness. None of them thought that they had won the war by themselves, or that wherever they were in the war was the most important place to have been, or that their job was the most critical in contributing to final victory. On the contrary, most of them, at the time, had a very personalized and narrow view of what was going on. Their war was right in front of them—the next hill to climb, the next strike to fly, the next watch to stand. Their only goal at the time was to survive the war and return home safely. What they did feel, though, was "camaraderie," the fact that they were a partner with millions of other Americans, all with the same purpose, all making the same kind of commitment. There was an incredible sense of unity in the United States during World War II, a feeling of common purpose where everyone was pulling on the same oar to achieve a common goal.

Perhaps one of their frustrations since the end of the war is their perception that this kind of unity and sense of purpose is not seen as much today. Lee Towne Adams, the retired County Court Judge, volunteered during his interview: "It's a crime what we have let happen to our cities. If we would have addressed the problems of our cities with the same vigor and commitment that we did in World War II, they wouldn't be in the bad condition they are today." That is an interesting observation coming from a country lawyer who has lived most of his life in a small town. These veterans have no nostalgia of wanting to go back and relive the war experiences themselves, but they do seem to yearn for those days of unified effort and common purpose. Somehow they feel that America has lost touch with that. They would like to recapture those years of camaraderie that they experienced during the war.

Some also seem concerned over a general lack of discipline in American society today. "When I was a boy," Vivian Taylor said, "right was right, and wrong was wrong. You never criticized your parents. You could trust a person's word. Where has that gone today?" Those young kids in 1941 knew that solutions to problems took a long time and that the commitment to win the war would take a long time. Most of them thought they would be in the Army for five or six years. They were prepared for the long haul. They had been taught that quick solutions and short cuts were a fool's trade. It took time, discipline and hard work to solve problems over the long term.

Many of them haven't spoken much about the war since coming home. Why? "Well, I didn't want to bore people with it. We all were in it one way or the other." In short, they didn't think anyone would be interested in listening, and they didn't want to impose themselves on someone else. Some had been quiet for other reasons: "I just wanted to forget it. There were a lot of bad memories too, you know." That sentiment came especially from those who had seen the worst of it: men like Bob Putney, who had survived Anzio, and George Elder, who had witnessed the slaughter at Iwo Jima. Once they started though, the stories flowed out, like some pent-up flood that had been waiting to burst. They were ready to talk. They just needed to be asked.

A wife of one of these veterans saw me on the street one day shortly after she had read my account of her husband's life during the war. "Thank you," she said, "I always wanted our kids and grandchildren to know what he did during the war. They hadn't known what he went through. Now, they do." That, I believe, is the unspoken reason that the stories came out. In their hearts, these old veterans knew that it was important for their kids and grandchildren to know what had happened.

When I asked Willard Perlee what reflections he might have on the war, his response was: "My generation has no future. We live our future day by day. Our children are our future. Maybe they can learn something." On another occasion, I was speaking with another veteran, Fred Johanson, trying to get more information on his experiences in Norway. We had been speaking for ten or fifteen minutes, when he said, "Let's talk about something else. I want to talk about our beautiful granddaughter, Lindsay. She is the delight of our lives." Fred's granddaughter, an attractive, smart, young lady of seventeen and an accomplished vocalist, had just won a local talent contest by singing an aria from the opera *Carmen.* It had been in the local newspaper and there had a been a lot of talk around town about the bright prospects for her future. That was more important to Fred than the war.

Vivian Taylor worries a lot, especially about his grandson, Michael. Vivian's daughter is a single parent and Vivian has had the obligation of acting as Michael's father as well as his grandfather. He doesn't really need to worry about Michael because Michael is now in college, having recently graduated from high school where he excelled in sports and scholastics and where, for three consecutive years, he was elected President of his class. Michael has vision. One day he told me, "My goal is to be the first African-American President of the United States." Yet Vivian still worries for Michael and the world he is going into. I imagine he hopes that his story of the war will teach Michael something about how things can change, but that they only change through perseverance and hard work.

Our own son, Bart, now 32, doesn't know much about World War II, but he has been learning about it as he has helped in preparing the maps and graphics for this book. He was visiting us early last fall at our place on the lake with his wife and two children. On one beautiful Saturday morning, I said to him, "Let's take the boat, go up the lake and see Sam Price. I want to talk with him some more about his experiences in World War II." When we arrived at Sam's house, we spent about five minutes talking about the war and the rest of the time talking about Sam's son, Norman, a friend of Bart's. Then a daughter-in-law walked in with two of her kids, and we spent the rest of the time talking about more family things.

I thought about what had happened as we headed back down the lake in the boat. It was obvious that Sam's family was his top priority. Nothing came in the way of that. Memories of World War II could wait until we finished talking about the important things. But part of that concern for family is passing on the experiences that count. Sam Price has raised his kids, taught them values and sent them off to college. However, you're never done with your kids. There is always something more that you can teach them while you still have the chance. There are good lessons and bad lessons that came out of the war. The kids will have to figure out which ones to hold on to. But it is good for them to know. That is why Sam Price and his fellow veterans wanted to tell their story.

Epilogue

I was a young boy when World War II ended, but I remember well the glory and exhilaration felt by everyone in our hometown. On V-J Day (victory over Japan), the whole town gathered at Third and Main Streets with horns blowing, people singing and confetti coming out of the second and third floor windows of the downtown buildings. Even kids my age were caught up in it. We didn't quite realize what was happening, but we danced around, hand-in-hand in circles, yelling "The war is over! The war is over!"

Later, probably in 1946, I vividly remember my excitement at seeing contrails high in the sky over our farm at the edge of the city as the bombers of the war flew by at such a high altitude that it looked like they were leaving streams of smoke. We had never seen that before. Then one day, the P-51 Mustangs came over–probably piloted by some fly-boys from our hometown. These fast, beautiful fighters twisted and turned over the city with barrel rolls and mock dog fights. Oh, did I want to be up in one of those! Maybe it was then that I realized that I had been left out of the big one, the war that really made the difference. I've often said since, "I guess I was born 20 years too late."

My generation's war was Vietnam. I was in the Navy then and, at first, served on a ship homeported in Japan. Periodically, we would get to Vietnam, stop at a few ports, do our job, and pick up our "hostile fire" pay as we steamed in and out of the combat zone. But that wasn't enough for me. I wanted to see it firsthand, and so I volunteered to go "in-country." The Navy quickly obliged and within a few months I was the captain of two small, fast patrol boats in the Mekong Delta called PBRs (Patrol Boat River). I saw my share of action, watched some friends die, and saw the power of the U.S. military. We had the best equipment and the best support a military organization could provide. We also had an ill-defined goal and an unwinnable mission. We were caught in the vise of a civil war. We were supporting a part of the country that believed in many of the freedoms and civil rights which we cherished, but we were also supporting a government which was essentially corrupt and whose leaders were getting rich from the American dollar. It wasn't a winning combination and, in the end, we lost the war.

Maybe that's why my generation had such a difficult time adjusting to life after the war. We hadn't won, we hadn't triumphed like our parents did in the big war. For example, it has always amazed me that so much has been made of the 2,483 MIAs (Missing in Action) from the Vietnam War. War is an ugly business and a lot of people end up just plain "missing." Nobody knows what happened to them. Aircraft would disappear over the Ho Chi Minh trail in dense jungles, men would disappear on patrols in areas with ill-defined borders. That's the way it is with war, with every war. In World War II, the United States had 79,000 MIAs. In one American cemetery alone, in Manila, where over 17,000 men and women who died in World War II are buried, there are an additonal 36,281 names on the wall of the missing. The Pacific theater was a huge area of water interspersed with islands. People disappeared and never came back.

Why wasn't there an outcry by the World War II veteran, similar to that of the Vietnam veteran, over the thousands who were missing in action? I can only surmise that it was because the end was different. World War II ended in total victory. People felt that a goal had been accomplished, and now it was time to return home, forget the past and get back to work. There was catharsis at the end of World War II. There was frustration and guilt at the end of the Vietnam war.

Since Vietnam is still only 20 years past, young people today tend to think of that conflict as representative of America's war record. That is unfortunate, because all that our country stood for and accomplished in the years 1941-1945 is often overlooked. Yes, there were 57,710 Americans who died fighting for their country in Vietnam. But there were 407,316 Americans who died fighting the Japanese and Germans in World War II. In the Vietnam conflict, 2,594,000 Americans served their country. However, more than 16,000,000 young people put on the uniform of their country during World War II. It is estimated that North Vietnam lost over 600,000 men and women in its fight against America and South Vietnam during that war. In World War II, Germany's military war dead were estimated at approximately 3,250,000, whereas Japan had approximately 1,270,000 killed in action. Just based upon the statistics, it is difficult to compare Vietnam with World War II.[1]

Certainly, the missions in the two conflicts were incomparable. In

World War II, America was fighting for its life and for its vision of what a democratic world should look like. In Vietnam, we weren't sure what we were fighting for and, for whatever it was, we hadn't been given an achievable goal. Acknowledging this may not make life easier for the Vietnam veteran, but it should lift him and his generation to a time before the 1960s, to the 1940s, when everything was on the line and when the best attributes of our democracy were put up against a horrifying and distorted view of civilization that had been forced on the world by the Axis powers.

The Vietnam war is now history and it taught us the limitations of American military power. It is time to put that war behind us, to bury those bad memories, and to let Vietnam and the Americans who fought there get on with a new and better life.

World War II did more than establish democracy as the future form of government for the industrialized countries of the world. It also changed the rules of warfare forever. Just after the dropping of the atomic bomb on Japan, Theodore White, the famous far-east correspondent for *Time-Life,* journeyed to Manila for an interview with General Douglas MacArthur. Always the consummate military strategist, MacArthur immediately got to the issue of the atomic bomb. "White," he said, "White, do you know what this means?" "What, sir?" White asked. It meant, he said, that all wars were over; wars were no longer matters of valor or judgment, but lay in the hands of scholars and scientists. "Men like me are obsolete," he said, pacing back and forth. "There will be no more wars, White, no more wars!"[2]

Of course, MacArthur knew that there would continue to be wars—little wars, brush-fire wars, limited wars—but he correctly sensed that there would never be another world war as he had experienced it. World War II had introduced the planet to the terrors of total war. It meant the destruction of whole cities, of entire populations. Civilians could no longer be protected from the horrors that had been reserved for armies and navies. Mankind, in World War II, had moved military conflict up to a new level... total annihilation. The next time it might not be just the Jews of Germany who would experience the holocaust, it could be all of Germany, it could be all of the United States.

And that's really where we are today, isn't it? As the Soviet Union has disintegrated, the control over nuclear weapons has become a problem. Nuclear material disappears from Russia and the former Soviet state as these former enemies seek hard currency to shore up their economies. Old ethnic and religious rivalries that we all thought had been buried by education and modernization come leaping back at us as chaos breaks out in the Balkans and missiles start flying in the polarized Middle East. There is still a dark side to human nature. Mankind is capable of incredible evil. Probably in my lifetime, and most assuredly in my children's lifetime, there will be a nuclear event somewhere. Ethnic and religious hatred will overcome the powers of morality and good sense. Someone or some country, a terrorist or a renegade state, will destroy an enemy with a nuclear bomb.

Who, then, will be the nuclear policeman who will step forward to save the world? If the world again drifts toward chaos and dictatorship, who or what country will mobilize to stop it? Will there be a generation of Americans who will come forth, as our parents and grandparents did in 1941, to pay the price to insure that the ways of democracy live on? We must hope so, for certainly this challenge will be upon us. The sacrifices of one generation lay the foundation for the next. Each new time requires a new commitment. As the children and grandchildren of those who fought in World War II read this book, I hope that they will find lessons in it which will help them face the challenges that inevitably lie ahead.

Rolland E. Kidder,
Lieutenant, U.S. Naval Reserve

Acknowledgements

This book could not have been written without the cooperation of my family. Everything worthwhile usually takes more time and effort than you originally estimate, and this book-writing project was no exception. It took me away from a lot of family time and household chores over the course of two years.

A special thanks to my wife Jane, who proofread each chapter looking for spelling and punctuation mistakes, of which there were many. To Bart Goodell, our son, who spent weekends and evenings designing and preparing this book for print, a special thanks. Also, I was fortunate in finding Vernon Crandall, a young Air Force veteran and son-in-law of one of those interviewed, who is an accomplished photographer and was able to retake pictures from the many old World War II black-and-white photos that were brought in by the veterans. I hope that his work is as appreciated by the readers as it has been by me. In addition, my colleagues at PB Sullivan & Co. were very supportive as veterans called or came into the office to deliver photographs or update a part of their story.

I also owe a debt to several friends who have had a long time interest in World War II, and who appreciate the significance of this period in American history. Marty Idzik and Greg Peterson had been taking World War II veterans to lunch to hear their stories, and suggested that I might want to do the same. Dan Bratton, Hadyn Williams, Jim Abdella, Bill Parment, Chuck Hannum and Barc Wellman all read the transcript, offered relevant suggestions, and recommended pertinent changes. One of these individuals, with total honesty, said: "It is a wonderful book but it needs substantial editing!" With that in mind, I was fortunate to find Joanne Schweik, who wielded her substantial editing skills. It was her dedicated and patient work that finally resulted in a manuscript ready for publishing.

However, my greatest thanks goes to the 28 World War II veterans who agreed to talk with me. I know that it was not easy for many of them to bring back these memories after so many years. But I hope they will conclude, after reading this book, that it was the right thing to do.

Without their willingness to tell us, those of us who were not there would never have known what it was like. We are better for having heard their stories. Their history has enriched our lives.

Endnotes

Introduction.

[1]Dwight D. Eisenhower, *Crusade in Europe,* (New York: Doubleday, 1948), 2; Doris Kearns Goodwin, *No Ordinary Time,* (New York: Simon & Schuster), 372.

Chapter 1.

[1]S.E. Smith, ed., *The United States Navy in World War II*, (New York: William Morrow, 1966).

[2]John Costello, *The Pacific War*, (New York: Rawson, Wade Publications, 1981).

[3]Samuel Eliot Morrison, *History of U.S. Naval Operations in World War II*, Vol. V, (Boston: Little Brown, 1949); Ralph Stone, ed., *John F. Kennedy 1917-1963,* (Dobbs Ferry, NY: Oceana Publications, 1971).

Chapter 2.

[1]Carlo D'Este, *World War II in the Mediterranean:* 1942-1945, (Chapel Hill, NC: Algonquin Books of Chapel Hill, 1990).

[4]Wesley Craven and James Cate, *The Army Airforces in World War II*, Vol. 1 ,6, 7, (Washington,DC: Office of Air Force History, 1983); C.L. Sulzberger, *The American Heritage Picture History of World War II*, (New York: American Heritage/Bonanza Books, 1966).

[5]Geoffrey Perret, *Winged Victory: The Army Air Forces in World War II*, (New York: Random House, 1993); Otha C. Spencer, *Flying the Hump,* (College Station, TX: Texas A & M University Press, 1992).

Chapter 3.

[1]"Berndt Balchen Obituary," *The New York Times*, October 19, 1973, 46.

[2]Craven and Cate, *Army Airforces*, Vol.1

[4]Sulzberger, *American Heritage Picture History*; Gerhard L. Weinberg, *A World at Arms: a Global History of World War II*, (Cambridge: Cambridge University Press, 1994).

Chapter 4.

[4]*Louis Snyder's Historical Guide to World War II*, (Westport, CT: Greenwood Press, 1982), 43.

[7]George S. Patton, Jr., *War As I Knew It*, (New York: Houghton

Mifflin Co., 1947), 317.

CHAPTER 5.

[1] *The 35th Infantry Division in World War II 1941-1945,* (Atlanta, GA: Albert Love Enterprises, circa 1946).

[2]Dwight D. Eisenhower, *Crusade in Europe,* (New York: Doubleday, 1948), 279.

[3]Weinberg, A *World at Arms.*

CHAPTER 6.

[1]Anne Bosanko Green, *One Woman's War,* (St. Paul: Minnesota Historical Society Press, 1989).

[2]Wyatt Blassingame, *Combat Nurses of World War II,* (New York: Random House, 1967), 155.

CHAPTER 7.

[2]*Louis L. Snyder's Historical Guide*, 720.

[3]Perret, *Winged Victory.*

[4]*Jane's Encyclopedia of Aviation,* (New York: Crescent Books, 1993).

[5]*Louis L. Snyder's Historical Guide,* 544.

CHAPTER 8.

[1]William K. Goolick and Ogden Tanner, *The Battle of the Bulge,* (Alexandria, VA: Time-Life Books, 1979).

[2]Jacquin Sanders, *A Night Before Christmas,* (New York: G.P. Putnam's Sons, 1963).

CHAPTER 9.

[1]Lou Potter, *Liberators, Fighting on Two Fronts in World War II,* (New York: Harcourt Brace Jovanovich, 1992).

[2]Ibid.

CHAPTER 10.

[1]Russell Miller, *The Resistance,* (Chicago: Time-Life Books, 1979).

[2]Ibid.

[3]William Colby, *Honorable Men: My Life in the CIA,* (New York: Simon & Schuster, 1978).

CHAPTER 11.

[1]D'Este, *World War II in the Mediterranean.*

[2]Eisenhower, *Crusade in Europe.*

[3]Martin Blumenson, *Anzio: The Gamble that Failed,* (New York: Dell Publishers, 1963).

[4]*Mud, Mules and Mountains,* copyright 1944, reprinted by permission of Bill Mauldin, March 17, 1996.

Chapter 12.

[1]Weinberg, A *World At Arms.*

[2]Marc' Antonio Bragadin, *The Italian Navy in World War II,* (Annapolis: United States Naval Institute, 1957).

Chapter 13.

[1]Simon Rigge, *War in the Outposts,* (Chicago: Time-Life Books, 1980).

[2]Ibid.

[3]Roger Cohen and Claudio Gatti, *In the Eye of the Storm: the Life of General H. Norman Schwarzkopf,* (New York: Farrar, Straus & Giroux, 1991).

Chapter 15.

[1]*Louis L. Snyder's Historical Guide,* 676-677.

[2]John Keegan, ed., *The Rand McNally Encyclopedia of World War II,* (Chicago: Rand McNally, 1977).

[4]Barrie Pitt, ed., *The Battle of the Atlantic,* (Chicago: Time-Life Books, 1980); Sulzberger, *American Heritage Picture History.*

Chapter 16.

[1]Jim Reardin, *Cracking the Zero Mystery,* (Harrisburg, PA:Stackpole Books, 1990); *Jane's Encyclopedia of Aviation.*

[3]John Costello, *The Pacific War,* (New York: Rawson, Wade Publishers, 1981); William Manchester, *Goodbye Darkness,* (Boston: Little, Brown & Co., 1980).

Chapter 17.

[1]*American Naval Fighting Ships Dictionary,* Vol. IV, (Washington: U.S. Government Printing Office, 1969).

[2]Costello, *The Pacific War,* 578.

[3]Pat Robinson, *The Fight for New Guinea,* (New York: Random House, 1943), 111; Manchester, *Goodbye Darkness,* 109.

[4]William J. Dunn, *Pacific Microphone,* (College Station, TX: Texas A & M University Press, 1988),300-303; *Louis L. Snyder's Historical Guide.*

Chapter 18.

[1]Clay Blair, Jr., *Silent Victory,* (New York: J.B. Lippincott, 1975);

[4]Robert E. Kuenne, *The Attack Submarine,* (New Haven: Yale

University Press, 1965).

CHAPTER 19.

[1]Richard O'Neill, *Suicide Squads: World War II,* (New York: St . Martin's Press, 1981), 11.

[2]Costello, *The Pacific War,* 518.

CHAPTER 20.

[2]Carl W. Proehl, ed., *The Fourth Marine Division in World War II,* (Washington: Infantry Journal Press, 1946); *Louis L. Snyder's Historical Guide,* 428-429.

CHAPTER 21.

[1]Michael Selzer, *Deliverance Day, The Last Hours at Dachau,* (Philadelphia: J.B. Lippincott, 1978), 188-193.

[2]Charles S. Desmond, *Mr. Justice Jackson,* (New York: Columbia University Press, 1969); *Louis Snyder's Historical Guide.*

CHAPTER 22.

[1]Perret, *Winged Victory.*

[2]Bill D. Ross, *Iwo Jima: Legacy of Valor,* (New York: The Vanguard Press, 1985).

[3]Richard Rhodes, *The Making of the Atomic Bomb,* (New York: Simon & Schuster, 1986); Weinberg, *A World at Arms.*

EPILOGUE.

[1]Statistics from: Louis L. Snyder, *The War: A Concise History, 1939-1945,* (New York: Julian Messmer, 1960); Harry G. Summer, Jr., *Vietnam War Almanac,* (New York: Facts on File Publications, 1985).

[2]Theodore White, *In Search of History,* (New York: Harper and Row, 1978), 224.

Bibliography

American Naval Fighting Ships Dictionary, Vol. 4, (Washington: U.S. Government Printing Office, 1969).

"Berndt Balchen Obituary," *The New York Times*, October 19, 1973, 46.

Blassingame, Wyatt, *Combat Nurses of World War II*, (New York: Random House, 1967).

Blair, Clay Jr., *Silent Victory*, (New York: J.B. Lippincott, 1975).

Blumenson, Martin, *Anzio: The Gamble that Failed*, (New York: Dell Publishers, 1963).

Bragadin, Marc' Antonio, *The Italian Navy in World War II*, (Annapolis: United States Naval Institute, 1957).

Cohen, Roger and Claudio Gatti, *In the Eye of the Storm: the Life of General H. Norman Schwarzkopf*, (New York: Farrar, Straus and Giroux, 1991).

Colby, William, Honorable Men: *My Life in the CIA*, (New York: Simon & Schuster, 1978).

Costello, John, *The Pacific War*, (New York: Rawson, Wade Publications, 1981).

Craven, Wesley and James Cate, *The Army Airforces in World War II*, Vol. 1, 6, 7, (Washington, D.C.: Office of Air Force History, 1983).

Desmond, Charles S., *Mr. Justice Jackson*, (New York: Columbia University Press, 1969).

D'Este, Carlo, *World War II in the Mediterranean: 1945-1945*, (Chapel Hill, NC: Algonquin Books of Chapel Hill, 1990).

Dunn, William J., *Pacific Microphone*, (College Station, TX: Texas A & M University Press, 1988).

Eisenhower, Dwight D., *Crusade in Europe*, (New York: Doubleday, 1948).

Goodwin, Doris Kearns, *No Ordinary Time*, (New York: Simon & Schuster, 1994).

Goolick, William K. and Ogden Tanner, *The Battle of the Bulge*, (Alexandria, VA: Time-Life Books, 1979).

Green, Anne Bosanko, *One Woman's War*, (St. Paul: Minnesota Historical Society Press, 1989).

Jane's Encyclopedia of Aviation, (New York: Crescent Books, 1993).

Keegan, John, ed., *The Rand McNally Encyclopedia of World War II*, (Chicago: Rand McNally, 1980).

Kuenne, Robert E., *The Attack Submarine*, (New Haven: Yale University Press, 1965).

Louis Snyder's Historical Guide to World War II, (Westport, CT: Greenwood Press, 1982).

Manchester, William, *Goodbye Darkness*, (Boston: Little, Brown & Co., 1980).

Mauldin, Bill, *Mud, Mules, and Mountains: Cartoons of the A.E.F. in Italy*, (Copyright 1944 by Bill Mauldin).

Miller, Russell, *The Resistance*, (Chicago: Time-Life Books, 1979).

Morrison, Samuel Eliot, *History of U.S. Naval Operations in World War II*, Vol. 5, (Boston: Little, Brown, 1949).

O'Neill, Richard, *Suicide Squads: World War II*, (New York: St. Martin's Press, 1981).

Patton, George S. Jr., *War As I Knew It*, (New York: Houghton Mifflin, 1947).

Perret, Geoffrey, *Winged Victory: The Army Air Forces in World War II*, (New York: Random House, 1993).

Pitt, Barrie, ed., *The Battle of the Atlantic*, (Chicago: Time-Life Books, 1980).

Potter, Lou, *Liberators, Fighting on Two Fronts in World War II*, (New York: Harcourt Brace Jovanovich, 1992).

Proehl, Carl W., ed., *The Fourth Marine Division in World War II*, (Washington: Infantry Journal Press, 1946).

Reardin, Jim, *Cracking the Zero Mystery*, (Harrisburg, PA: Stackpole Books, 1990).

Rhodes, Richard, *The Making of the Atomic Bomb*, (New York: Simon & Schuster, 1986).

Rigge, Simon, *War in the Outposts*, (Chicago: Time-Life Books, 1980).

Ross, Bill D., *Iwo Jima: Legacy of Valor*, (New York: The Vanguard Press, 1985).

Robinson, Pat, *The Fight for New Guinea*, (New York: Random House, 1943).

Sanders, Jacquin, *A Night Before Christmas*, (New York: G.P. Putnam's Sons, 1963).

Selzer, Michael, *Deliverance Day, The Last Hours at Dachau*, (Philadaelplhia: J.B. Lippincott, 1978).
Smith, S.E., ed., *The United States Navy in World War II*, (New York: William Morrow, 1966).
Snyder, Louis. L., *The War: A Concise History, 1939-1945*, (New York: Julian Messmer, 1960).
Spencer, Otha C., *Flying the Hump*, (College Station, TX: Texas A & M University Press, 1992).
Stone, Ralph, ed., *John F. Kennedy 1917-1963*, (Dobbs Ferry, NY: Oceana Publications, 1971).
Sulzberger, C.L., *The American Heritage Picture History of World War II*, (New York: American Heritage Books, 1966).
Summer, Harry G. Jr., *Vietnam War Almanac*, (New York: Facts on File Publications, 1985).
The 35th Infantry Division in World War II 1941-1945, (Atlanta, GA: Albert Love Enterprises, circa 1946).
Weinberg, G. L., *A World at Arms: a Global History of World War II*, (Cambridge: Cambridge University Press, 1994).
White, Theodore, *In Search of History*, (New York: Harper and Row, 1978).

Index